Genocide and the Eur

CW00493862

Genocide is one of the most heinous abuses of human rights imaginable, yet reaction to it by European governments in the post-Cold War world has been criticised for not matching the severity of the crime. European governments rarely agree on whether to call a situation genocide, and their responses to purported genocides have often been limited to delivering humanitarian aid to victims and supporting prosecution of perpetrators in international criminal tribunals. More coercive measures – including sanctions or military intervention – are usually rejected as infeasible or unnecessary. This book explores the European approach to genocide, reviewing government attitudes towards the negotiation and ratification of the 1948 Genocide Convention and analysing responses to purported genocides since the end of the Second World War. Karen E. Smith considers why some European governments were hostile to the Genocide Convention and why European governments have been reluctant to use the term genocide to describe atrocities ever since.

KAREN E. SMITH is Reader in International Relations at the London School of Economics and Political Science. She has written extensively about the European Union's foreign relations, including the role that human rights may play in those relations, and is the winner of the 2007 Anna Lindh Award for excellence in research on European foreign and security policy. Her most recent books include *European Union Foreign Policy in a Changing World* (2nd edition, 2008) and *The European Union at the United Nations: Intersecting Multilateralisms* (with Katie Verlin Laatikainen, 2006).

Genocide and the Europeans

KAREN E. SMITH

CAMBRIDGE
UNIVERSITY PRESS

CAMBRIDGE UNIVERSITY PRESS
Cambridge, New York, Melbourne, Madrid, Cape Town, Singapore,
São Paulo, Delhi, Dubai, Tokyo, Mexico City

Cambridge University Press
The Edinburgh Building, Cambridge CB2 8RU, UK

Published in the United States of America by Cambridge University Press,
New York

www.cambridge.org
Information on this title: www.cambridge.org/9780521133296

First published 2010

Printed in the United Kingdom at the University Press, Cambridge

A catalogue record for this publication is available from the British Library

Library of Congress Cataloguing in Publication data
Smith, Karen Elizabeth.
Genocide and the Europeans / Karen E. Smith.
p. cm.
Includes bibliographical references and index.
ISBN 978-0-521-11635-0 – ISBN 978-0-521-13329-6 (pbk.)
1. Genocide–History–21st century. 2. Genocide–Case studies.
3. Europeans–Attitudes. I. Title.
HV6322.7.S64 2010
364.15′1094–dc22
2010022035

ISBN 978-0-521-11635-0 Hardback
ISBN 978-0-521-13329-6 Paperback

Contents

Tables and boxes

Tables

Box

Acknowledgements

I researched and wrote this book during a year-long period of sabbatical and research leave. The research leave was made possible by a grant I received as part of the 2007 Anna Lindh Award for excellence in research on European foreign and security policy, awarded by the Volkswagen Foundation (Hannover), the Riksbankens Jubileumsfond (Stockholm) and the Compagnia di San Paolo (Turin). I am extremely grateful to the three foundations for their support.

Three LSE students translated material into English from Dutch, Luxembourgish and German: Tine van Criekinge, Isabelle Nicolay and David Maleki. I am grateful to them all for their help, and especially for David Maleki's expert research assistance for much of the time I was researching this book.

The staff of the National Archives of the UK, the Irish National Archives, archives at the School of Oriental and African Studies, the New York Public Library and the American Jewish Historical Society also helped me to track down relevant documents and other materials. UK parliamentary material is reproduced with the permission of the Controller of HMSO on behalf of Parliament. Material obtained under the UK Freedom of Information Act is reproduced under the terms of the Click-Use Licence. Material from the National Archives of Ireland is reproduced with permission from the Director of the National Archives of Ireland.

Several colleagues kindly read and commented on parts of the draft manuscript; many thanks to Elizabeth Stubbins-Bates, Christopher Hill, and Katie Verlin Laatikainen for helping me to refine my arguments. Thanks also to several people who took the time to answer my queries relating to all manner of subjects, from Dutch and German human rights policy to international criminal justice, and from activism on the Darfur case to Genocide Studies: Herbert Hirsch, Hilde Reiding, Christian Schaller, Gerry Simpson, James Smith, Theo van Boven, Willem van Genugten, and Jan Wouters.

Abbreviations

AU	African Union
BBC	British Broadcasting Corporation
CDU	Christian Democratic Union (Germany)
CHR	Commission on Human Rights (of the United Nations)
CSCE	Conference on Security and Cooperation in Europe
CSU	Christian Social Union (Germany)
DPKO	Department of Peacekeeping Operations (United Nations)
DRC	Democratic Republic of Congo
ECCC	Extraordinary Chambers in the Courts of Cambodia
ECOSOC	Economic and Social Council (of the United Nations)
EU	European Union
FAC	Foreign Affairs Council (of the European Union)
FCO	Foreign and Commonwealth Office
FDP	Free Democrats Party (Germany)
FMG	Federal Military Government (of Nigeria)
FRG	Federal Republic of Germany
FRY	Federal Republic of Yugoslavia
GDR	German Democratic Republic
ICC	International Criminal Court
ICJ	International Court of Justice
ICTR	International Criminal Tribunal for Rwanda
ICTY	International Criminal Tribunal for the former Yugoslavia
IFOR	Implementation Force
INA	Irish National Archives
JEM	Justice and Equality Movement

KLA	Kosovo Liberation Army
MP	Member of Parliament
MSF	Médecins sans Frontières
NATO	North Atlantic Treaty Organization
NGO	non-governmental organisation
NIOD	Netherlands Institute for War Documentation
OAU	Organisation of African Unity
OSCE	Organization for Security and Cooperation in Europe
P5	five permanent members of the UN Security Council
PDS	Party of Democratic Socialism (Germany)
RPF	Rwandan Patriotic Front
RPR	Rassemblement pour la République (French political party)
SAA	Stabilisation and Association Agreement
SPD	Social Democratic Party (Germany)
SHZ	Safe Humanitarian Zone (in Rwanda)
SLM/A	Sudanese Liberation Movement/Army
SPLA	Sudan People's Liberation Army
UDF	Union des Démocrates pour la République (French political party)
UK	United Kingdom
UKNA	United Kingdom National Archives
UMP	Union pour un Mouvement Populaire (French political party)
UN	United Nations
UNAMID	United Nations African Mission in Darfur
UNAMIR	United Nations Assistance Mission for Rwanda
UNHCR	United Nations High Commissioner for Refugees
UNPROFOR	United Nations Protection Force
US	United States
USA	United States of America
USSR	Union of Soviet Socialist Republics
WEOG	Western Europe and Other Group (at the United Nations)
WEU	Western European Union

1 *The norms against genocide*

'Never again Auschwitz' is a powerful, emotive cry, laden with the guilt of the past, but replete with the promise of redemption by taking action, this time, to stop the extermination of our fellow human beings. The promise was embedded in the very first United Nations human rights treaty, the Convention on the Prevention and Punishment of the Crime of Genocide in December 1948, concluded almost four years after the Auschwitz-Birkenau concentration camps were liberated. The speed with which this Convention was agreed reflected the deeply-felt need to reset the world's moral bearings after the Nazis' monstrous plans to wipe out entire populations had been revealed. This 'odious scourge' – in the words of the Convention's preamble – had to be eliminated.

Over sixty years later, and 'never again Auschwitz' is more replete with irony than redemption. Again and again genocide has been carried out, and again and again, little has been done by the United Nations (UN) – and its member states – in response. And yet, again and again, the promise of 'never again' is repeated. This book asks why such a strong and apparently deeply-felt moral imperative remains, for the most part, rhetorical. It does so by concentrating on European governments' response to genocide. Given the historical legacy of the Holocaust (or Shoah) in Europe, and the general importance given to international law and the protection of human rights by European states, it would be reasonable to assume that European states have similar views on how they should respond to a genocide being perpetrated in another country, and that their response would be a forceful one.

Very little has been written about the attitudes of European governments towards either the 1948 Genocide Convention or genocide in general. In fact, I could find only one article on the views of one European government, the United Kingdom (UK), on the

Genocide Convention,[1] and only indications of the views of some European governments regarding the negotiation of the Convention in William Schabas' seminal study of the Convention (*Genocide in International Law*).[2] There are no works that consider the attitude of European governments, other than the UK, to the Convention *after* it was signed – though there are comparisons of the legislation implementing the Convention in various European states.[3] Moreover, while there is a growing body of literature on the attitudes of this or that European government towards this or that genocide, there is no work that considers European views on genocide in general.[4] This contrasts with the extensive body of literature on the attitude of the US government regarding genocide. Samantha Power's book, *'A Problem from Hell': America and the Age of Genocide* won the Pulitzer Prize for non-fiction in 2003.[5] The forty-year debate in the USA on whether to ratify the 1948 Genocide Convention has also been covered amply by historians, political scientists and legal scholars.[6]

Genocide and the Europeans aims to fill the gap in the literature on European responses to genocide. As it turns out, quite a few European governments were hostile to the Genocide Convention, and some took decades to ratify it. Furthermore, European governments are not keen on using the term to describe atrocities. This books considers why this is the case. It analyses how European governments have reacted to four cases of proven or purported

1 A.W. Brian Simpson, 'Britain and the Genocide Convention', *British Yearbook of International Law*, vol. 73 (2003), 5–64.

2 William A. Schabas, *Genocide in International Law: The Crime of Crimes*, 2nd edition (Cambridge: Cambridge University Press, 2009). The first edition was published in 2000.

3 See the special issue of *International Criminal Law Review*, vol. 5, no. 3 (2005).

4 Of course a book entitled *Genocide and the Europeans* could also take as its starting point European perpetration of genocide, or complicity in its perpetration. For trenchant criticism of western involvement in genocide and war crimes, see Adam Jones, ed., *Genocide, War Crimes and the West: History and Complicity* (London: Zed Books, 2004).

5 Samantha Power, *'A Problem from Hell': America and the Age of Genocide* (New York: Perennial, 2002).

6 See Lawrence J. LeBlanc, *The United States and the Genocide Convention* (Durham: Duke University Press, 1991). The issue has been debated or analysed in the pages of numerous journals including *The American Journal of International Law, Yale Law Journal*, and *Journal of Genocide Research*.

genocides in the post-Cold War era: Bosnia and Herzegovina (1992–95), Rwanda (1994), Kosovo (1998–99), and Darfur, Sudan (2003–). In two cases, Bosnia and Rwanda, genocide is now widely agreed to have taken place; in the other two, Kosovo and Darfur, this is a more controversial question. European governments have been heavily involved in debates and/or action in all four cases. The focus here is on three governments in particular: France and the UK, both permanent members of the Security Council (one of the UN's 'competent organs' that may take action to prevent and suppress acts of genocide under the 1948 Genocide Convention) and endowed with the most extensive diplomatic and military capabilities in Europe, and Germany, which, given its past as the country that carried out the Holocaust, considers itself to have a particular moral responsibility to ensure that such a man-made cataclysm never happens again. Where other European governments – such as Belgium and the Czech Republic (with respect to Rwanda) or the Netherlands (with respect particularly to Srebrenica, Bosnia) – have taken a notable position or played a significant role, then they are included in the analysis, but it is not possible to cover the debates in all European countries in one book.

Norms and their influence

This book gauges whether and how European governments have been affected by the international legal framework against genocide and in particular the 1948 Genocide Convention. It is contended first of all that this framework is a 'legal norm', in the sense that it codifies expectations for state behaviour, firstly not to commit genocide and secondly to prevent and punish genocide.

The study of norms in international relations has largely been undertaken within the framework of 'constructivism', and hence the starting point of this book is the constructivist work on international norms. Constructivism puts forward three propositions regarding international relations: (1) 'to the extent that structures shape the behaviour of states and other actors, normative and ideational structures are as important as material structures'; (2) the social identities of states condition state interests and actions; (3) normative and ideational structures exist because of the 'practices of knowledgeable social agents, which makes them human artefacts amenable to transformation'.[7] These three propositions differentiate constructivism from two other mainstream approaches to international relations. Realism stresses the influence of material structures, and particularly that of the distribution of power in an anarchical international system, on state behaviour and interactions between states, which produces latent or outright conflict between them; constructivists instead specify that 'anarchy is what states make of it' and that cooperation rather than conflict can be an outcome of such interactions.[8] Liberal (or rational) institutionalism posits that security and the pursuit of power may not necessarily top a hierarchy of individual state interests (so economic wealth and other interests may be more important), but does not draw the connection between interests and the identity of states that constructivism does.

The role of international law is interpreted quite differently in the three approaches. Realism is the most dismissive: norms, legal rules, institutions are merely masks for state power, and states comply with them only insofar as they do not damage national interests. In liberal institutionalism, law, norms and institutions are very important – they are created by states to help foster or 'lock in' cooperation, by reducing transaction costs and enabling reciprocity. But rules and institutions operate in areas of 'low politics'; when it comes to 'high politics' (issues of security) they are much less likely to constrain states. In constructivism, international law is part of the social structure of the international system. Furthermore, international law affects state identity and interests: states begin to see themselves as compliers with international law, and interpret their interests accordingly. However, states may interpret law and its 'power' differently, and have different views on the legitimacy of different rules, an issue that has not been dealt with at length by constructivists.[9]

In neither liberal institutionalism nor constructivism has much work been done on the potential impact of different types of rules or

[7] Christian Reus-Smit, 'The Politics of International Law', in Christian Reus-Smit, ed., *The Politics of International Law* (Cambridge: Cambridge University Press, 2004), pp. 21–22.

[8] Alexander Wendt, 'Anarchy is What States Make of It: The Social Construction of Power Politics', *International Organization*, vol. 46, no. 2 (1992).

[9] See the discussion in Anthony Clark Arend, 'Do Legal Rules Matter? International Law and International Politics', *Virginia Journal of International Law*, vol. 38, no. 2 (1998).

norms. Norms are 'collective expectations about proper behavior for a given identity'.[10] But, as Martha Finnemore notes, there are different types of norms and they may have different influences on states. She points to professional, moral, and cultural norms, as well as legal norms, and suggests that legal norms could have distinctive effects. This could be because states use their coercive powers when norms have a legal status; or because many foreign policy-makers have legal training; or because western, bureaucratic culture invests particular authority in law. She then suggests a research question: 'Do legal norms, in fact, receive more deference and command more compliance than other kinds of norms independent of state enforcement'?[11] Christian Reus-Smit notes that many constructivists argue that since legal norms are more codified than social norms, 'they more powerfully constitute actors' identities, interests and actions'. However, he argues that 'the distinction constructivists draw between social and legal norms is inconsistent and underdeveloped', with some denying a distinction and others emphasising it.[12]

In this study, norms are seen as having three possible impacts on states: requiring action (to comply with the norm), constraining action (again, to comply with the norm), and enabling action (which could be justified as in compliance with the norm). The last two impacts follow Nicholas Wheeler's argument that norms can both constrain *and* enable actors. That is, 'decision-makers are inhibited by legitimation concerns', which constrain action that cannot be legitimised as conforming with a norm; norms can also provide actors 'with public legitimating reasons to justify actions, but they do not determine that an action will take place.'[13] In addition, there can be obligations to take action to comply with a norm (to change domestic legislation, for example). In other words, there are things states must do, cannot do, and could justify doing, in accordance with the norm.

[10] Ronald L. Jepperson, Alexander Wendt and Peter J. Katzenstein, 'Norms, Identity, and Culture in National Security', in Peter J. Katzenstein, ed., *The Culture of National Security: Norms and Identity in World Politics* (New York: Columbia University Press, 1996), p. 54.

[11] Martha Finnemore, 'Are Legal Norms Distinctive?', *New York University Journal of International Law and Politics*, vol. 32, no.3 (Spring 2000), quote on p. 704.

[12] Reus-Smit, 'The Politics of International Law', pp. 3–4.

[13] Nicholas Wheeler, *Saving Strangers: Humanitarian Intervention in International Society* (Oxford: Oxford University Press, 2000), p. 9.

This book argues that there are actually two norms against genocide: a legal one and a social one. In the case of the Genocide Convention, we have the legal norm: that is, we have a definition of genocide and a set of rules by which states are to punish and prevent genocide which have been codified in a treaty. The legal norm can evolve (and has, to a limited extent), but is defined by the text of the convention and the various interpretations of that text provided in the case law developed in national and international tribunals.

We also have a social norm – with a wider definition of genocide, and a different, more demanding, conception of what states should do in the case of genocide, which goes beyond what is codified in the Genocide Convention. The social norm is consistent with a cosmopolitan moral perspective, and is espoused by cosmopolitan theorists, but is also widely shared by commentators, journalists, NGOs, and the like – which is why the term 'social norm' is used here rather than 'moral norm'. To some extent, the Genocide Convention (the legal norm) codifies the social norm – the Convention would not have come into being were it not for the widely-felt imperative to ensure the Holocaust never again happened. But the social norm is broader than the legal norm, and in some uses, reflects subsequent disappointment with the Genocide Convention's limited provisions to 'prevent and punish' genocide. A brief illustration of the differences between the legal and social norms is given here; the differences are expanded upon further below.

The first difference is the definition of genocide. As Martin Shaw notes, there is much 'theoretical confusion surrounding the concept.'[14] The definition in the Genocide Convention is widely taken as the authoritative definition (especially by policy-makers) but it has been harshly criticised by many as being so narrow and constricting as to exclude most atrocities. Application of the Convention's definition is also not always a straightforward matter when it comes to concrete cases. However, the theoretical confusion derives also from the fact that there is wider definition of genocide common in public parlance, which is broader than that of the Convention. For example, it is common to refer to the 'Cambodian genocide', which took place under the Khmer Rouge between 1975 and 1979, but the use of the term genocide is contested in policy-making and academic circles on the

[14] Martin Shaw, *What is Genocide?* (Cambridge: Polity Press, 2007), p. 37.

grounds that the killing of the Cambodian people does not properly fit the definition in the 1948 Convention.

The second difference is what action is required of states in the event of genocide. Under the Genocide Convention, states 'undertake to prevent and punish' genocide. What 'prevent and punish' means in practice is very much a matter for debate: the Convention itself does not mandate any *particular* action with respect to 'prevention', but it does set out certain requirements regarding the punishment of genocide. Thus the legal norm is clear only with respect to the obligation to punish, in a court of law, perpetrators of genocide. However, the social norm requires a response going beyond the legal norm: genocide is seen as raising 'a legal, political and moral obligation, an irrevocable imperative that cannot be pushed aside but must be acted on ...'[15] Particularly since the end of the Cold War, the social norm entails an expectation, if not an obligation, that states will take measures to *stop* genocide, measures which ultimately should include the use of coercive military force if that is what it takes to stop the killing. The social norm calls for whatever it takes to ensure 'Never again Auschwitz'. In sum, the legal norm against genocide constrains action (the carrying out of genocide), enables it (to prevent genocide), and requires it (to punish genocide); the social norm goes further by requiring some sort of intervention to try to stop a genocide that is ongoing.

The questions at the heart of this book, then, are do the legal and social norms against genocide have an impact on European state behaviour, interests or even identity? Or do European states ignore them when it is in their interests to do so? And do the legal and social norms have different impacts on European states, with the legal norm 'more powerfully constituting their identities, interests and actions' (to use Reus-Smit's phrase)? One possibility explored in this book is that governments avoid using the term genocide not because they wish to avoid the obligations arising under the Genocide Convention but because they wish to avoid the obligations arising from the social norm. While the obligations under the social norm may be indeterminate, certainly compared to the clarity of the obligation to punish genocide in the Genocide Convention, it is that indeterminacy that also frightens governments: they could be pushed into

[15] Lene Hansen, *Security as Practice: Discourse Analysis and the Bosnian War* (London: Routledge, 2006), p. 140.

taking actions they do not wish to take. But if they must recognise genocide – because the facts simply cannot be ignored – then they could 'take refuge' under the legal norm and cite their compliance with the Genocide Convention, thus deflecting pressures to comply with the social norm.

Genocide and the Europeans seeks to unpack the influence of the two norms against genocide on European governments. It first reviews European attitudes towards the negotiation and ratification of the Genocide Convention and considers whether and how European states sought to ensure that they were in compliance with the Convention. Most of the book then focuses on the role the legal and social norms against genocide have played in the foreign policy of European states, that is, in their responses to possible genocides in other countries. In so doing, it first considers whether they have used the term genocide, and if so, does it fit the definition of the Genocide Convention, or the wider definition of the social norm? It then analyses the action taken by European governments in response to suspected or apparent acts of genocide. How have European governments justified their positions, and have they referred to the legal or the social norm? Have they argued that either norm enables (or requires) action to be taken to prevent or punish or stop genocide? Have they argued that the norm does not apply because the case is not one of genocide, and is that a justification for not taking action? Is the social norm used instrumentally, when governments want to justify intervention, or do governments perceive there to be an 'irrevocable imperative', so they must act in the event of genocide? Research on US policy has illustrated that in the 1990s, the reluctance to name the Rwandan genocide stemmed from a desire to avoid creating a moral imperative to act to stop it, but that under the Bush Administration, naming the Darfur genocide was seen as a substitute for coercive action.[16] Have European governments followed similar reasoning? Is naming a genocide now seen as a substitute for action?

The emphasis is on the positions and arguments presented by governments publicly – to national audiences (including parliaments and the media) and international audiences (including the UN and the European Union). The research thus relies above all on primary

[16] Eric A. Heinze, 'The Rhetoric of Genocide in U.S. Foreign Policy: Rwanda and Darfur Compared', *Political Science Quarterly*, vol. 122, no. 3 (2007).

sources such as official government papers, speeches and declarations by foreign policy-makers and diplomats.

The rest of this chapter provides a brief historical account of the origins of the word 'genocide' and of the Genocide Convention – both of which can be attributed to one extraordinary individual, Raphael Lemkin. The chapter then elaborates on some of the key issues raised by the Convention and subsequent development of the legal framework, including the thorny issue of the definition of genocide and the obligations on states that arise from the Convention.

Raphael Lemkin and the push for an international convention on genocide

Rarely can we so clearly point to the pivotal role of one individual in developing an international norm as we can in the case of the prevention and punishment of genocide. Raphael Lemkin (1900–1959), a lawyer, linguist, and Polish-Jewish refugee in the United States, not only invented the term 'genocide', but was the driving force behind the approval of a United Nations General Assembly resolution on genocide as a crime in international law (on 11 December 1946), the drafting and approval of the United Nations Convention on the Prevention and Punishment of the Crime of Genocide (9 December 1948), and the subsequent attempts to have the convention ratified by as many states as possible. The inscription on Lemkin's grave in Mount Hebron, New York City is succinct but entirely apt: 'Dr Raphael Lemkin (1900–1959), the Father of the Genocide Convention'.[17]

[17] Until the beginning of this decade, Lemkin's role was only occasionally acknowledged – perhaps because the Genocide Convention was rarely invoked during the Cold War, perhaps because Lemkin was not the easiest individual to get along with, given his single-minded concentration (some would say obsession) on the issue of genocide. He was called a 'crank', 'pest', 'nag', 'dreamer', 'fanatic', and worse. In 2001, William Korey published an *Epitaph for Raphael Lemkin* (Jacob Blaustein Institute for the Advancement of Human Rights of the American Jewish Committee) which contains some biographical information (available at www.ajcarchives.org/main.php?GroupingId=3861 [last accessed 13 April 2010]). There is only one full-length biography of him: John Cooper, *Raphael Lemkin and the Struggle for the Genocide Convention* (Houndmills: Palgrave, 2008). Samantha Power devoted four chapters of her book, *'A Problem from Hell'* to Lemkin's work. A previous biography, James J. Martin, *The Man Who Invented Genocide: The Public Career and Consequences of Raphael Lemkin*

The term 'genocide' was introduced in Lemkin's book, *Axis Rule in Occupied Europe*, published in 1944.[18] He invented it because he was not satisfied with any other term to describe the precise phenomenon: barbarity, race murder or mass murder didn't capture the motivation for the crime, which is based on racial, ethnic, or religious considerations. The term more accurately described the 'attempt to destroy a nation and obliterate its cultural personality.'[19] He created the word from the Greek word *genos* (race, tribe) and the Latin *cide* (killing), to indicate the 'destruction of a nation or of an ethnic group'. The term is thus similar to terms such as tyrannicide, infanticide, and homicide. Clearly mindful of the practices of the German occupiers in much of Europe (particularly Poland), he intended it

> to signify a coordinated plan of different actions aiming at the destruction of essential foundations of the life of national groups, with the aim of annihilating the groups themselves. The objectives of such a plan would be disintegration of the political and social institutions, of culture, language, national feelings, religion, and the economic existence of national groups, and the destruction of the personal security, liberty, health, dignity, and even the lives of the individuals belonging to such groups. Genocide is directed against the national group as an entity, and the actions involved are directed against individuals, not in their individual capacity, but as members of the national group.[20]

(Torrance, CA: Institute for Historical Review, 1984), was written by a Holocaust denier, and cannot be taken as a serious piece of research: it is highly anti-Semitic and Martin consulted none of Lemkin's papers (Cooper, *Raphael Lemkin*, 2008, pp. 2–3). There is some doubt about the year of Lemkin's birth: his gravestone indicates 1900, but other sources state 1901. Lemkin's papers are spread across three archives (though much material also appears to have been lost): the New York Public Library, the American Jewish Historical Society, and the American Jewish Archives. See Tanya Elder, 'What You See Before Your Eyes; Documenting Raphael Lemkin's Life by Exploring his Archival Papers, 1900–1959', *Journal of Genocide Research*, vol. 7, no. 4 (2005).

[18] Raphael Lemkin, *Axis Rule in Occupied Europe: Laws of Occupation, Analysis of Government, Proposals for Redress* (Washington, DC: Carnegie Endowment for International Peace, 1944).

[19] See the discussion in Korey, *Epitaph for Raphael Lemkin*, part 1, 2001, quote on p. 21.

[20] Lemkin, *Axis Rule*, p. 79. The book is almost entirely devoted to reproducing the various laws and decrees issued by the occupiers, analysis of which unveils their genocidal policies.

In August 1941, British Prime Minister Winston Churchill decried the 'barbaric fury' of the Nazis, whose armies were exterminating whole districts as they advanced: 'we are in the presence of a crime without a name'. By inventing the term 'genocide', Lemkin gave the crime a name.[21] As is evident from his definition above, Lemkin did not consider the Nazi extermination of European Jews as the only case of genocide; in fact from 1947 until his death he was researching and writing a book on the history of genocide, which included cases from antiquity (the destruction of Carthage by Rome) and colonial rule (including the Spanish conquest of Latin America, the Belgian reign in Congo, and the annihilation of the Hereros of south-west Africa by Germany).

Lemkin's work influenced the officials working on preparing indictments for the Nuremberg trials, because genocide was included under one of the counts of the indictment: defendants were charged with conducting genocide.[22] The Nuremberg trial of major war criminals, though, never used the term genocide.[23] Instead, it convicted Nazi leaders of 'crimes against humanity' perpetrated after the war began on 1 September 1939; therefore, 'only group extermination carried out during the war was held punishable.'[24] The crimes against humanity perpetrated by the Nazis were inextricably linked to the aggressive war they waged in Europe; 'inhuman acts and persecutions of the civilian population were punishable only when committed during or in connection with the war.'[25]

This, for Lemkin, was bitterly disappointing. In *Axis Rule in Occupied Europe*, Lemkin had argued that genocide was a problem not just of war, but of peacetime as well. He had also called for an international treaty requiring states to enact provisions protecting minority

[21] Raphael Lemkin, 'Genocide', *The American Scholar*, vol. 15, part 2 (1946), 227.

[22] Though Lemkin did not claim to have directly influenced the prosecutors to include a charge on genocide. Cooper, *Raphael Lemkin*, p. 62.

[23] Schabas, *Genocide in International Law*, 2nd edition, p. 44. 'Genocide' was used in later trials and judgments (pp. 48–52).

[24] 'Genocide: A Commentary on the Convention', *The Yale Law Journal*, vol. 58, no. 7 (1949), 1143.

[25] Raphael Lemkin, 'Genocide as a Crime under International Law', *The American Journal of International Law*, vol. 41, no. 1 (1947), 148. The differences between crimes against humanity and genocide are discussed further in the next section.

groups and punishing genocidal practices. After the Nuremberg judgment, he pressed for the 'necessity of establishing a rule of international law which would make sure that "revolting and horrible acts" committed by a government on its own citizens, to use the words of the Nuremberg Tribunal, should in future not go unpunished.'[26] In a proposal for an international treaty, Lemkin suggested that 'the crime of genocide should be recognized therein as a conspiracy to exterminate national, religious or racial groups. The overt acts of such a conspiracy may consist of attacks against life, liberty or property of members of such groups merely because of their affiliation with such groups.'[27] As William Schabas notes, 'it was Nuremberg's failure to recognize the international criminality of atrocities committed in peacetime that prompted the first initiatives at codifying the crime of genocide.'[28]

Quickly identifying the new United Nations General Assembly as the most appropriate place to start lobbying for a new rule, he lobbied member state delegates in the hallways of the then meeting place at Lake Success, New York (it is inconceivable that today a member of the public would have such access to diplomats at the UN). He drafted a resolution in October 1946, and convinced the delegates of Cuba, India and Panama to sponsor it in the General Assembly.[29] After a couple of months of discussion in the Legal Committee (Sixth Committee) the resolution was approved by the General Assembly unanimously, on 11 December 1946 (see Appendix 1). The resolution (no. 96 (I)) declared genocide to be a crime under international law, and that 'genocide is a denial of the right of existence of entire human groups, as homicide is the denial of the right to live of individual human beings'. It acknowledged that 'many instances of such crimes of genocide have occurred when racial, religious, political or other

[26] Lemkin, 'Genocide as a Crime', 148.

[27] Lemkin, 'Genocide', 230.

[28] William A. Schabas, 'Origins of the Genocide Convention: From Nuremberg to Paris', *Case Western Reserve Journal of International Law*, vol. 40, nos. 1 and 2 (2007–08), 36.

[29] He approached small countries for their support, believing that large countries had bureaucratic processes which meant they already had taken decisions regarding the first UN General Assembly meeting. Cooper, *Raphael Lemkin*, p. 79. See also Lemkin's own account of the push for the resolution in 'Genocide as a Crime', 148–9. According to Korey, the US Ambassador told Lemkin he would support the resolution, but that he should approach other smaller countries to sponsor it. The British (notably unenthusiastic) and the French gave him a similar answer. Korey, *Epitaph*, p. 27.

groups have been destroyed, entirely or in part.' More importantly, the resolution requested that the Economic and Social Council draw up a draft convention on the crime of genocide.

Over the next two years, the Genocide Convention took shape. First UN Secretary-General Trygve Lie asked three experts, including Lemkin, to help write a draft. This draft was then considered by an Ad Hoc Committee established by the Economic and Social Council (ECOSOC), the Sixth Committee, and the General Assembly as a whole. On 9 December 1948, the General Assembly adopted the Convention for the Prevention and Punishment of the Crime of Genocide, by a vote of 55 to none, with three countries absent: Costa Rica, El Salvador and South Africa. Thus Lemkin invented the term genocide (now universally used, even if the precise definition of the term is contested) and successfully pressed for an international treaty outlawing the practice, which, as discussed further in this book, has had a profound impact on state behaviour.

The Genocide Convention has nineteen articles, of which about half are substantive (see Appendix 2). In article 1, the parties confirm that genocide, 'whether committed in time of peace or in time of war', is an international crime which 'they undertake to prevent and punish'. Article 2 contains the definition of genocide:

> any of the following acts committed with intent to destroy, in whole or in part, a national, ethnical, racial or religious group, as such:
>
> - killing members of the group;
> - causing serious bodily or mental harm to members of the group;
> - deliberately inflicting on the group conditions of life calculated to bring about its physical destruction in whole or in part;
> - imposing measures intended to prevent births within the group;
> - forcibly transferring children of the group to another group.

This definition is notably more limited than Lemkin's original conception, which included the notion of 'cultural genocide'. It is also more restricted than the definition implied in the 1946 General Assembly resolution, which included political groups. In part, the narrowness of this definition has sparked the debates about naming genocide. For now, it is important to record that the definition arose out of a process of intergovernmental negotiation: it was the lowest common denominator of what the negotiating states could agree.

Under article 4, persons committing genocide or other acts (as set out in article 3) including conspiracy to commit genocide or complicity in genocide, shall be punished, regardless of whether they are constitutionally responsible rulers, officials or private individuals. The convention thus indicates that individuals, not states or governments, are to be held responsible for committing the crime – a conception that generated much dissent among some European governments.

States are to enact domestic legislation implementing the convention, under article 5. Enforcement of the convention is then provided in three articles. Under article 6, persons charged with genocide shall be tried by a tribunal of the state in whose territory the act was committed, or by an 'international penal tribunal' (yet to be established). Under article 8, any contracting party can call upon the competent organs of the UN to take action appropriate for the prevention and suppression of acts of genocide. And in article 9, contracting parties can submit disputes relating to the interpretation, application or fulfilment of the convention to the International Court of Justice.

Forty-one states signed the Convention by the deadline of 31 December 1949; states that had not signed the Convention could still accede to it after that date.[30] In December 1949, a General Assembly resolution called upon states which were not members of the UN to accede to the Genocide Convention.[31] By October 1950, over twenty states had ratified the Convention, the number required to bring it into force, and the Convention entered into force on 12 January 1951.

The Genocide Convention is the first international human rights instrument to have been agreed in the post-Second World War era, but it is not considered to be one of the core international human rights treaties nor was it negotiated in any of the UN's machinery on human rights (the General Assembly's Third Committee, or the Human Rights Commission).[32] The Convention was over-shadowed right at the start by the adoption, on the following day, 10 December

[30] After it was approved by the General Assembly on 9 December 1948, the Convention was opened for signature until 31 December 1949 (article 11); signatories could then 'ratify' it. Any state after 1 January 1950 which had not signed it could 'accede' to the convention.

[31] UN General Assembly Resolution 368 (IV), 3 December 1949.

[32] The notion that the Genocide Convention is a human rights treaty needs to be nuanced: Human rights treaties don't typically define crimes, and a 'typical human rights treaty prohibits certain conduct by states but does not provide for the punishment of individuals'. John Quigley, *The Genocide*

1948, of the Universal Declaration of Human Rights. It is also one of the least widely ratified human rights treaties, with 141 parties thus far.[33] William Schabas maintains that this is because of unease with the 'onerous obligations that the treaty imposes, such as prosecution or extradition of individuals, including heads of State.'[34] Nonetheless, the International Court of Justice in 1951 emphasised that the prohibition on genocide was binding, even on states that were not parties to the Convention, because the prohibition on genocide was vested in the principles of civilised nations.[35]

Throughout the Cold War, the Genocide Convention was rarely invoked by states – though accusations of genocide were made fairly frequently by various non-governmental organisations and occasionally government officials and members of parliament (MPs), as Chapter 3 shows. But the Convention acquired new relevance with the end

Convention: An International Law Analysis (Aldershot: Ashgate, 2006), p. 79. Lemkin himself had been very concerned to keep genocide separate from human rights issues – he feared that the proposed UN Human Rights Covenant, and particularly the general formulation regarding the deprivation of life therein, would dilute the legal prohibition against genocide. '[T]he dividing line between the crime of Genocide, which changes the course of civilization on one hand, and uncivilized behaviour of individuals on the other hand – disappears.' He argued that not every matter of internal legislation (such as against murder) should become a matter of international concern: 'international jurisdiction is exceptional'. If this distinction is not kept, then international tensions will arise over interference in domestic affairs – and confusion will result. The value of the Genocide Convention was that it overrode the UN Charter's prohibition against intervention in domestic affairs. Raphael Lemkin, 'The U.N. is Killing its Own Child: The Danger to the Genocide Convention' (no date), in New York Public Library, Lemkin papers, reel 4.

33 As of 28 September 2009. Compare with other treaties: International Covenant on Civil and Political Rights (165 parties); International Covenant on Economic, Social and Cultural Rights (160 parties), Convention against Torture (146 parties, but it entered into force only in 1987), Convention on the Elimination of all Forms of Racial Discrimination (173 parties), Convention on the Elimination of all Forms of Discrimination against Women (186 parties), and Convention on the Rights of the Child (193 parties).

34 Schabas, *Genocide in International Law*, 2nd edition, p. 3.

35 See Jan Wouters and Sten Verhoeven, 'The Prohibition of Genocide as a Norm of *Ius Cogens* and its Implications for the Enforcement of the Law of Genocide', *International Criminal Law Review*, vol. 5, no. 3 (2005), 404. The case is Reservations to the Genocide Convention, Advisory Opinion of 28 May 1951.

of the bipolar confrontation and the concurrent outbreak of shocking violence in several areas of the world. Genocide was included as one of the crimes punishable by the two ad hoc international criminal tribunals created to deal with the violence in the former Yugoslavia and Rwanda. And it was included as one of the three core crimes punishable by the International Criminal Court (ICC), which began operating in July 2002.[36] In all three cases, the definition of genocide remained that of the 1948 Convention, and in all three cases, it was made clear that genocide was a separate category of crime, not reducible to crimes against humanity or war crimes.

Furthermore, the debates throughout the 1990s about how the international community should respond to mass atrocities, genocide, crimes against humanity and the like, led to the development – and apparent universal acceptance – of the principle of 'the responsibility to protect'. In September 2005, a UN summit that considered various reform issues, backed the principle.[37] Specifically, the UN members declared: 'Each individual state has the responsibility to protect its populations from genocide, war crimes, ethnic cleansing and crimes against humanity ... We are prepared to take collective action, in a timely and decisive manner, through the Security Council, in accordance with the Charter, including Chapter VII, on a case-by-case basis and in cooperation with relevant regional organizations as appropriate, should peaceful means be inadequate and national authorities manifestly fail to protect their populations from genocide,

[36] A fourth crime, aggression, will also be covered by the ICC, once it has been defined (no definition could be agreed during the negotiations to create the ICC).

[37] This principle originated in the Canadian-sponsored International Commission on Intervention and State Sovereignty, which issued a report in 2001 including it. Rather than focus on the rights and wrongs of humanitarian intervention, the Commission suggested focussing instead on the responsibility of all states to protect their own populations, and on the responsibility of the international community to take appropriate action if a state fails to do so. That appropriate action could entail coercive humanitarian intervention, but only as a last resort. See, for example, Gareth Evans, 'The Responsibility to Protect: An Idea Whose Time Has Come ... and Gone?', *International Relations*, vol. 22, no. 3 (2008); and Alex J. Bellamy, *Responsibility to Protect* (Cambridge: Polity, 2009). In 2004, the principle was backed by the UN Secretary-General's High-Level Panel on Threats, Challenges and Change, which informed the debates on reform at the 2005 World Summit.

war crimes, ethnic cleansing and crimes against humanity.'[38] The extent to which this principle augments the legal norm against genocide is dubious, but it can be seen as a development of the social norm, as discussed further below.

Issues for governments

The Genocide Convention and further legal developments, as well as the case law generated by the two ad hoc international criminal tribunals and the International Court of Justice, have clarified some issues relating to the legal norm against genocide, but left others open to debate. In particular, there is still no consensus on what governments are expected or required to do in case of a genocide occurring outside their territory. Three issues are discussed in this section, and all three involve competing or intersecting conceptions of treaty law, customary law and the social norm.

The first is the existence or not of a hierarchy of international crimes. Three crimes have been considered serious enough to merit definition in the statute of the International Criminal Court: genocide, crimes against humanity and war crimes. War crimes are generally understood to be violations of the laws of war as set out particularly in the four Geneva Conventions of 1949. The Nuremberg Charter (the basis for the Nuremberg trials) first defined crimes against humanity, but they have not been codified in a treaty. The ICC statute defines crimes against humanity as acts that occur during an attack on a civilian population such as murder, extermination, torture, rape and persecution 'against any identifiable group or collectivity on political, racial, national, ethnic, cultural, religious, gender ... or other grounds.' There is an obvious overlap with the concept of genocide, but until recently, the understanding had been that genocide could occur during times of peace or war, while crimes against humanity occurred during war. Judgments of international criminal tribunals have eroded this distinction, in that crimes against humanity are not only associated with armed conflict, though there is still the broad view that genocide and crimes against humanity are distinct crimes.[39]

[38] UN General Assembly Resolution 60/1, 2005 World Summit outcome, A/RES/60/1 (24 October 2005), paragraphs 138–9.

[39] See the discussion in Schabas, 'Origins of the Genocide Convention', 49–55.

But is genocide the worst crime of all? William Schabas maintains that genocide belongs at the apex of a pyramid of international crimes: it is the 'crime of crimes'.[40] In a 1985 report on prevention and punishment of genocide for the UN Commission on Human Rights, Benjamin Whitaker argued:

> Genocide is the ultimate crime and the gravest violation of human rights it is possible to commit. Consequently, it is difficult to conceive of a heavier responsibility for the international community and the Human Rights bodies of the United Nations than to undertake any effective steps possible to prevent and punish genocide in order to deter its recurrence.[41]

Likewise, the preparatory work on the International Criminal Court, conducted by the International Law Commission, reinforced this point. The rapporteur noted that, 'Among what were described as "crime of crimes", genocide was the worst of all. Moreover, it was a crime that was still being committed.'[42]

If genocide is considered to be graver, or even just different, than other crimes, then the reactions of governments should presumably be differentiated, with genocide attracting an appropriately graver response. Alain Destexhe has argued that genocide 'is the first and greatest of the crimes against humanity both because of its scale and the intent behind it: the destruction of a group. It is, therefore, a crime that obliges the international community to respond: The elimination of any group that is representative of the human race must affect the whole human race.'[43] Or, as Henry Shue has argued:

> The commission of genocidal massacre seems more heinous than the commission of the same number of random killings because, perhaps, of the diabolically evil character of systematic, calculated murders combined with a conviction of one's own superiority to other human beings so strong as to permit one to adopt a conscious policy of exterminating them. Thus, in my view, it would be preposterous to suggest that there is a universal

[40] Schabas, *Genocide in International Law*, 2nd edition, p. 11.

[41] United Nations Economic and Social Council, Revised and updated report on the question of the prevention and punishment of genocide prepared by Mr B. Whitaker, (2 July 1985, p. 5) document no. E/CN.4/Sub.2/1985/6.

[42] Cited in Schabas, *Genocide in International Law*, 2nd edition, p. 104.

[43] Alain Destexhe, 'The Third Genocide', *Foreign Policy*, no. 97 (Winter 1994/95), 4.

negative duty not to commit genocide but that there is no positive duty to protect intended victims.[44]

But as Schabas notes now, 'there are almost no distinctions to be made in terms of the legal consequences that flow from characterizing a crime as "genocide" or "crimes against humanity" or "war crimes"'.[45] Van den Herik finds that 'both ad hoc tribunals have maintained that there is no abstract hierarchy between genocide and crimes against humanity ... Hence, from a legal perspective, genocide is not a graver crime than crimes against humanity.' A residual feeling is nonetheless apparent that the judges feel there is something special about genocide that makes it more serious – the destruction of human groups not just people.[46] David Scheffer has argued that the three crimes (genocide, crimes against humanity, war crimes) should be folded into the larger category of 'atrocity crime', which would thus eliminate the need to try to distinguish genocide from the other two crimes – and thus eliminate much of the controversy regarding use of the term genocide.[47] While there may be a legal argument for this, it should be noted that the social norm against genocide certainly articulates that genocide is not only different, but more serious, which demands a different, more serious response.

This book considers the views and practices of European governments. Do they view genocide as different and/or as a graver crime than other serious crimes? Do their responses to atrocities differ if genocide is alleged or not?

[44] Henry Shue, 'Limiting Sovereignty', in Jennifer Welsh, ed., *Humanitarian Intervention and International Relations* (Oxford: Oxford University Press, 2004), p. 18.

[45] William A. Schabas, 'Semantics of Substance? David Scheffer's Welcome Proposal to Strengthen Criminal Accountability for Atrocities', *Genocide Studies and Prevention*, vol. 2, no. 1 (2007), 34–5. A member of the German Bundestag whom I interviewed in October 2008 insisted that one should not try to separate out the three crimes of genocide, crimes against humanity and war crimes; doing so was a useless exercise and only led to disputes about exact definitions.

[46] Larissa van den Herik, 'The Schism between the Legal and the Social Concept of Genocide in Light of the Responsibility to Protect', in Ralph Henham and Paul Behrens, eds., *The Criminal Law of Genocide: International, Comparative and Contextual Aspects* (Aldershot: Ashgate, 2007), p. 91.

[47] David Scheffer, 'Genocide and Atrocity Crimes', *Genocide Studies and Prevention*, vol. 1, no. 3 (2006).

The second issue for governments is the definition of genocide, which highlights a distinction between the legal and social norms. As already noted above, the legal norm – the definition in the Convention – is more limited than Lemkin's original conception, in that it excludes the notion of 'cultural genocide', and contains a quite limited conception of 'groups'. And when it comes to applying the norm in actual cases, there is disagreement about the exact definition. Judges, prosecutors, defence lawyers, government legal advisers, and so on, may disagree on whether the evidence adequately shows that this or that individual can be held responsible for committing acts of genocide. The notion of 'intent' in particular – and what indicates evidence of it – is a large bone of contention in such legal debates.[48] As Antje Wiener argues, 'contestation is to be expected', even in the case of legal norms, 'which require social institutions to enhance understanding and identify meaning that is normative practice.'[49]

Case law has addressed issues such as '*intent* to *destroy*, in whole or *in part*'. One of the biggest legal controversies of the 1990s was whether 'ethnic cleansing' was an act of genocide. The ad hoc tribunals and the International Court of Justice have ruled that it is not: expulsion of a group from a given territory is not the same as physical destruction of the group. In 2007, the ICJ put it as thus:

> [n]either the intent, as a matter of policy, to render an area 'ethnically homogenous' nor the operations that may be carried out to implement such policy, can *as such* be designated as genocide: the intent that characterizes genocide is 'to destroy, in whole or in part' a particular group, and deportation or displacement of the members of a group, even if effected by force, is not necessarily equivalent to destruction of that group, nor is such destruction an automatic consequence of the displacement.[50]

Schabas warns that there would be 'undesirable consequences to enlarging or diluting the definition of genocide. This weakens the terrible stigma associated with the crime and demeans the suffering of

[48] I am grateful to Gerry Simpson for pointing this out to me.

[49] Antje Wiener, 'Enacting Meaning-In-Use: Qualitative Research on Norms and International Relations', *Review of International Studies*, vol. 35, no. 1 (2009), 179.

[50] Cited in William A. Schabas, 'Genocide and the International Court of Justice: Finally a Duty to Prevent the Crime of Crimes', *Genocide Studies and Prevention*, vol. 2, no. 2 (2007), 109.

its victims. It is also likely to enfeeble whatever commitment States may believe they have to prevent the crime. The broader and more uncertain the definition, the less responsibility States will be prepared to assume.'[51]

But this position is controversial. Numerous social scientists and other observers, as well as victims, contest the legal definition. Caroline Fournet is particularly scathing about the definition of genocide in the Convention: 'it is nevertheless doubtful whether the crime had to be so narrowly defined that its definition would in fact not cover one single case of genocide'.[52] The requirements of genocide 'are unduly restrictive, so much so that they constitute a clear obstacle to the qualification of the crime of genocide and, in turn, a clear obstacle to its adequate prosecution and effective punishment'.[53] She argues that the definition of genocide referred to in the UN General Assembly's 1946 Resolution – which is broader than the Convention's – should be seen as the more accurate reflection of customary international law. 'Resolution 96 (I) did nothing less than codify an existing peremptory norm of international law'.[54] The Genocide Convention thus weakened and unduly restricted the customary law, and the prohibition in the Resolution should apply instead. However, customary law is generally identified as a mix of state practice conforming to the norm and the belief that there is a legal obligation (*opinion juris*).[55] If *state* practice does not conform to a wider definition of genocide, then it would be difficult to establish that there is a different definition in customary law. As will be seen throughout this book, the definition of genocide used by European governments is most often that of the

[51] Schabas, *Genocide in International Law*, 2nd edition, p. 10, and see pp. 221–34 on ethnic cleansing and genocide.

[52] Caroline Fournet, *The Crime of Destruction and the Law of Genocide: Their Impact on Collective Memory* (Aldershot: Ashgate, 2007), p. 37. Likewise, Leila Sadat has argued that of the more than 100 million civilians killed in the past 70 years, only six to eight million of them have fallen within the reach of the Genocide Convention, as applied by international courts and tribunals. Sadat, 'The Crime against Humanity Initiative', in Nick Donovan, ed., *The Enforcement of International Criminal Law* (Laxton, Nottinghamshire: Aegis Trust, 2009), p. 21.

[53] Fournet, *The Crime of Destruction*, p. 40.

[54] Fournet, *The Crime of Destruction*, p. 104.

[55] Identifying these features, however, is a matter of debate. See Richard Price, 'Emerging Customary Norms and Anti-Personnel Landmines', in Reus-Smit,

Genocide Convention; only the German government has used a wider definition of the term (encompassing ethnic cleansing).

Many social scientists have taken a different starting point when defining genocide, sometimes elaborating on Lemkin's original conception.[56] As Jacques Semelin argues, why should social scientists start with a definition that was reached by a process of intergovernmental bargaining in 1948?[57] If this is a recurring social phenomenon that should be distinguished from other similar phenomenon, then social scientists could start the conceptualisation process from a different standpoint. Two alternative definitions are worth repeating here. Mark Levene defines genocide as such:

> Genocide occurs when a state, perceiving the integrity of its agenda to be threatened by an aggregate population – defined by the state as an organic collectivity, or series of collectivities – seeks to remedy the situation by the systematic, *en masse*, physical elimination of that aggregate, *in toto*, or until it is no longer perceived to represent a threat.[58]

For Levene, the state is clearly central, and the development of the international system of states is crucial in the occurrence of genocide: 'This study thus sees in the processes whereby that system was created both the primary well-springs and continuing motor to genocide.'[59]

Martin Shaw emphasises instead the connection between war and genocide and deliberately widens the definition of perpetrators beyond states. Thus he defines genocide as 'a form of violent social conflict, or war, between armed power organizations that aim to destroy civilian social groups and those groups and other actors who resist this destruction.' Genocidal action is 'action in which armed power organizations treat civilian social groups as enemies and aim to destroy their real or putative social power, by means of killing,

ed., *The Politics of International Law* (Cambridge: Cambridge University Press, 2004).

[56] A fair few abandon the term genocide altogether and substitute others: 'politicide', 'gendercide', 'ethnocide', 'democide', and 'auto-genocide' (this last one invented particularly to apply to the case of Cambodia under the Khmer Rouge). See Shaw, *What is Genocide?*, pp. 63–78.

[57] Jacques Semelin, 'What is "Genocide"?', *European Review of History – Revue européenne d'Histoire*, vol. 12, no. 1 (2005).

[58] Mark Levene, *The Meaning of Genocide* (London: I.B.Tauris, 2005), p. 35.

[59] Levene, *The Meaning of Genocide*, p. 205.

violence and coercion against individuals whom they regard as members of the groups.'[60] Furthermore, Shaw explicitly rejects attempts to separate out 'cleansing' from 'genocide': 'Expulsion of populations, so readily distinguished *from* genocide, turns out to be a central feature *of* it, and non-genocidal expulsion an illusory category.'[61]

Both Levene and Shaw extend the notion of 'groups': 'collectivity' in Levene's conception; 'civilian social group' in Shaw's. Their definitions are thus clearly closer to those of Lemkin, and of the 1946 UN General Assembly Resolution.

In public discourse, there is arguably an even wider understanding of the term. In 2008, the 'Genocide Prevention Task Force' – a group consisting of, among others, a former US Secretary of State (Madeleine Albright), a former US Defence Secretary (William S. Cohen) and a former US ambassador to the UN (Thomas R. Pickering) – put forth an expansive definition of genocide. Their concern was to avoid 'debates about its definition or application to constrain or distract policymakers from addressing the core problems it describes'. Therefore 'genocide and mass atrocities' was the preferred term, defined as 'large-scale and deliberate attacks on civilians'.[62]

'Genocide' as used in common parlance – the language of journalists and MPs and non-governmental organisations (NGOs) and activists and concerned members of the public – comes closer to these more expansive notions than that of the Genocide Convention. As we shall see in the European discourse surrounding particular purported genocides, the term is used much more often by those who are not in government than by those who are in government. The position of many observers, including journalists and activists, is that genocide does have a wider meaning and thus has occurred and occurs more often than is acknowledged by governments, or courts.[63]

60 Shaw, *What is Genocide?*, p. 154.

61 Shaw, *What is Genocide?*, p. 61.

62 Genocide Prevention Task Force, *Preventing Genocide: A Blueprint for U.S. Policymakers* (United States Holocaust Memorial Museum, the American Academy of Diplomacy and the Endowment of the United States Institute of Peace, 2008), pp. xxi-xxii. There is also a minority strain in public debates which objects to the use of the term genocide in particular cases because the only case of genocide is the Shoah. But the dominant discourse is one that uses a wider definition of the term.

63 Though clearly it is problematic when accusations of 'genocide' are tossed around as easily as happened, for example, when Russia accused Georgia of genocide against South Ossetians in August 2007.

The purpose of this book is not to take a stance on this or that particular definition. The point here is that there are other definitions of genocide, some of which date back to before the Genocide Convention was agreed. The relatively narrow definition of genocide in the Convention constitutes the legal norm. A more extensive definition constitutes the social norm. This book considers whether European governments use the definition in the Convention, or the wider definition of the social norm, when and if they use the term at all.

The third issue left open by the Genocide Convention is what obligations are required of governments to prevent genocide. The obligations regarding punishment are fairly clear cut. The Convention requires that individuals charged with genocide 'be tried by a competent tribunal of the State in the territory of which the act was committed', or by a future international criminal tribunal. The obligation on states parties is thus to try individuals for crimes committed within their territory. It is generally understood that this obligation does not prohibit states from trying their own nationals for crimes of genocide. States must also extradite suspects to the state that has jurisdiction. However, the Convention rules out universal jurisdiction, which means that states can prosecute offenders wherever the offence was committed, and whether the offender is a national or not. The Sixth Committee negotiations on the Convention explicitly rejected universal jurisdiction.[64] The statute of the International Criminal Court recognises only territorial and personal jurisdiction (that is, the Court has jurisdiction if the state on which the offence was committed is a party to the Statute, or if the person accused is a national of a state which is a party to the Statute). But customary law on this is evolving,

[64] Schabas, *Genocide in International Law*, 2nd edition, pp. 409–16. The Eichmann case is not considered to establish a precedent for universal jurisdiction. In 1960, Mossad agents captured the leading Nazi in Argentina, brought him back to Israel, where he was tried for 'crimes against the Jewish people', found guilty and executed. The Israeli court adopted a principle of universal jurisdiction, to justify trying him in Israel. Fournet argues that the fact that Israel did not use the Genocide Convention (though the definition of crimes committed against the Jewish people is similar to the Convention's definition of genocide, with the important additions of cultural genocide and incitement to hatred of Jews), illustrates the uselessness of the Convention: it simply cannot capture the specificity even of the Shoah. Fournet, *The Crime of Destruction*, pp. 113–16.

as many states have enacted legislation which allows universal jurisdiction for genocide, with no protest from other states.[65] Chapter 2 will review the situation in European states.

It has to be noted here as well that any prosecution for genocide happens after the fact – well after people have been murdered. Thus, if governments wait until there has been some sort of legal pronouncement on whether mass murder is a genocide or not, then it is too late to do much about it. The 'power of law' here may be such that it prevents any meaningful response to a purported genocide.

'Prevention' is much less clear, and there is little indication in the Genocide Convention as to what this entails. Under article 8, states parties 'may call upon the competent organs of the United Nations to take such action under the Charter of the United Nations as they consider appropriate for the prevention and suppression of acts of genocide'. Until 2004, this had never occurred. And what action the UN should take is also not clear: what is 'appropriate action'? What is certainly not spelled out is any obligation or right to intervene coercively to prevent or suppress genocide.

The situation under treaty law, the Genocide Convention, was clarified somewhat by the International Court of Justice (ICJ) in its recent ruling on *Bosnia* v. *Serbia*. The ICJ first established that, although not so explicitly stated, the effect of article 1 of the Convention is to prohibit states from themselves committing genocide. Furthermore, it confirmed that any state party to the Convention has an obligation to prevent genocide if it is happening outside its territory, where 'it has it in its power to contribute to restraining in any degree the commission of genocide.'[66] More specifically, the Court argued that:

> it is clear that the obligation in question is one of conduct and not one of result, in the sense that a State cannot be under an obligation to succeed, whatever the circumstances, in preventing the commission of genocide: the obligation of States parties is rather to employ all means reasonably available to them, so as to prevent genocide so far as possible. A State does not incur responsibility simply because the desired result is not achieved;

[65] Schabas, *Genocide in International Law*, 2nd edition, pp. 434–5.
[66] Cited in Schabas, 'Genocide and the International Court of Justice', 115.

responsibility is however incurred if the State manifestly failed to take all measures to prevent genocide which were within its power, and which might have contributed to preventing the genocide.[67]

But 'all means reasonably available to them' are not defined. The debate since the 1990s has centred on whether there is a right – or even a duty – to intervene coercively to stop atrocities from being committed. For some cosmopolitan political theorists the issue is clear. Terry Nardin has argued:

Failing to resist those who commit the crimes – genocide and other 'crimes against humanity' – that warrant international intervention is unjust in the same way that that [*sic*] failing to resist an international aggressor is unjust. It fails to uphold the laws of civilized existence against the rule of violence.[68]

Furthermore, the duty to do something falls not just on the 'international community' but on individual states:

Even if an international organization like the UN has a duty to intervene, it does not follow that no individual state has such a duty. On the contrary, if a state is in a position to provide assistance and no other state or organization is able to do so, it should provide that assistance. If it fails to act, it has acted unjustly and may be held responsible for its failure.[69]

Henry Shue notes that the weakness of the Genocide Convention is that it binds no one to anything: 'genocide is in theory punishable but in practice usually unchallenged while underway by anyone who could stop it. Morally this is intolerable. It is no way to run a "civilization".'[70] The Convention gives the UN Security Council permanent members the 'putative right, not to do wrong, but to permit wrong – to allow the commission of genocide'.[71] Shue puts the case

[67] International Court of Justice, 'Application of the Convention on the Prevention and Punishment of the Crime of Genocide (*Bosnia and Herzegovina* v. *Serbia and Montenegro*), Summary of the Judgment of 26 February 2007', Summary 2007/2 (26 February 2007), p. 16.
[68] Terry Nardin, 'International Political Theory and the Question of Justice', *International Affairs*, vol. 82, no. 3 (2006), 460.
[69] Nardin, 'International Political Theory', 464.
[70] Shue, 'Limiting Sovereignty', 19.
[71] Shue, 'Limiting Sovereignty', 20.

for 'limiting the sovereignty of powerful states to stand idly by, while genocidal states massacre their own people'.[72]

There seems to be support among publics across the world for intervention to stop genocide. An international public opinion poll conducted in 2006–7 found clear majorities in twelve countries around the world in favour of the statement that the 'UN Security Council has the right to authorize the use of military force to protect people from severe human rights violations, such as genocide, even against the will of the government committing such abuses'. And there were majorities in eight countries and a plurality in four countries favouring the contention that the UN Security Council had the 'responsibility' to authorise the use of military force in such circumstances. An earlier poll (2005) in eight African countries found similar levels of support for the 'right' of the UN Security Council to authorise intervention to stop human rights abuses such as genocide.[73] This is further evidence of the social norm against genocide.

For some legal commentators too, the norm against genocide is so strong that it justifies coercive armed intervention to try to stop it. Geoffrey Robertson argues:

> The most basic right of all is that to life – guaranteed by Article 8 of the Universal Declaration. At its highest, namely when the State takes life pursuant to a policy of genocide, this right is so forcefully protected by international law (it carries every Latin tag from *jus gentium* and *jus cogens* to *opinio juris* and *erga omnes*) that it justifies armed intervention by other states, whether pursuant to Chapter VII or by way of a unilateral humanitarian mission, and the ICJ may order 'provisional measures' against a government under the Genocide Convention.[74]

For Jan Wouters and Sten Verhoeven, the prohibition against genocide meets the criteria for *ius cogens*, as it is a norm of general international law, which means it is binding for the great majority of states; it is accepted and recognised by the international community of states as non-derogatory because it is about protection of fundamental interests

[72] Shue, 'Limiting Sovereignty', 28.
[73] The Chicago Council on Global Affairs and WorldPublicOpinion.org, 'Publics Around the World Say UN Has Responsibility to Protect Against Genocide', 4 April 2007 (available at www.worldpublicopinion.org).
[74] Geoffrey Robertson, *Crimes against Humanity: The Struggle for Global Justice*, 2nd edition (London: Penguin Books, 2002), pp. 102–3.

of the international community and not the particular interests of certain states; and no derogation is permitted from the peremptory norm. A 'breach of a norm of *ius cogens* violates a norm which is so fundamental for the international community that every member of that community can be regarded as having a legal interest in compliance with this norm. As a result, when a violation occurs, every member of the international community, even if it is not directly affected by the breach, has a legal interest in protecting these norms, and can take steps to enforce them.'[75] Such steps could mean bringing a case against the culprit state before the ICJ, or taking counter-measures against it, or taking action through the channels of the UN. 'If, however, the UN fails to act against violations of fundamental norms of the international community, every State should take its responsibility and react for the sake of the international community and for its own sake.'[76] Similarly, Lori Lyman Bruun has argued that international customary law has evolved such that 'it becomes clear that customary international law now permits an aggressive outside response to governmental policies of genocide.'[77] Such a response is justified because genocide has international consequences.

But this is controversial, and it is certainly dubious that there is a customary international law allowing intervention in the absence of UN Security Council authorisation. The UN Charter itself (treaty law) prohibits the use of force except in self-defence and under Chapter VII. In 2008, the then UN High Commissioner for Human Rights, Louise Arbour, argued forcefully that not only neighbouring or regional states must try to prevent genocide, but that the five permanent (P5) members of the Security Council hold an even heavier responsibility to do so. The P5 should agree not to use their veto powers in such situations. But she specified that the Security Council can react to a potential genocide using 'the range of diplomatic, dissuasive and coercive measures that the Security Council is empowered to deploy, *assuming that the situation has reached the point of*

[75] Wouters and Verhoeven, 'The Prohibition of Genocide as a Norm of *Ius Cogens* ', 404.

[76] Wouters and Verhoeven, 'The Prohibition of Genocide as a Norm of *Ius Cogens*', 409.

[77] Lori Lyman Bruun, 'Beyond the 1948 Convention: Emerging Principles of Genocide in Customary Law', *Maryland Journal of International Law and Trade*, vol. 17, no. 2 (1993).

constituting a threat to international peace and security'.[78] Thus it is the Security Council that should act, or authorise action, and only if there is a threat to international peace and security – which could be very hard to demonstrate. This is a view that by and large coincides with that of most states.

The 2005 World Summit Outcome Document (a political, not legal, document) specifically states that when the responsibility to protect requires enforcement action, the UN Security Council is the appropriate body to authorise such action. And more recently, it is clear that there is quite substantial opposition at the UN to the responsibility to protect principle in general – a reflection of a strong aversion, particularly among developing countries, to 'humanitarian intervention' by western countries.[79] Thomas Weiss notes that even among developed countries, 'there still is appallingly sparse responsibility to protect those suffering from atrocities that shock the human conscience – "unhumanitarian non-intervention"'.[80] The custom is *not* to intervene.

In sum, the social norm against genocide would require states to act to stop genocide when it is occurring, possibly even in the absence of UN Security Council authorisation. The legal norm requires them to take action to punish individuals responsible for genocide, and to 'prevent' it, but this does not necessarily entail the use of force (and certainly does not entail force that has not been authorised by the UN Security Council). An analysis of the position of European governments on this issue is at the heart of this book.

Outline of the book

Chapter 2 analyses the role of European governments in the origins and development of the international legal and normative framework on preventing and punishing genocide. What were their positions

[78] Louise Arbour, 'The Responsibility to Protect as a Duty of Care in International Law and Practice', *Review of International Studies*, vol. 34, no. 3 (2008), 456. Emphasis added.

[79] See van den Herik, 'The Schism between the Legal and the Social Concept of Genocide', 93; Evans, 'The Responsibility to Protect'. For many developing countries, humanitarian intervention is just a politically-correct version of old-fashioned colonial rule or neo-imperialism.

[80] Thomas Weiss, *Humanitarian Intervention* (Cambridge: Polity Press, 2007), p. 122.

during the drafting of the 1948 Genocide Convention, on ratifying the Convention, on making or accepting reservations to the Convention? It then reviews their positions on implementing the Convention domestically. It also considers the role of European governments in the creation and support of international tribunals (International Criminal Tribunal for the Former Yugoslavia, International Criminal Tribunal for Rwanda, International Criminal Court) and specifically for the inclusion of 'genocide' within their remits. Finally, it analyses the positions of European governments regarding the recent articulation of the principle of 'the responsibility to protect'.

Chapter 3 considers whether European governments used the term genocide during the Cold War period to describe events in Nigeria, Bangladesh, Cambodia, and other places. It considers whether there has been a change in the discourse about genocide over time.

The rest of the book is organised into chapters based on four purported or confirmed genocides in the post-Cold War period, Bosnia, Rwanda, Kosovo and Darfur. Each chapter first examines the politics of 'naming' genocide in France, Germany and the UK, with additional consideration of other European states where relevant. The four chapters seek to answer three sets of questions about the politics of naming genocide: (1) Did European governments state that a genocide was occurring or had occurred, and at what point during or after the events did they do so?; (2) What public justifications (if any) did they give for using or not using the term, and did these justifications refer to the legal or social norm?; (3) What were the debates within the national context surrounding the use of the term, and were governments under pressure from domestic actors to use or not to use the term?

Each chapter then analyses the policy responses of European governments to the four suspected or alleged cases of genocide. What were the official 'policies' (aims and instruments)? To what extent did governments seek to intervene to stop or punish genocide? What policy instruments were used, considered for use, or rejected? Policy responses could range from declarations condemning the violence/genocide to military intervention to try to stop the violence, as well as attempts to block such responses. Did they seek to punish the perpetrators of genocide, and in what way? What material and rhetorical support have they given to the international tribunals prosecuting the crime of genocide? How readily have they been willing to capture and extradite individuals indicted for the crime of genocide?

Each chapter also considers why the European governments took the positions that they did, by analysing which actors won the arguments for action or non-action and why. In line with much constructivist international relations theory, the 'weight' of ideational forces in decision-making will be contrasted with the weight of material forces. For example, did material interests – trading links, strategic partnerships – trump normative considerations?

The final chapter of the book considers the question, is there a 'European' way of responding to genocide? Are there more similarities than differences in the national debates about naming and responding to genocide? The research will show that in most cases of purported genocide, the inclination *not* to name genocide as such and *not* to intervene has been strong. Why have European governments repeatedly expressed their conviction that genocide must be halted, and yet when faced with particular cases of suspected genocide, hesitated to use the term 'genocide' and then to take action to prevent, suppress or punish genocide? What do the responses of European governments tell us about the development of a common European 'strategic culture' as regards intervention to prevent genocide? Finally, the impact that such responses may be having on the legal and social norms is analysed. What does European state practice tell us about how the norms might develop in future? Are European states becoming more willing to assume a 'responsibility to protect' others from genocide?

2 *European governments and the development of the international legal framework on genocide*

This chapter analyses the role of European governments in the origins and development of the international legal and normative framework on preventing and punishing genocide. It cannot be said that European governments were among those leading the international community towards agreement on the Genocide Convention: smaller countries and the USA and Australia arguably played much more leading roles in this respect. And perhaps surprisingly, while some West European countries readily accepted the Genocide Convention, others were much more critical: several West European states were not among those countries that first signed, ratified or acceded to the Convention, and some took over twenty years to accede to it. Eventually European governments 'came round' to the legal norm, and have since espoused a stronger response to genocide.

European states and the drafting of the Genocide Convention[1]

During the process of drafting the Convention, there was by no means a common viewpoint shared by the various European countries present. In fact, from the start of the negotiating process, two countries were generally hostile to the Convention: the United Kingdom and the USSR. Both had voted for the Genocide Resolution, but neither were

[1] At the time of the negotiations on the Convention, several European states were not yet members of the UN; they could only join the UN once the USA and USSR finally agreed a package deal and lifted their vetoes on countries joining from the opposing side. Thus in 1955, Hungary, Austria, Finland, Ireland, Italy, Portugal and Spain joined. But both Germanys joined only in 1973, after the approval of the Basic Treaty between the FRG and GDR.

enthusiastic about the idea of an international convention. The USSR's stance will not be discussed at length here, as this book is focused principally on the positions of France, Germany and the UK.

The UK's hostility was evident right from the start of the drafting process. Its opposition was based on several grounds, not all of them coherent with each other. The first is that the UN had better things to get on with doing, and that a Convention on genocide would not contribute anything to international law. On 26 February 1947, Eric Beckett, a legal advisor to the Foreign Office, wrote in a minute:

> This Assembly resolution on genocide is a useless resolution, and I think our attitude to it generally must be that we should not mind if it got lost somewhere and died a natural death, and at the most we do not want much time and expense being wasted in drawing up a perfectly useless convention ... It is all a complete waste of time, seeing that, if genocide takes place anywhere, it will take place under conditions where no international convention will be observed.[2]

A Foreign Office note for the Cabinet Steering Committee on International Organisations, which was responsible for providing the negotiating mandates for the UK delegation at the UN, stated that the Convention 'could do no good, and indeed might do harm if it failed, by throwing doubt on a principle which we regard as already well established in international law.'[3] The Nuremberg judgment had stated genocide was an international crime, therefore there was no need to risk having a Convention drawn up to which not all states might adhere.[4] The general UK view was that the issue of genocide would be more properly dealt with by the International Law Commission,

[2] In document UN 1658, in UK National Archives (hereinafter UKNA) file FO 371/67573. The British attitude of 'scepticism as to the value of international agreements' (and this one in particular) was defended by one of the UK's premier international lawyers, Professor J. L. Brierly, on the BBC in 1949. He warned against allowing the Genocide Convention to be seen as an 'important advance' when in fact nothing important had happened and this would add 'to those feelings of disillusion and cynicism about the possibilities of progress through international co-operation'. Brierly, 'The Genocide Convention', *The Listener* (10 March 1949).

[3] Foreign Office note of 12 July 1948, document UN 1481, in UKNA file FO 371/72693.

[4] Of course the UK then didn't sign up to the Convention for over twenty years. The British argument that genocide had been illegal since the Nuremberg trial

in conjunction with the codification of the Nuremberg principles. This was rightly viewed by other UN member states as an attempt to 'kill the Convention by committee', though the Netherlands also supported such a referral.[5]

In the UK, there was a general dislike of the new term 'genocide' (evident also in the views of some MPs[6]). And the initial definition of genocide in article 1 of the Convention was viewed as too extensive, leaving open the possibility that the UK could be considered guilty of genocide against the Germans in the British zone, colonial peoples, the Welsh ('as we don't allow Welsh to be used in Law Courts'), and the Jews in Palestine.[7]

The Foreign Office was, however, keenly aware that 'a large body of public opinion in many countries had shown itself in favour of a Convention ... Consequently His Majesty's Government might be severely criticized for standing aside from a Convention on the grounds that it would mark no progress in International Law and therefore do no good.' However, even if the draft text 'were considerably amended, we should need to make a number of changes in our domestic legislation before we could accede to it, and it is at least doubtful whether Parliament would be prepared to devote the necessary time to this.'[8] But if the UK's proposal that the Convention be

has been criticised as 'not tenable'. The Nuremberg Charter only created a *lex specialis* against a named group of men. While genocide was condemned, the tribunal acknowledged that how a state treats its own citizens is not a matter with which international law concerns itself. Josef Kunz, 'The United Nations Convention on Genocide', *The American Journal of International Law*, vol. 43, no. 4 (1949), 742. The UK's position is somewhat resonant with Fournet's argument (see Chapter 1) that genocide has always been illegal, that the General Assembly Resolution expressed this in law, and that the Convention unduly restricted the customary law.

5 The Netherlands formally proposed that the Sixth Committee refer the Convention to the International Law Commission. Schabas, *Genocide in International Law*, 2nd edition, p. 63.

6 In one exchange in the House of Commons in October 1949, the word was described as 'horrible', and 'horribly illiterate'. Hansard (19 October 1949), col. 533. Two decades later, in the House of Lords debate on the Genocide Bill, one lord complained about 'the illiteracy of the word "genocide"'. Hansard, House of Lords (12 November 1968), col. 431.

7 Minute by C. D. W O'Neill (29 July 1947), in document UN 3792 in UKNA file FO 371/67519.

8 Foreign Office note of 12 July 1948, document UN 1481, in UKNA file FO 371/72693.

referred to the International Law Commission and the Human Rights Commission was rejected (as happened), then the delegation should still take part in negotiations on it.

The British government – supported strongly by the Netherlands – argued that the Convention was useless because genocide was a crime committed by states, not by individuals. And no state that was committing genocide would be restrained by an international convention, or surrender itself for international trial. The Attorney General, Sir Hartley Shawcross, stated at the UN: 'The obvious truth was that individual genocide was already punishable by the laws of all countries, whereas genocide committed by States was punishable only by war.'[9] A UK attempt to introduce an amendment recognising state responsibility for genocide was defeated, narrowly, in the Sixth Committee. While France shared the view that national courts could not be counted on to prosecute genocide, it came to the conclusion that the Convention should provide for individuals to be held accountable before an international court.[10] Individuals were to be the focus of the Convention, with some provision made, in article 6, for trial by an international penal tribunal, should one be created in the future.

The British particularly disapproved of the notion of 'cultural genocide' (destruction of the specific characteristics of a group), as opposed to 'physical genocide' (killing members of the group) or 'biological genocide' (attempting to prevent births within the group). Cultural genocide was particularly dear to Lemkin's heart however. He argued that the right of a racial, national or religious group's existence was also linked to 'the value of the contribution made by such a group to civilization generally. If the diversity of cultures were destroyed, it would be as disastrous for civilization as the physical destruction of nations.'[11] An initial draft of the Convention had prohibited destroying the language, religion or culture of a group by 'prohibiting the use of the language of the group in daily intercourse or in schools, or the printing and circulation of publications in the language of the group; destroying or preventing the use of libraries, museums, schools, historical monuments, places of worship or other cultural

[9] In Sixth Committee, Sixty-fourth meeting (1 October 1948), UN document A/C.6/SR.64, p. 18.

[10] Schabas, *Genocide in International Law*, 2nd edition, pp. 492–4.

[11] Cited in Cooper, *Raphael Lemkin*, p. 91.

institutions and objects of the group.'[12] The UK argued that cultural genocide really involved issues regarding the treatment of minorities, and should therefore be referred to the sub-committee of the Human Rights Commission dealing with the protection of minorities. Its opposition to the inclusion of cultural genocide in the Convention was shared by western countries, including France and the Netherlands. Ultimately these countries were successful, as cultural genocide was dropped in late October 1948 when the draft was being considered by the Sixth Committee.[13]

But the UK did support the inclusion of 'political groups' in the definition of groups in article 1. Its position was that 'exclusion of political groups in a convention of this kind is tantamount to condoning their slaughter.'[14] France too favoured the inclusion of political groups, as did the Netherlands.[15] But they were up against the even stronger opposition of the Soviet bloc and several Latin American countries, as well as Belgium. The main arguments against the inclusion of political groups were that political groups were not 'stable', as opposed to racial, national and religious groups which had an inalienable character; the term 'genocide' itself did not include political groups (a point made by Belgium); the protection of political groups should come within the scope of the Human Rights Commission instead (a point made by Sweden, though it later switched sides); and the inclusion of political groups would

[12] Article III of the Ad Hoc Committee draft, reprinted in the appendix of Schabas, *Genocide in International Law*, 2nd edition.

[13] Supporters of the inclusion of cultural genocide included the Soviet bloc, China and several predominantly Muslim countries such as Pakistan and Egypt (who argued that cultural genocide was being committed in the Holy Land). Cooper, *Raphael Lemkin*, pp. 168–9.

[14] Annex IV of the brief for the UK delegation from the Cabinet Steering Committee on International Organizations (15 September 1948), in UKNA file CO 936/19/2. The UK's insistence that political groups be included was seen by Lemkin as another attempt to smother the convention, because including political groups would mean that either the Assembly would not pass the convention, or that few countries would then ratify it. He thus successfully lobbied the US delegation to propose dropping the reference to political groups. Korey, *Epitaph for Raphael Lemkin*, p. 39.

[15] An initial vote, on 15 October 1948, on retaining political groups in the definition favoured doing so. Most West European countries voted in favour of this, including the UK, Netherlands, Luxembourg, France, Norway Denmark and Sweden; Belgium voted against. Sixth Committee, Seventy-fifth meeting (15 October 1948), UN document A/C.6/SR.75.

inhibit ratification by many states. As a result, the USA – hitherto a strong supporter of the inclusion of political groups – agreed, in the interests of ensuring wide ratification of the Convention, to support exclusion of political groups, and the Sixth Committee so agreed.[16]

The Netherlands remained bitter about this decision. The UK Foreign Office files contain a translation of a speech given by the Dutch Foreign Minister in parliament on 4 July 1951. Dirk Stikker was responding to an MP's question as to why the Dutch government had not yet acceded to the Genocide Convention. Stikker stated:

> The principal reason for the Government's hesitation in this matter is that, in the opinion of the Government, this treaty shows a serious hiatus, namely, that the definition of the offence does not make any mention of 'political genocide', that is, the extermination of political groups. In the discussions on this treaty the Netherlands delegation pleaded very strongly in favour of including political genocide in the definition. In the opinion of the Government the treaty loses much of its value by the non-inclusion of political genocide, because we have in past years, and particularly in the second World War, been witnesses of this form of genocide, consisting in the extermination of certain political parties, measures against political persons as such, etc.[17]

In the UK, the Home Office was absolutely opposed to the Convention and initially insisted that the UK not vote in favour of the Convention, though it could abstain rather than oppose it.[18] The main reason for its objection was that the Convention contained, in article 7, the provision that genocide shall not be considered as a political crime for the purpose of extradition. The Home Office argued that this would require changing UK legislation, and doing away with its traditional

[16] On this occasion, on 29 November 1948, those West European countries in favour of excluding political groups were Belgium, Denmark, UK, and Greece; the Netherlands opposed the motion; France, Sweden, Luxembourg and Norway abstained. Sixth Committee, Hundred and twenty-eighth meeting (29 November 1948), UN document A/C.6/SR.128. See the account of the negotiations on political groups in Schabas, *Genocide in International Law*, 2nd edition, pp. 153–65.

[17] Letter from the British Embassy in The Hague to the Foreign Office (17 August 1951), document UP 254/38 in UKNA file FO 371/95709.

[18] Letter from the Home Office to the delegation (27 November 1948), document UN 3245, in UKNA file FO 371/72693.

stance of offering asylum to those charged with 'political offences'.[19] Yet during the negotiations, the UK delegate, Gerald Fitzmaurice, had argued that the crime of genocide was political and that 'It was precisely because of the political nature of the crime that it was necessary to state that, for purposes of extradition, it should be considered as non-political.'[20] As seen below, this issue divided the Home Office and Foreign Office for twenty years, and essentially prevented the UK from acceding to the Convention until 1970. Similar considerations also concerned other European countries, as discussed further below.

Because of the Home Office objection, the UK abstained in the Sixth Committee vote on the Genocide Convention. It was quite isolated, joined in its abstention by the Soviet bloc countries and South Africa. The UK delegation reported to the Foreign Office that the abstention 'went very much against the grain', and they urged consideration of the possibility of supporting the Convention when it was voted on in the General Assembly.[21] This prompted a very stern reply from the Foreign Office reminding the delegation of the 'strength of Home Office objections', because UK legislation would need to be changed, and the Home Office regarded it 'as virtually impossible, even if it were desirable, to put the necessary legislation through Parliament.'[22] This reply in turn prompted an extraordinary outburst from Sir Hartley Shawcross, the UK Attorney General and member of the UK delegation, to the Foreign Secretary:

> I must say in the most emphatic terms that I am shocked to find that it is proposed that the United Kingdom should abstain from supporting the draft Convention on genocide ... In adopting this course we shall find ourselves in a minority consisting of the Slav States and South Africa and we

[19] The UK position regarding international treaties was that domestic law needed to comply with international treaty law; therefore if domestic law was not already in compliance with an international treaty, the government should only give its assent to that treaty once parliament had agreed to the necessary implementing legislation. See Simpson, 'Britain and the Genocide Convention', 14–19.

[20] Cited in Schabas, *Genocide in International Law*, 2nd edition, p. 449.

[21] Telegram from the UK delegation to the Foreign Office (1 December 1948), document UN 3267, in UKNA file FO 371/72693.

[22] Telegram from the Foreign Office to the UK delegation (3 December 1948), in UKNA file FO 371/72693.

shall lay ourselves open to severe and, I think myself, justified criticism both in the Assembly and at home.

Shawcross argued that all of the acts of genocide proposed in the Convention were already criminal under existing UK law, and so therefore there were no grounds for justifying abstention.[23] The Home Office relented, and the Home Secretary agreed that the UK delegation could vote in favour of the Convention as long as it also noted the reservation that the UK were not committed to amending UK law accordingly and that the vote was without prejudice to the right to grant asylum. This the UK did, and the Convention was approved unanimously (with even the 'Slav States' voting in favour).

In stark contrast to the UK, France was more supportive of the Genocide Convention, though it had initially described the term 'genocide' as a 'useless and even dangerous neologism'. Instead, it persistently argued that the issue of genocide should be considered as one aspect of crimes against humanity, and therefore initially rejected the idea that genocide was a crime of war and of peacetime. For example, it wanted the preamble to describe genocide as a crime against humanity. But other states successfully argued that the two concepts were distinct and separate.[24]

France was also firmly in favour of the setting up of an international criminal court – in fact, it declared that because the Convention left open the possibility of doing so, France could therefore sign the Convention despite reservations it had about other provisions.[25] It had submitted a draft convention to the Ad Hoc committee in February 1948, containing quite detailed provisions regarding the creation of an international criminal court.[26] France's insistence on including a reference to an international criminal tribunal stemmed from its belief that genocide was a crime perpetrated by states or government officials, and therefore prosecution by national courts

23 Document UN 3305, in UKNA file FO 371/72693. This is all the more extraordinary because Shawcross was not enthusiastic about the Convention at all. His intervention indicates the extent to which he was aware of the blow to the UK's reputation and standing that an abstention could make.

24 Schabas, 'Origins of the Genocide Convention', 38–9.

25 Schabas, *Genocide in International Law*, 2nd edition, p. 89.

26 Schabas, *Genocide in International Law*, 2nd edition, p. 446.

would be inconceivable.[27] The British also argued that genocide was a crime committed by states (a principal reason why it considered an international convention to be a useless way of trying to stop genocide), but it did not favour the creation of an international criminal court because it would nonetheless require force to bring perpetrators of genocide before an international criminal court. Instead, the International Court of Justice should be able to award compensation for damages to victims.[28] France was ultimately successful in having a reference made to an international criminal court in the Genocide Convention (in article 6), though it took until 1999 for one to be set up.

Ratification of or accession to the Convention

In spite of the USSR's stance during the negotiations, the Soviet bloc countries were among the first to sign and ratify or accede to the Genocide Convention, even though the Convention did not make the connection between Nazi fascism and genocide that the Soviet Union had persistently demanded throughout the drafting process.[29] However, the USSR, Ukrainian Soviet Socialist Republic, the Byelorussian Soviet

27 Cooper, *Raphael Lemkin*, p. 139. Lemkin appears to have viewed the French position as an attempt to limit genocide. In a chronology (presumably written or at least approved by Lemkin) in his papers at the NYPL (reel 4), it is stated that in May 1948, 'un projet Français de *limiter le Genocide* a la destruction de la vie par les gouvernements ou par des indivus instigués par les gouvernements, ou quand ces acts sont toleres par les gouvernements est rejetté par le Comité de redaction' (emphasis added). In a memorandum entitled 'To avoid responsibility for genocide in Algeria the French are destroying the Genocide Convention' (Lemkin papers, reel 4, NYPL), Lemkin accuses the French government of trying to evade responsibility for genocide in Algeria because of the stance it was taking in negotiations on a Draft Code of Offences against Peace and Security of Mankind. Crimes against humanity were to be defined as being conducted by state authorities or by individuals acting at the instigation of such authorities, which, Lemkin argued, meant that individual colonists in Algeria would not be held responsible for crimes committed against Algerians. Lemkin argued this destroyed the principle of criminal responsibility, for corporate bodies cannot be held responsible under criminal law. Algeria's rebels did accuse France of conducting a 'war of genocide'. See, for example, 'Rebels Insist on Free Algeria', *The Times* (31 October 1957).

28 Schabas, *Genocide in International Law*, 2nd edition, p. 450.

29 Right from the beginning of the attempt to push the Genocide Resolution through the General Assembly, Lemkin had recognised the need to counter any potential Soviet opposition. In the fall of 1946 Lemkin approached Jan Masaryk, the Foreign Minister of Czechoslovakia, asking him to try to

Socialist Republic, Albania, Bulgaria, Czechoslovakia, Hungary, Poland and Romania all made reservations to several articles when they signed the Convention; that which generated most opposition was the reservation to article 9, which allows state parties to submit disputes regarding the interpretation, application or fulfilment of the Convention to the International Court of Justice.[30]

The Soviet bloc reservations sparked a move by several states, including the UK, to have the question of reservations to the convention referred to the International Court of Justice. The UK argued that a state that insisted on the reservation in the face of objection from other states could not be regarded as a party to the convention.[31] The ICJ opinion was issued on 28 May 1951, and the majority view did not agree with the UK's position: if a party objects to a reservation that it considers incompatible with the object and purpose of the Convention, then it can consider the reserving state not to be a party; if it accepts the reservation as being compatible with the Convention, then it can consider the reserving party to be a party to the Convention. From then on, most states who objected to reservations by other parties did so without considering the reserving states not to be parties to the Convention.[32]

convince the Russian Foreign Minister, Andrei Vishinsky, to support the resolution. Masaryk apparently met Vishinsky the following day, and the USSR did support the resolution. Little more than a year later, on 10 March 1948, Masaryk was dead, having 'jumped' or 'been pushed' from a window in the Czechoslovak foreign ministry following the communist takeover of Czechoslovakia in February 1948 (we will probably never know what actually happened).

30 Following the collapse of communism, these states or their successors mostly withdrew their reservations to article 9, though they maintained an objection to article 12, on the grounds that the Convention should extend to all non-self-governing territories. The most controversial reservations of all, however, are those made by the USA when it finally ratified the Convention (in November 1988), as the USA stated that no case involving it may be referred to the ICJ without its prior consent, and that nothing in the Convention requires legislation which is prohibited by the US constitution (in other words, the constitution is the highest law of the land and cannot be subordinated to international law).

31 On the UK's views, see Simpson, 'Britain and the Genocide Convention', 39–43.

32 One important exception is the Netherlands, which did not accept the reservations made to article 9 and did not consider any state that made such reservations to be a party to the Convention (thus the Soviet bloc countries were not considered to be parties, and the USA is still not considered to be a party).

The first West European countries to sign the Convention were France (11 December 1948), Norway (11 December 1948), Denmark (28 September 1949), Belgium (12 December 1949), Greece (29 December 1949), and Sweden (30 December 1949). They were also among the first to ratify the Convention (see Table 2.1). In December 1949, the General Assembly called on non-members of the UN to accede to the Convention, and in January 1950, the Secretary-General sent out invitations to various countries including Italy, the Federal Republic of Germany, Bulgaria, Hungary and Romania.[33]

For the three Scandinavian states, the issue was completely uncontroversial. For example, in a 1952 explanatory memorandum on the Convention for the Swedish parliament, the government stated: 'The desirability that Sweden should join all the other nations in ratifying the convention and so contributing to make it legally binding needs no special emphasizing.' Furthermore, the fact that Swedish law prohibited extradition for political crimes was not seen as an obstacle at all: political crime was not defined in the law, and 'accordingly, there is nothing to prevent us in the application of the law from complying with the prohibition in the convention against regarding genocide as a political crime. Indeed this would appear to agree very well with the spirit of Swedish law.'[34] The Danish law enacting the Convention was

[33] Cooper, *Raphael Lemkin*, p. 180. The General Assembly resolution requests the Secretary-General to send invitations to non-UN members which are active members of UN specialised agencies or parties to the International Court of Justice (Resolution 368 (IV)). Therefore, the list excludes the German Democratic Republic and Spain. The GDR did not accede to the Genocide Convention until 1973, when it joined the UN. Western states blocked its membership in international organisations until West Germany recognised the GDR in 1972 (part of *Ostpolitik*). In contrast, the Federal Republic of Germany had become a member of FAO in 1950, as well as numerous European and Atlantic organisations (chief among them NATO and the European Coal and Steel Community). Wilhelm Bruns, *Die UNO-Politik der DDR* (Stuttgart: Verlag Bonn Aktuell, 1978). I am grateful to my research assistant David Maleki (DM) for having translated the relevant parts of this book for me. The exclusion of Spain (isolated as well as isolationist under the Franco regime) had been explicitly mentioned in the General Assembly's debate. See 'L'Espagne ne pourra signer la convention internationale contre le génocide', *Le Monde* (6 December 1949). Spain joined the UN in 1955, and acceded to the Genocide Convention in September 1968.

[34] Translation of the memorandum in Irish Ministry of Foreign Affairs file 417/65 I, in the Irish National Archives.

Table 2.1. ***Ratifications (r) and accessions (a) to the Genocide Convention: selected European countries***

Austria	19 March 1958 (a)
Belgium	5 September 1951 (r)
Denmark	15 June 1951 (r)
France	14 October 1950 (r)
(West) Germany	24 November 1954 (a)
Greece	8 December 1954 (r)
Ireland	22 June 1976 (a)
Italy	4 June 1952 (a)
Luxembourg	7 October 1981 (a)
Netherlands	20 June 1966 (a)
Norway	22 July 1949 (r)
Portugal	9 February 1999 (a)
Spain	13 September 1968 (a)
Sweden	27 May 1952 (r)
Switzerland	7 September 2000 (a)
United Kingdom	30 January 1970 (a)

considered by Raphael Lemkin to be 'far superior to all the domestic laws which have been enacted prior to this time', and an example for other countries to follow.[35]

One issue that, somewhat curiously, did not really arise during the negotiations or ratification process is concern that European colonial powers could be accused of genocide themselves. Several countries still had colonies after the Second World War, including Belgium, France, the Netherlands, Portugal and the UK. Those countries might thus have reason not to accede or ratify the Convention, not because they were intent on committing genocide but because they feared being accused of having committed genocide in their colonies. Yet two colonial powers, Belgium and France, ratified the Convention almost immediately; the Netherlands, Portugal and the UK did not.

Instead, another issue proved problematic in several countries. The Convention states that for the purposes of extradition, genocide

[35] See his views on the Danish law in, among other letters, a letter to Agda Rossel of Sweden, the newly-elected chair of the UN Commission on the Status of Women (22 June 1956), in Lemkin papers, NYPL, reel 1.

cannot be considered a political crime, and thus laws that protect individuals fleeing 'political persecution' (and the like) cannot extend to those accused of genocide. Extradition would prove to be quite controversial – though the extent to which this controversy actually reflected concerns about extradition rather than the Convention itself must be left open to question. The Belgian delegate to the General Assembly, for example, declared that he had voted for the Genocide Convention but that he would have to reserve the position of his government as regards the provisions relating to extradition. The Belgian government would only be able to implement the convention to the extent allowed by Belgian legislation, until such time as changes could be made to the law.[36] In the event, however, Belgium was one of the first countries to ratify the Convention.

France also signed and ratified the Convention quite quickly and without controversy. The French National Assembly adopted the Convention on 28 April 1950, with no debate considered necessary.[37] However, only in March 1994 was the crime of genocide incorporated into the French national penal code.[38] Under the French constitution, international treaties have superiority over domestic law, so the Convention was directly applicable in France. But as Caroline Fournet has shown, individuals (notably Klaus Barbie, Paul Touvier, Maurice Papon, and Aloïs Brunner) in the decades following the Second World War were never charged with the crime of genocide, but instead with crimes against humanity. French courts, she argues, have been reluctant to apply the Genocide Convention, not only by refusing to classify the Holocaust as genocide, but also by avoiding applying the Genocide Convention in more recent cases.[39]

[36] See statement by Mr Kaeckenbeeck, in Sixth Committee, Hundred and thirty-third meeting (2 December 1948), UN document A/C.6/SR.133, p. 704.

[37] Lemkin was quite active in writing to various French parliamentarians to press for early ratification, and was apparently told by Pierre Montel, the chair of the commission on military affairs in the National Assembly, that it was a 'matter of national honour' that the Convention would be 'ratified without one word of discussion'. This episode is recounted in drafts of a chapter of his autobiography, 'Climbing a Mountain Again', in reel 2 of the Lemkin papers in the NYPL.

[38] The definition of the crime of genocide is wider than that of the Convention's, and includes the destruction 'of a group determined by any other arbitrary criterion' (Article 211–1, French Penal Code, 1 March 1994).

[39] Caroline Fournet, 'Reflection on the Separation of Powers: The Law of Genocide and the Symptomatic French Paradox', in Henham and Behrens, eds., *The Criminal Law of Genocide*, especially pp. 216–22.

The Federal Republic of Germany also had little hesitation about acceding to the Convention. Although work had to be done to fit the provisions of the Convention into German law, the bill was passed by the Bundestag unanimously. In the debates on the accession to the Convention, members of the Bundestag noted the strong moral imperatives incumbent upon Germany to ensure the prevention and punishment of genocide. The Convention was seen as a significant contribution to the development of international law – and an apt commemoration of the crimes committed by the Nazi regime.[40]

Like the Federal Republic of Germany, Italy also responded rapidly to the UN's call for non-member states to accede to the Genocide Convention. In 1952, the Italian parliament authorised the government to accede to it, and in June 1952, the government did so. However, the law authorising accession did not actually implement the Convention – that would have to wait until an implementing law came into force, which did not happen until 1967. The long delay was due to an extended debate on how to reconcile the Genocide Convention's provisions on extradition with the Italian constitution, according to which non-citizens may not be extradited for political crimes. In 1963, a court in Bologna refused to extradite a German citizen indicted for genocide, because it considered genocide to be a political crime. Only then could agreement first be reached to amend the Italian constitution, so as to avoid more such cases in future, by stating that the Constitution's provisions do not apply to crimes of genocide, and then to enact the implementation law on prevention and punishment of the crime of genocide, in 1967.[41]

In contrast, other European states were much less enthusiastic about acceding to the Convention in the first place, notably the

[40] Interestingly, the Bundestag debates also brought up the expulsion of Germans from East European countries after the war – with some members arguing this too was a crime of genocide. *Stenographischer Bericht: Plenarprotokoll*, Deutscher Bundestag: First Reading (Session 10; Bonn, 21.01.1954); Second and Third Reading (Session 37; Bonn, 08.07.1954). Translations by DM. There are a few copies of letters (in German) from Lemkin to German parliamentarians (Thomas Dehler and Franz Seidl), all from 1954, in which he critiques the German implementation law; he was particularly exercised by the use of the term 'annihilation' rather than 'destruction' (groups can disappear even if individual members do not). He viewed the former term as being too close to the Nuremberg judgment. Lemkin papers, NYPL, reel 1; translation from the German by DM.

[41] Michela Miraglia, 'Genocide: The Italian Perspective', *International Criminal Law Review*, vol. 5, no. 3 (2005).

UK, the Netherlands, Ireland and Luxembourg.[42] The UK government's official and public attitude on the question of accession to the Convention was that it was 'still studying the legal implications'; this was repeated time and again in answers to questions from MPs and civil society organisations for fourteen years. In 1962, the UK finally announced that it would not accede to the Convention after all, only to reverse that position a few years later, after the Labour government of Harold Wilson entered office. The behind-the-scenes story is only apparent from a reading of the various documents on the matter held in the UK National Archives.[43] These documents show that the lukewarm (though gradually warmer) attitude of the Foreign Office was met by complete stonewalling by a hostile Home Office.

After an initial period in which the Foreign Office was quite content to let the matter languish,[44] it became more active in supporting UK accession. The Foreign Office view can be summed up in three points:

(1) The Genocide Convention, though a 'miserable' document, is also a fairly harmless one, and would not really require much of the

[42] Given time and space constraints as well as linguistic limitations, two other 'latecomers' are not discussed here, Portugal or Switzerland. I have been unable to find any secondary literature, or much in the press, about why these two countries did not accede to the Convention until 1999 and 2000 respectively. In Portugal, authoritarian rule ended in the 1970s, at which point it also divested itself of its colonies. This might explain why it had not acceded before then, but does not explain why the wait until 1999. Switzerland did not join the UN until 2002, but it had ratified other international human rights treaties much earlier (the two International Covenants, for example, in 1992).

[43] And since those documents entered the public record, only one article has thus far been written about the UK's position: Simpson, 'Britain and the Genocide Convention'. Cooper's *Raphael Lemkin* also contains much about the UK's attitude towards the Convention, relying on the documents from the National Archives.

[44] Thus a minute from D.H.T. Hildyard in the UN Department on 30 March 1950 argued that although the Home Office's case was not very strong, the Convention makes so little contribution to human progress that the UK should not be put off by any criticisms that non-accession might bring. In fact, UK non-accession might set a good example, and thus the Convention would never come into force. Document UP 252/25, in UKNA file FO 371/88599. When, however, the Convention did gather enough ratifications/accessions to enter into force, and more countries began to accede to it (particularly from the Commonwealth), the UK's stance became more uncomfortable – inevitably affecting Foreign Office attitudes towards the Convention.

UK by way of implementing it.[45] Home Office points regarding extradition (see below) can be overcome. In any event, it would be unthinkable for the UK to want to protect anyone who might be guilty of genocide.

(2) There is pressure on the government to accede to the Convention from inside the UK and the government must at least give a straight answer to the question of why it has not acceded. However, pressure from civil society organisations was relatively short-lived: between 1948 and 1954, the UK government was urged to accede to the Convention by a wide variety of religious, peace, and women's organisations. Lemkin himself also wrote to the Home Secretary, in January 1952, urging the UK to accede to the Convention, if necessary by making a reservation to article 7. He implored, 'We need badly the humanitarian leadership of Great Britain in the matter of the genocide convention.'[46] After 1954, the civil society groups appear to have given up pressing the government on the issue. But Members of Parliament did not. In particular, the MP from Leicester, Barnett Janner (later Sir Barnett Janner) raised the issue regularly in the House of Commons, though he too was silent on the issue between 1956 and 1960. Such periods of silence made it difficult for the Foreign Office to argue its case with the Home Office; from 1961 onwards, when Janner resumed his persistent questioning, the Foreign Office could more legitimately press the Home Office for a decision to be made.

(3) The Convention may be useless, but not acceding to it gives an unfortunate impression on the international scene: 'the crime of genocide is so clearly abominable that we shall always be open to criticism so long as we do not accede ... there may be some who will see behind our reluctance to accede some unspoken intention to use weapons of mass destruction, or some other sinister reason for not acceding ... This would give a useful propaganda weapon to the Soviet *bloc*.'[47] As more and more states acceded to

[45] See, for example, minute by G. Fitzmaurice (15 July 1949), in document UN 1324, in UKNA file FO 371/78849.

[46] Letter from Lemkin to Sir David Maxwell Fyfe, in UKNA file FO 371/10149. He received the same sort of response as did all the civil society organisations: the government is studying the implications of accession.

[47] Memorandum for the Cabinet Home Affairs Committee by the Secretary of State for Foreign Affairs and the Secretary of State for the Home

the Convention, the Foreign Office became increasingly aware of the UK's isolation and more concerned at the impression that it was giving in international circles.

What does not appear in the Foreign Office arguments is concern that the UK could be held in breach of the Convention because of its colonial policies. There is no indication that this was ever a worry, even though, for example, the brutality with which the British repressed the 'Mau Mau' insurgency in Kenya in the 1950s sparked outrage in the UK. Clearly it was too farfetched to consider that such massacres (and the associated racism) might appear to others to be genocidal.[48] There was thus no concern about whether the UK was actually in compliance with the main provisions of the Convention.

Instead, the problem centred on the extradition issue. For its part, the Home Office argued that accession to the Convention would require the UK to change its legislation regarding political asylum, because article 7 states that genocide cannot be considered a political crime for the purposes of extradition. The Extradition Act of 1870 prohibits the extradition of a fugitive criminal if the offence is of a political character. The Home Office argued that making an exception for genocide would not only destroy the absolute character of the extradition rule, but would make it difficult if not impossible to refuse extradition in cases where spurious accusations of genocide were made against someone benefitting from asylum in the UK. This would be controversial, and thus stood no chance of passage by Parliament. To some extent, there was sympathy with this view in the Foreign Office too. In a response to a 1953 letter from the Ethical Union urging accession to the Convention, M.S. Williams from the Foreign Office wrote that the tradition of not extraditing for political offences was 'a point of morality hardly less important than that involved in genocide itself'.[49]

Department on the Genocide Convention, in UKNA file FO 371/166847. The memorandum was prepared for a meeting of the Cabinet committee on 16 March 1962.

[48] See Piers Brendon, *The Decline and Fall of the British Empire 1781–1997* (London: Vintage, 2008), chapter 19. Brendon notes that the UK was incredulous when at the Council of Europe Greece sought to raise British human rights violations in its colony Cyprus in 1957: 'human rights were for foreigners' (p. 623).

[49] Letter of 21 December 1953, in UKNA file FO 371/107080.

On 28 July 1953, the Cabinet could only agree to defer a decision on accession.[50] For several years, the issue remained more or less dormant, though the Foreign Office tried on various occasions to challenge the Home Office view. The Foreign Office then agreed to refer the issue to the Law Officers, to ask for their opinion. That opinion, issued on 22 November 1961, indicated that if the UK was to accede to the Genocide Convention, it would indeed be necessary to amend the Extradition Acts.[51] At around the same time, Sir Barnett Janner began to urge accession in a series of parliamentary questions. The Home Office and Foreign Office then put the issue before the Cabinet Home Affairs Committee in March 1962, and that committee agreed that the UK should not accede to the Convention. The government's position was stated in the House of Commons in an answer to a question from Sir Barnett Janner on 18 July 1962: accession would involve amending the Extradition Acts, and would be 'a derogation from this country's traditional right to grant political asylum which the Government do not think it right to accept'.[52] The government's statement made it clear that it abhors genocide, would never commit it, and that those who commit it should be brought to justice. But as *The Times* noted the following day, the government's objections are 'not quite substantial enough to warrant taking a position so open to misinterpretation. The problem of extradition could probably be overcome with some minor changes.'[53] Janner also did not give up, asking several more parliamentary questions in the following years.

With a change of government in 1964, the UK reversed its stance. This had been signalled prior to the elections: in October 1962, in

[50] In the meantime, the UK's non-accession and sceptical attitude regarding 'genocide' and the Convention did not prevent the Foreign Office's 'Information Research Department' from identifying a rather useful propaganda purpose of the Convention. They proposed that the term be used to describe the policies of the USSR towards certain nations such as the Chechens, and that any time the communist bloc attacked the British colonial system, officials should recall the treatment of the Chechens (and other nations within the USSR). See minute by R. Conquest of 18 January 1951 on 'The Genocide Theme', and the memorandum on Soviet genocide of 24 November 1951, both in UKNA file FO 11/421. This propaganda campaign apparently did not last long, as there are no further documents on it beyond 1951.

[51] In UKNA file FO 371/160917.

[52] Hansard (18 July 1962), cols. 423–4.

[53] 'Convention Worth Improving', *The Times* (19 July 1962).

the debate on the Queen's speech, Harold Wilson, then the shadow Foreign Secretary, asked why the UK had not ratified the Genocide Convention, and argued that it was all the more urgent to do so because of the 'resurgence of evil, Nazi anti-social doctrines in this country'.[54] During the 1964 election campaign Wilson indicated on two occasions that the UK should accede to the Genocide Convention.[55] While the Labour Party's 1964 election manifesto did not specifically mention the Genocide Convention, it did strongly state that:

> our most important effort will be concerned to revive the morale and increase the powers of the United Nations. Every year that has passed since the Conservatives came to power has seen Britain's influence in the United Nations decline. At home the Prime Minister and others have voiced their nagging criticisms while in the General Assembly, time and time again Britain is to be found among the ranks of the abstentionists on vital issues of freedom and racial equality.[56]

Even then, the Wilson government did not present the Genocide Bill in parliament until 1968 (symbolically, during the International Year for Human Rights). The main debate in the House of Commons took place on 5 February 1969, where the government noted that the extradition issue had prevented UK accession until now, but: 'One cannot, however, overlook the fact that up to now 73 countries, many of whom are no less liberal in their outlook than ourselves, countries like Australia and Canada, the Netherlands and Sweden, have felt able to accept this restriction.'[57] Further,

> The importance of this legislation does not lie so much in the number of prosecutions to which it will give rise, or in the number of persons whose extradition for offences of genocide it will secure, as in the proof which it affords that the United Kingdom, as a civilised nation and a firm defender of human rights, condemns this barbaric crime and undertakes to prevent and to punish it.[58]

[54] Hansard (31 October 1962), vol. 666, col. 151.

[55] In a speech to the Society of Labour Lawyers in the Temple on 20 April 1964, and in an answer to a number of questions put forward by the Jewish Chronicle on 2 October 1964. UKNA file FO 371/183639.

[56] Labour Party 1964 election manifesto, 'The New Britain', available at www.politicsresources.net/area/uk/man/lab64.htm [last accessed 14 April 2010]

[57] Hansard (5 February 1969), col. 483.

[58] Hansard (5 February 1969), col. 485.

While a few MPs raised the extradition issue during the debate, the Genocide Bill passed smoothly through parliament, and received the royal assent on 27 March 1969.[59] On 30 January 1970 the UK notified the UN of its accession to the Convention. As is clear in the justifications presented for acceding to the Convention, the principal concern of the UK was its reputation as a 'civilised nation'. Civilised nations condemn genocide to the point of accepting the Convention. However, it is more than an odd juxtaposition that at the same time the UK government was pushing for approval of the Genocide Bill, and arguing that civilised nations condemn, prevent and punish genocide, it was very busy refuting, rather than seriously investigating, allegations that genocide against the Igbos was taking place in Nigeria (see chapter 3).

The Netherlands initially took quite a principled stand against acceding to the Convention. In addition to the dismay regarding the exclusion of political groups (noted above), the Dutch government argued that the Convention would not be effective:

> It is to be anticipated that the worst offences of this kind will be committed by totalitarian States ... This means that the principal offenders will go unpunished. One can hardly imagine that totalitarian States would be willing to apply a convention of this kind to their subjects, a fact that is already finding expression in various reserves with respect to the authority of the International Court of Justice ... The treaty would thus have little effect where it is most needed and would be abused for purposes of propaganda where it is needed least.[60]

Given the manifest unhappiness with the Convention, the Netherlands did not rush to accede to it. It was under some domestic pressure

[59] Again, the absence of concern as to whether the UK was fully in compliance with the Convention is notable. In December 1968, Auberon Waugh had suggested in *The Spectator* that British ministers could be answerable in the courts to charges of genocide in Nigeria (Biafra). But the Foreign Office was confident it could rebut any concerns about this on the grounds that it had been proven that Nigeria was not committing genocide (see chapter 3); in the end the issue was only mentioned in passing during the debate. See Note from A. J. Collins (3 February 1969), on Genocide and Nigeria, in UKNA file FCO 61/520.

[60] Letter from the British Embassy in The Hague to the Foreign Office (17 August 1951), document UP 254/38 in UKNA file FO 371/95709, containing translation of Stikker's speech in the Dutch parliament.

to do so: in August 1952, the First International Humanist congress of Amsterdam called on all governments to ratify the Genocide Convention immediately.[61] But there was also domestic criticism of the Convention. One of the first monographs on the Genocide Convention was written by Pieter N. Drost, a leading Dutch international lawyer. Drost's views on the Convention were quite trenchant: 'The Genocide Convention as a partial and provisional realization of international criminal law does not substantially contribute to the promotion of either peoples' rights or human rights.'[62] In a section entitled 'Final criticisms', he grouped his critique under subtitles such as 'pointless preamble', 'purposeless Article I', 'deficient definition in Article II', and 'puny provisions of Article VII'.[63] Much of his criticism was similar to the criticisms of the Dutch Government as noted above. Thus, the exclusion of 'political groups' was considered to be 'a wide and dangerous loophole for any government to escape the human duties under the Convention'.[64] Instead, he argued, genocide 'is the deliberate destruction of physical life of individual human beings by reason of their membership of *any* human collectivity as such.'[65] Drost's views thus seem to echo (if they did not directly influence) the Dutch government's concerns about the Convention.[66]

The Dutch position, though, seems to be at odds with the importance it currently places on international law and human rights. But two factors probably played a role in the delay in ratifying the Convention. The first is that the Netherlands has often been late in ratifying human rights

[61] 'International Humanist and Ethical Union is established: Congress in Amsterdam adopts resolution', *De Leeuwarder Courant*, 27 August 1952 (translation by Tine van Criekinge (TvC)).

[62] Pieter N. Drost, *The Crime of State: Penal Protection for Fundamental Freedoms of Persons and Peoples, Book II Genocide* (Leyden: A. W. Sythoff, 1959), pp. i–ii. Book I was on Humanicide: Human Rights as Legal Rights. The Netherlands has never been enthusiastic about drafting new human rights standards which it feels do not add much to existing standards (including as set out in UN General Assembly declarations), and which could even risk watering down previously-agreed standards. See Hilde Reiding, *The Netherlands and the Development of International Human Rights Instruments* (Antwerp and Oxford: Intersentia, 2007), pp. 400–1.

[63] Drost, *The Crime of State*, pp. 119–136.

[64] Drost, *The Crime of State*, p. 123.

[65] Drost, *The Crime of State*, p. 125. Emphasis added.

[66] Ward Churchill charges that Drost was a 'solid member of the Dutch establishment', who supported Dutch colonial policies, and that his

conventions because the legal system is monist, so the specific provisions of any treaty could be used in court cases directly and immediately upon ratification. This leads to caution in proceeding to ratification.[67]

The second factor is the domestic environment. Contrary to its later reputation as a 'leading country' on human rights, the Netherlands was not enthusiastic about the creation of international human rights instruments from 1945 until the 1960s. This has been attributed primarily to its interests in maintaining its colonial empire (which lasted until 1963).[68] Thus, in the Dutch case, the incongruity between colonial rule and human rights, including the legal norm against genocide, does seem to have occurred to policy-makers. In addition, for the first couple of decades after the end of the Second World War there was very little 'national memory' of the destruction of Dutch (and European) Jews in the Shoah. As Pieter Lagrou has shown, the suffering that the Netherlands as a whole endured from October 1944 to May 1945 'greatly reduced the public's capacity to commiserate with particular groups of martyrs'.[69] Furthermore, the general chaos and financial hardship in the immediate aftermath of liberation led the government to refuse to categorise victims of the war, and thus give them particular assistance. 'Any group claiming special merit or special suffering not only threatened to be a burden on the national budget, but also endangered the national consensus that heroism and martyrdom had been the collective experience of the Dutch people'.[70] This policy of 'national consensus' then prohibited official commemoration of the Holocaust. Two Prime Ministers, Jan de Quay (May 1959 – July 1963) and Victor Marijnen (July 1963 – April 1965), instructed their cabinets not to participate in Auschwitz commemoration ceremonies, and the government

motivation for writing *The Crime of State* was to 'create as comprehensive and sophisticated an intellectual barrier as possible against characterisations of Dutch imperialism as being inherently genocidal.' Ward Churchill, *A Little Matter of Genocide* (San Francisco: City Lights Books, 1997), p. 415.

67 Correspondence with Professor Willem van Genugten, Tilburg University (16 January 2009), and with Theo van Boven, former Dutch Foreign Ministry official (5 March 2009). The Netherlands did not ratify the two International Covenants (on Civil and Political Rights, and on Economic, Cultural and Social Rights) for more than ten years after they had been signed.

68 Reiding, *The Netherlands*, p. 13.

69 Pieter Lagrou, 'Victims of Genocide and National Memory: Belgium, France and the Netherlands, 1945–65', in Gordon Martel, ed., *The World War Two Reader* (London: Routledge, 2004), p. 404.

70 Lagrou, 'Victims of Genocide', p. 404.

refused to donate money to construct an international monument at Auschwitz.[71] But in the 1960s, the Dutch role in the Shoah became more of a subject for public discussion and debate. There was embarrassment over the refusal to contribute to the Auschwitz monument, and in 1964 a television documentary on the Nazi occupation discussed the Dutch part in the genocide of the Jews.[72] This coincided with the general liberalisation of Dutch society and political system in the 1960s (the so-called process of 'depillarization'), in which issues such as civil and political rights became much more prominent. Accession to the Genocide Convention (the law was approved on 2 July 1964) appears to be much less of a controversial step in this changing context.

Ireland had a similar attitude towards the Convention as the UK, but its government never came under the sort of domestic pressure to accede that the British government did. No parliamentarians pressed for accession (and no parliamentary questions were asked on the issue until 1973, when the government made moves to ratify several human rights conventions), the Department of Foreign Affairs files contain just three letters from civil society organisations pushing for accession, and there was almost nothing in the press about the issue. Following the General Assembly resolution inviting states that were not yet members of the UN to accede to the Convention, the Irish government did consider the question, but as in the UK, there was a conflict between the Foreign Affairs and Justice Departments.

The Foreign Affairs Department was not enthusiastic about the Convention: it was considered to be useless and superfluous, and inadequate because its purpose is penal rather than preventative. But

> although the Convention cannot be said to inspire any feeling of security, its condemnation of the crime of genocide, which includes religious persecution, is a healty [sic] indication of the abhorrence with which it is viewed by civilized states. Genocide is an international crime and any action against it must be by international accord and the Convention, while it might not go far enough, is at least a step in the right direction.[73]

[71] Lagrou, 'Victims of Genocide', p. 409.

[72] Lagrou, 'Victims of Genocide', p. 409. The Anne Frank house became a museum in 1960; the Hollandsche Schouwburg (a theatre that became a deportation centre for Jews) became a monument in 1962.

[73] 'Convention on Genocide' (4 August 1951), in Irish National Archives (hereinafter INA), Department of Foreign Affairs file 417/65/I.

The Department of Justice was hostile. On 22 September 1950, the department wrote to the Foreign Affairs Department, indicating: 'The [Justice] Minister is strongly of opinion that Ireland should not become a party to this Convention unless and until it is found that this is the only country not ratifying or acceding to it.'[74] The government's official reasons for non-accession were 'the difficulty of giving legislative effect to the definition of genocide, which was drawn in very wide terms. Some hesitation was felt about the extradition provisions, as to whether they would require an unjustifiable derogation from the exception from extradition of political offences.'[75]

But as was the case in the UK, as more and more countries acceded to the Convention – including the UK itself – Ireland began to feel more isolated. In the Department of Foreign Affairs, there was a desire to improve the country's human rights record – especially as 'Human Rights Year 1968' loomed.[76] And by 1972, when Ireland was about to join the European Community, the Department was keen to point out that Ireland was virtually alone amongst the EC member states in not having acceded to the Genocide Convention.[77] In 1973, the Foreign Affairs Minister indicated that he wished Ireland to accede to those UN human rights agreements to which Ireland was not already a party, given that 1973 was the twenty-fifth anniversary of the UN Declaration of Human Rights. In a letter to the Secretary of the Department of Justice, the fact that almost every European country had become a party to the Genocide Convention was highlighted.[78]

In November 1968, under a new Prime Minister (Jack Lynch), the government approved the drafting of a bill to implement the Convention – and specifically stated that it was 'mindful of the impression of lack of respect for the objects of the Convention to which our continued

[74] Letter in INA, Department of Foreign Affairs file 417/65/I.

[75] Oifig an Aire Gnothai Eachtracha, 'Memorandum for the government: accession to the United Nations Convention on the Prevention and Punishment of the Crime of Genocide' (23 December 1975), in INA, Department of Foreign Affairs file 417/65/II.

[76] In a minute of 30 September 1966, in INA, Department of Foreign Affairs file 417/65/II.

[77] In a minute of 25 January 1972, in INA, Department of Foreign Affairs file 417/65/II.

[78] Letter of 28 March 1973, from Hugh McCann (Foreign Affairs) to A. Ward (Justice), in INA, Department of Foreign Affairs file 417/65/II.

non-accession could give rise.'[79] But the Justice Department still stalled. A Genocide Bill was only presented to parliament (Tithe an Oireachtais) in late 1973. The Genocide Act was signed on 18 December 1973. Even then, there were still delays (an indication of the relatively low priority given to the Genocide Convention). The government did not take a decision to accede to the Convention until January 1976.[80]

In the case of Luxembourg, it appears that it did not accede to the Genocide Convention until 1981 because the issue simply was not enough of a priority for successive governments to push it through parliament. In September 1952, the proposal to accede to the Convention was directed to the Council of State (Conseil d'Etat), an advisory body of 21 citizens appointed by the Grand Duke. The Council of State did not issue its opinion on the proposal until 1969. It did not reach the Chamber of Deputies until May 1981. It had been on the agenda of the previous government in the late 1970s but 'other things were given priority due to adverse circumstances (particularly the difficulties in the steel industry)'.[81] Numerous deputies commented negatively on the delay, as Luxembourg stood out amongst its EC partners as the only country not to have acceded to the Convention, and the Convention was approved unanimously. Four years later, in July 1985, the law implementing the Convention's provisions was debated in the Chamber of Deputies. In that debate, it was noted that national law did have to be modified in accordance with the Convention, but that this nonetheless was not an acceptable excuse for the delay. The law implementing the Convention was also approved unanimously.[82]

European attitudes towards the Genocide Convention were thus quite complex and varied. While some governments – notably the Scandinavians – embraced the drafting process and the outcome of the Convention itself, and had little difficulty in accepting its provisions, other European governments had serious concerns. Some of

[79] 'Memorandum for the government' (23 December 1975).

[80] Cabinet minutes of 9 January 1976, in INA, Department of Taoiseach files 2006/133/398.

[81] Discourse of the rapporteur, M. Dondelinger, on the proposal no. 433 to approve the Genocide Convention, in the Chamber of Deputies, 14 May 1981 (C-1980–0-55–0007). Translation by Isabelle Nicolay (IN). The transcripts of the debates in the Chamber are available at www.chd.lu/archives/ArchivesPortlet.

[82] Debate on proposal no. 2547 (C-1984–0–073–0007) on 3 July 1985. Translation by IN.

these concerns came out during the negotiations on the Convention; others manifested themselves later, in a reticence either to accede to the Convention or to enact legislation implementing the Convention.

In any event, as time went on, it became increasingly uncomfortable for European states to remain aloof and constructivist insights help show why: states were not comfortable with the identity associated with non-accession or non-ratification of the Convention. In some cases there was domestic pressure to accept the Convention, but in all cases, there was a clear awareness of the implications for a state's international reputation and standing if it were to remain a non-party, or in non-conformity with the provisions of the Convention (as in the case of Italy). In other words, many European states did not sign up to the Convention out of an ingrained conviction that it was the right thing to do; they had to come round to the idea as the reputational costs of not doing so became more apparent ('civilised' countries abhor genocide which means acceding to or ratifying the Convention; remaining outside such a group became increasingly unacceptable). A notable exception here is the Federal Republic of Germany, where German responsibility for the Holocaust undeniably was a key factor in its speedy acceptance of the Convention. However, it is noteworthy that none of the major European countries (especially France, Germany[83] and the UK) and none of the EU institutions issued a declaration on the sixtieth anniversary of the Genocide Convention on 9 December 2008 – though there were declarations aplenty regarding the sixtieth anniversary of the Universal Declaration of Human Rights, which fell on the following day.

National provisions for punishment of the crime of genocide

Under the Genocide Convention, state parties are to enact domestic legislation outlawing genocide, and providing for its punishment. All European states have done so (eventually), but this raises jurisdictional issues: how far have European states stretched their jurisdiction

[83] Though the German Human Rights Commissioner, Günter Nooke, did speak at a conference in Marburg/Frankfurt commemorating the 60th anniversary of the Convention (www.auswaertiges-amt.de/diplo/en/Infoservice/Presse/Reden/2008/081206-Nooke-GenocideConvention.html [last accessed 13 April 2010]).

over genocide committed in another country by nationals or residents or foreigners? Jan Wouters and Sten Verhoeven have shown that while some European states have assumed extraterritorial jurisdiction over genocide, there are still quite a number of differences between them.[84]

In Austria, universal jurisdiction is possible under certain circumstances; in 1994, the Supreme Court ruled that there was no duty to extradite a Bosnian Serb to Bosnia and Herzegovina because of the war there, and no international criminal tribunal either, so therefore universal jurisdiction could be exercised.[85] Belgium had allowed universal jurisdiction for serious violations of international humanitarian law, but in 2003 it repealed this 1993 law. The new law allows Belgium to prosecute any national or resident of Belgium for allegedly perpetrating genocide outside Belgium. France has jurisdiction to prosecute if the perpetrator or victim have French nationality. Under a 2002 law, Germany can prosecute alleged perpetrators of genocide, war crimes, and crimes against humanity without any requirement of a territorial link to Germany – essentially, Germany has adopted a position of universal jurisdiction. The Netherlands can prosecute if the alleged perpetrators are arrested on Dutch soil, though only if they cannot be extradited to the state on whose territory genocide was committed or surrendered to the International Criminal Court. Spain has universal jurisdiction under a 1985 law.

The UK's Genocide Act of 1969 only permitted it to exercise territorial jurisdiction over genocide, strictly following article 6; in 2001, this act was superseded by the International Criminal Court Act, which determines that the UK can prosecute for genocide, crimes against humanity and war crimes if they are committed in the UK, or outside the UK by a UK national or resident (or by a foreigner who becomes a UK resident). The UK law was, however, criticised because it did not allow for prosecutions of UK residents for crimes of genocide committed before the 2001 act entered into force, and did not allow

[84] Jan Wouters and Sten Verhoeven, 'The Prosecution of Genocide – in Search of a European Perspective', in Henham and Behrens, eds., *The Criminal Law of Genocide: International*, pp. 197–205. See also Helmut Kreicker, 'National Prosecution of Genocide from a Comparative Perspective', *International Criminal Law Review*, vol. 5, no. 3 (2005).

[85] The accused was found not guilty for lack of evidence. Wouters and Verhoeven, 'The Prosecution of Genocide', p. 198.

for prosecutions of non-residents (even if present in the UK) at all. The Aegis Trust, an advocacy group campaigning against genocide, pushed for the law to be amended, arguing that Rwandan *genocidaires* living in Britain could not be prosecuted in the UK, but may not be extradited to Rwanda because of concerns about whether they would receive a fair trial there. It also noted that the ICC has the capacity to hold only a few trials a year.[86] As noted in Chapter 5, four Rwandan genocide suspects were released because they could not be extradited to Rwanda nor prosecuted in the UK. In April 2010, the government's proposals to close the loopholes were approved by parliament: crimes are now covered if committed since 1991, and the law now also covers all those entering the UK for work, study or to claim asylum.

In addition to legislation implementing the Genocide Convention, Caroline Fournet argues that states should go further and outlaw genocide denial – which, she maintains, is a form of incitement to genocide, though the Genocide Convention does not specifically address this issue.[87] Several European states have outlawed Holocaust denial (and stipulated prison sentences for it): Austria (1992), Belgium (1995), Czech Republic (2001), France (1990); Germany (1985), Luxembourg (1997), Poland (1998), Romania (2005), and Switzerland (1995). With the exception of Luxembourg and Switzerland, whose laws cover genocide and other crimes against humanity in general, and Poland, whose law includes denial of 'communist crimes', the laws specifically outlaw denial of the Holocaust.[88] But other countries such as Denmark, Sweden and the UK do not have such laws, as they are seen to be contrary to the freedom of speech.

In early 2007, at the start of its EU presidency, Germany began pushing for the European Union as a whole to outlaw Holocaust denial; a previous attempt to do so had been scuppered in 2005 by the UK, among other states. The German proposal was controversial – particularly for member states (and others) which consider freedom

[86] Anna Macdonald, 'Strengthening UK Law on Genocide, War Crimes and Crimes against Humanity', in Nick Donovan, ed., *The Enforcement of International Criminal Law*, (Laxton, Nottinghamshire: Aegis Trust, 2009). See Aegis website on this (www.aegistrust.org/index.php) and Ken Macdonald, 'Our Haven for War Criminals', *The Guardian* (8 November 2008).

[87] Fournet, *The Crime of Destruction and the Law of Genocide*, p. 83.

[88] See the list of laws on the website of the Coordinating Forum for Countering Antisemitism, www.antisemitism.org.il/eng [last accessed 13 April 2010].

of speech to be more important.[89] And some member states wanted to go even further, outlawing denial of 'communist crimes'. Armenian groups lobbied for inclusion of the Armenian genocide.[90] In the end, the EU framework decision requires member states to punish 'publicly condoning, denying or grossly trivialising crimes of genocide, crimes against humanity and war crimes as defined in Articles 6, 7, and 8 of the Statute of the International Criminal Court ... when the conduct is carried out in a manner likely to incite to violence or hatred against such a group or a member of such a group'. However, states can limit this to specific crimes that have been established by a final decision of a national court and/or an international court. In other words, national laws could cover the Holocaust and incidents of genocide as determined by the UN tribunals or the ICC – which thus leaves out the case of the Armenian genocide.[91]

Denial of the Armenian genocide is particularly controversial and merits a brief discussion here because it has been a major issue in several European countries, and in relations between Europe and Turkey. Turkey denies that it was a genocide while Armenia – and the Armenian expatriate communities in several countries – maintain that it was. The Turkish denial has driven attempts to have the Armenian genocide 'recognised' as such. A few parliaments across Europe have declared that there was a genocide in Armenia, and have pressed their governments to raise the issue with Turkey – notably Belgium (1998), Bulgaria (1995), Cyprus (1990), France (2001), Germany (2005), Greece (1996), Italy (2000), Sweden (2000), and Switzerland (2003).[92] Several of these declarations (such as those of Greece and Cyprus) must be seen as reflecting a desire to score political points

[89] *The Economist*, for example, argued that 'Holocaust denial laws are wrong whoever imposes them. But they are at least understandable in countries where Nazism had indigenous roots. No such excuse can be made for the European Union as a whole'. 'Slippery slope', *The Economist* (27 January 2007).

[90] Tobias Buck, 'Holocaust Law Leaves Many Dissatisfied', *Financial Times* (20 April 2007).

[91] Council Framework Decision 2008/913/JHA of 28 November 2008 on combating certain forms and expressions of racism and xenophobia by means of criminal law, in Official Journal of the European Union L 328/55 (6 December 2008).

[92] Donald Bloxham, *The Great Game of Genocide: Imperialism, Nationalism and the Destruction of the Ottoman Armenians* (Oxford: Oxford University

against Turkey. As Donald Bloxham notes, 'the notion of states passing resolutions on the character of historical events in undoubtedly an odd one in any circumstances.' But 'the Turkish state has sought to play the game of denial on the international political stage and has therefore invited a response in kind.'[93]

The Turkish refusal to recognise the Armenian genocide coupled with its persecution of historians or intellectuals who have tried to raise the issue (most notably the Nobel prize winner Orhan Pamuk) has emboldened some critics of Turkey to go further than just issuing declarations of recognition. In October 2006, the French National Assembly outlawed denial of the Armenian genocide; the French government opposed the law, however, and it did not enter into effect. The Turkish government expressed considerable dismay over the National Assembly move, and across Turkey there were numerous protests against France. The European Commissioner for Enlargement, Olli Rehn, also condemned the draft law because it could have serious consequences for EU-Turkey relations, and would damage EU attempts to push Turkey to allow free speech (the Turkish penal code penalises 'insulting Turkishness').[94] The French move is virtually impossible to separate out from the widespread opposition to Turkish membership of the EU in France. More ominously for Turkish membership prospects, the European Parliament, which must approve EU membership applications, considers Turkish recognition of the genocide to be a prerequisite for EU membership.[95]

The further development of the legal norm

In Europe, the legal norm had a rather inauspicious beginning, but by the time the 1990s began, European governments were quite

Press, 2005), p. 223. He notes further (p. 224) that the French parliament's declaration is odd in that it simply recognises the 'Armenian genocide of 1915', but does not attribute any responsibility to any perpetrator (and certainly not to the Turkish state).

93 Bloxham, *The Great Game of Genocide*, p. 226.

94 Mark Beunderman, 'Rehn Warns France Against Adopting Armenia Genocide Law', *EUObserver.com* (10 October 2006), and Honor Mahony, 'Brussels and Ankara Condemn French Law on Armenia Genocide', *EUObserver.com* (12 October 2006).

95 European Parliament resolution on the opening of accession negotiations with Turkey, P6_TA(2005)0350 (28 September 2005), paragraph 5.

outspoken proponents of it. As discussed further in Chapters 4 and 5, European governments helped create the International Criminal Tribunals for the former Yugoslavia and Rwanda (though not without ambivalence), and are (now) amongst their foremost supporters. The definition of genocide in the statutes of those tribunals is the same as that of the Genocide Convention.

And while European governments did have differing positions regarding the International Criminal Court, there were no disagreements regarding the inclusion of genocide or the definition of genocide in the ICC statute. Only one state, Cuba, tried, unsuccessfully, to expand the definition of genocide during the negotiations on the ICC statute, arguing for the inclusion of social and political groups.[96] But despite the strong support that some European governments had shown for such an expansion during the drafting of the Genocide Convention, no other state supported the Cuban effort. The definition of genocide is the same as that in the Genocide Convention. Furthermore, genocide was clearly considered to be a separate crime, not a crime against humanity (as France had tried to argue during the Genocide Convention negotiations).

European governments also came out (rhetorically) in favour of taking strong action to prevent genocide from occurring in the first place – and even of intervening to stop genocide. In 2004, fifty-five countries, including all the member states of the European Union plus numerous other European countries, gathered for an intergovernmental conference on preventing genocide, part of a series of related conferences under the auspices of the Stockholm International Forum, sponsored by the Swedish government. The Forum produced a declaration, in which the various governments declared that they would seek to develop mechanisms to identify and report genocidal threats as early as possible, so as to prevent genocide, mass murder, and ethnic cleansing; they would protect groups identified as potential victims of genocide, mass murder or ethnic cleansing, in accordance with international law; they would ensure that perpetrators of genocidal acts were brought to justice; they would support research into genocide prevention, and education against genocidal dangers; and they would consider various options for action against genocidal

[96] Schabas, *Genocide in International Law*, 2nd edition, p. 109.

threats, mass murders and ethnic cleansing.[97] The Forum suggested that the UN Secretary-General create a post of 'Special Adviser for the Prevention of Genocide', which he did shortly afterwards.[98]

All the European governments have strongly supported the principle of the responsibility to protect, included in the 2005 UN World Summit Outcome Document.[99] But as Alex Bellamy notes, the UN summit version of 'responsibility to protect' is a weaker one than that originally proposed by an International Commission on Intervention and State Sovereignty. 'Thus UN member states recognised their responsibility to protect their own citizens but *did not* recognise a *responsibility to act* beyond using peaceful means in cases of mass killing, genocide and ethnic cleansing.'[100] They merely state they are 'prepared to take collective action'.

There are some differences between France, the UK and Germany on this. France and the UK have 'flatly rejected the view that unauthorised intervention should be prohibited in all circumstances';[101] Germany argues that the use of force without the consent of the host government could only be sanctioned by the Security Council – in accordance with its traditional reverence for the primacy of international law and the UN Charter.[102] Since the summit, European governments have repeatedly stressed that the international community has a 'shared responsibility' to protect civilians from genocide and crimes against humanity.[103] In December 2008, the EU declared

97 Declaration of the Stockholm International Forum 2004, available at: www.manskligarattigheter.gov.se/stockholmforum/2004/page1617.html [last accessed 13 April 2010].

98 The Special Adviser can only propose steps to prevent genocide, not determine whether or not it is occurring. He is to gather information, provide early warning of situations that could result in genocide, and make recommendations for action. See Juan E. Méndez (the first Special Adviser), 'The United Nations and the Prevention of Genocide', in Henham and Behrens, eds., *The Criminal Law of Genocide*.

99 United Nations General Assembly, Resolution 60/1, 'World Summit Outcome', A/RES/60/1.

100 Bellamy, *Responsibility to Protect*, p. 90.

101 Bellamy, *Responsibility to Protect*, p. 67.

102 Bellamy, *Responsibility to Protect*, p. 69. See also the German government's 7th Human Rights Report (15/5800), of 17 June 2005, which again emphasises the German advocacy of the UN Security Council's right to act in the case of massive human rights violations. Translation by DM.

103 See 'Excerpts of Government Statements on the Responsibility to Protect: Europe 2005–2007', Institute for Global Policy (New York),

that 'sovereign governments ... hold a shared responsibility to protect populations from genocide, war crimes, ethnic cleansing and crimes against humanity'.[104] A key question is the extent to which European governments are willing to push the rest of the international community to act (and if so, how), and to contribute themselves to any such action, in the event that a government does not fulfil the responsibility to protect its population from genocide. Do European governments fully accept *their* responsibility to protect, or just that the 'international community' has such a responsibility?

Conclusion

European attitudes towards the legal norm have evolved over time, in some cases from outright hostility, to a fairly strong rhetorical stance that even favours coercive military intervention as a last resort to stop genocide from occurring, though this would have to be approved by the UN Security Council if all European governments were to support it. The next chapter analyses the evolution of the Cold War European discourse and response to purported or actual genocides. Of particular importance will be the extent to which European governments relied on the definition of genocide in the Genocide Convention (the legal norm) or a wider definition that includes political groups (which many European governments supported during the negotiations on the Convention). How did European governments interpret their obligation to 'prevent and punish genocide' under the Convention – was this obligation seen to over-ride the predominant norm of non-interference in the internal affairs of countries?

available at: www.responsibilitytoprotect.org/index.php/government_statements/c133 [last accessed 13 April 2010].

104 European Council, 'Report on the implementation of the European Security Strategy: providing security in a changing world', document S407/08, Brussels (11 December 2008), p. 2.

3 *European discourses on genocide during the Cold War*

This chapter analyses European debates on genocide from the end of the Second World War through to the end of the Cold War. It considers whether European governments used the term genocide (and came under domestic pressure to use the term) during the Cold War period to describe massive human rights violations in a wide variety of countries. Has there been a change in the discourse about genocide over time, from less use to more use? This chapter also analyses how governments interpreted the definition of genocide and their obligations under the Genocide Convention. Did the definition they used stem from the legal norm of the Convention, or the social norm? And if genocide was perceived to be ongoing, how did European governments respond?

From the 1960s, the term was used quite frequently in public discourse – by opposition (or even backbench) MPs, by civil society groups, by journalists – to describe events, and as a call for action.[1] In this usage, the term was interpreted quite widely, to cover numerous episodes of genocide during the Cold War. In contrast, European *governments* rarely labelled atrocities as genocide. Although European governments may have become convinced that they had to sign up to the Genocide Convention because it was what 'civilised nations' do, or because they found the isolation of not signing up too uncomfortable, they were clearly not willing to use the term 'genocide' freely during the Cold War. In fact they sometimes sought actively to prove that a genocide was not occurring. In public, governments gave only

[1] The 1950s was a relatively quiet decade for use of the term – as can be seen by doing a search for the term in a database of articles from *The Times*, and the Hansard record of debates in the UK Houses of Parliament. While Raphael Lemkin certainly felt that the Soviet Union was committing genocide in the 1950s, particularly in Lithuania, the word was not widely used in public parlance regarding the Soviet Union. See, for example, Cooper, *Raphael Lemkin*, p. 210.

a minimal indication of what they considered to be the limits of the definition in the Convention and of their obligations under the Convention.

The avoidance of the term genocide is puzzling. After all, once the extradition issue was taken care of in domestic legislation, the obligations on European governments under the Convention were not onerous: there being no international tribunal, it would be up to the courts of the country where genocide had taken place to prosecute individuals for the crime. If a case of genocide was referred to the Security Council, it was unlikely much would happen, given Cold War divisions at the UN. It is odd then that governments avoided even suggesting in public that genocide was being perpetrated, by Cold War allies *or* rivals. One explanation could be that European governments feared that if they used the term, they could be accused in turn of violating the Convention, as several European colonial powers were fighting rebellions in their colonies in the first twenty or so years after the Second World War. But this simply didn't seem to be a serious worry. Another explanation could be that the word genocide was considered with such reverence that it would not be used lightly (and should never be politicised). This is possible, though such a consideration does not appear to have played an explicit role in policy-making in the cases here. Another explanation is that governments avoided the use of the word because to do so would invoke the social norm against genocide and increase the pressure on them to take action they did not want to take.

There are three cases of purported genocide during the Cold War that prompted not only widespread public concern but also a government response: the fate of Biafrans in Nigeria, atrocities in East Pakistan (now Bangladesh), and the horrors in Cambodia under Khmer Rouge rule. There were other cases in which genocide was alleged to have occurred, but in these the level of public concern was not as high and/or European governments easily brushed aside such allegations. This chapter first analyses the three cases, and then considers the use of the term to describe events in other countries.

The Nigerian Civil War, 1967–1970

On 30 May 1967, the military ruler of the eastern regions of Nigeria ('Biafra'), Odumegwu Ojukwu, announced the secession of Biafra from the Nigerian federation, and its independence as a sovereign state. In response, the Federal Government imposed a blockade and shortly thereafter launched an attempt to regain control of the region by military means. It did not succeed until January 1970. Estimates of the number of people who died in the Nigerian Civil War vary widely, though one million dead is an oft-cited figure. Many died of starvation. The war – and European governments' policies towards it – provoked considerable unease across Europe, to the extent that polling showed it was the second, and sometimes even the first, most important international issue after the Vietnam War. Across Europe there were street demonstrations and protests, campaigns to write letters to MPs, persistent media and editorial interest, and a huge effort, mainly organised by churches, to send humanitarian aid to Biafra.[2]

Of interest here is that accusations of genocide were made by the Biafrans against the Nigerian Federal Government and/or its armed forces, and were widely repeated in European discourse, though never by governments. Such accusations fed considerable public opposition to official government positions on Biafra and above all, to that of the UK, which continued to sell arms and ammunition to the Nigerian Federal Government throughout the war. What sets the Biafra case apart from other Cold War instances of purported genocide is not just the extent of the public alarm regarding the possibility that a genocide was ongoing, but that European governments – particularly the UK – considered it necessary to prove that no genocide was in fact occurring. An unprecedented 'International Observer Team', made up of representatives from Canada, Poland, Sweden, the UK, the Organisation of African Unity and the United Nations, was sent to Nigeria to counter – rather than to investigate impartially – the genocide accusations. The Biafra case is thus given most attention in this chapter.

[2] The Nigerian Civil War prompted the founding of new humanitarian aid agencies, including Africa Concern (now Concern), based in Ireland, and Médecins Sans Frontières, which was founded in 1971 by doctors (including the current French Foreign Minister Bernard Kouchner) who felt that the Red Cross had not been independent enough of the Nigerian government during the war. In Ireland alone the joint Africa Concern/Biafra Famine Appeal raised over £300,000. Enda Staunton, 'The Case of Biafra: Ireland and the Nigerian Civil War', *Irish Historical Studies*, vol. 31, no. 124 (November 1999), table 2, 534.

Nigeria became independent in 1960, and initially consisted of three regions (four, from 1963). Each region had a majority ethnic group; in the eastern region Igbos (or Ibos[3]) predominated. In January 1966, a group of officers (mainly Igbo) carried out a coup attempt, in which the prime minister and two regional premiers were killed. The general commanding officer, Johnson Ironsi, established control and appointed five military governors, one for each of the four regions plus Lagos. Ojukwu was appointed the military governor of the eastern region. The 1966 coup attempt was seen elsewhere in the country as an attempt to establish Igbo domination. In July 1966, a revolt by army elements from the northern region led to Ironsi's murder. He was replaced by Major-General Yakubu Gowon. But the coup attempt failed in the east, where Ojukwu remained in control and refused to recognise Gowon as the new head of state. At the end of September, perhaps 30,000 Igbos living mainly in the northern region were massacred.[4]

Relations between the eastern region and the Federal Military Government (FMG) deteriorated sharply. On 30 May 1967, Ojukwu announced Biafran independence to the 'people of Eastern Nigeria', 'aware that you can no longer be protected in your lives and in your property by any government based outside Eastern Nigeria'.[5] The FMG immediately imposed a blockade on the region. In August 1967, Biafran forces invaded the neighbouring mid-western region, but then withdrew. In the wake of their withdrawal Igbo civilians were killed. As more and more of Biafra's territory was lost to Federal forces, food supplies in the agriculturally-poor region grew scarce. In May 1968, Port Harcourt, Biafra's only link to the outside world, was captured by Nigerian forces. The facts that Igbo civilians had been killed and that malnutrition and starvation claimed increasing numbers of victims gave the accusations of genocide enough force to generate widespread public concern in Europe. In the wake of the fall of Port

[3] Ibo is the Anglicised spelling.

[4] The number of dead was initially given as 30,000 by the eastern region after the names of dead and missing were listed. In 1969, the British government stated that 7000 had died; in later stages of the war, the Biafran government claimed that 50,000 had been killed. Suzanne Cronje, *The World and Nigeria: The Diplomatic History of the Biafran War 1967–1970* (London: Sidgwick and Jackson, 1972), p. 18.

[5] Cited in John J. Stremlau, *The International Politics of the Nigerian Civil War, 1967–1970* (Princeton: Princeton University Press, 1977), p. 60.

Harcourt, several British newspapers used Holocaust imagery: 'worse than Belsen'; 'fate could be as dreadful as that of the victims of the Nazi concentration camps'.[6] It was widely believed that because Igbos believed they would be at risk if they were defeated by the FMG, they had every incentive to continue fighting. The war would not end until the safety of Igbos could be assured.[7]

It is also the case that the Biafran 'government' was skilled at propaganda, and did use the accusations about genocide to try to gain diplomatic recognition.[8] On 5 August 1968, Ojukwu accused the FMG of genocide in a speech to the OAU in Addis Ababa, in a clear attempt to garner diplomatic support. He alleged that the massacres of eastern Nigerians in 1966 were a genocide, and accused Gowon of 'aspiring to be the Hitler of Africa'. Further, he argued that 'this palpable genocide' was being financed and directed by non-African countries.[9]

While some (or most, depending on your point of view) of the information coming out of Biafra was 'spin', it did resonate. For supporters of the Federal Military Government of Nigeria, the propaganda was the reason for pro-Biafran sentiment – not identification with the cause of self-determination or horror at the carnage of the war.

[6] Cronje, *The World and Nigeria*, p. 75.

[7] For example, see the view of UK MP, James Griffiths, expressed in the debate on UK arms supplies to Nigeria, in the House of Commons, 12 June 1968, Hansard, vol. 766, cols. 248–50. Such fears seemed justified if one listened to one of Nigeria's top military commanders: in August 1968, Col Adekunle told *The Economist*: 'I want to prevent even one Ibo having even one piece to eat before their capitulation. We shoot at everything that moves, and when our forces march into the center of Ibo territory, we shoot at everything, even at things do not move.' Quote in Stremlau, *The International Politics*, p. 331. In 1968, the 'International Committee for the Study of the Crimes of Genocide', a Paris-based unofficial organisation of lawyers from several countries, investigated the case of a possible genocide by Nigeria and apparently determined that genocide was occurring. But this sort of finding could be easily ignored by governments. Cronje, *The World and Nigeria*, pp. 277–8.

[8] Only four African countries recognised Biafra: Tanzania, Gabon, Ivory Coast, and Zambia between April and May 1968; Haiti also did so in March 1969. The OAU as a whole backed Nigerian unity, and were quite suspicious of any European support for Biafra, which they likened to Belgian, French and UK backing for secessionist Katanga (in Congo) earlier in the decade.

[9] Republic of Biafra, Address by Ojukwu to Organisation of African Unity, Addis Ababa, 5 August 1968, in 'Nigerian Civil War Collection' (archives of Suzanne Cronje), at the School of Oriental and Asian Studies, London, MS321463, vol. 65.

British Prime Minister Harold Wilson was scathing about Biafran propaganda, while at the same time recognising its persuasive power. He wrote:

> The purveyors of Biafran propaganda flooded the Western press and Western legislatures with literature, and secured a degree of moral control over Western broadcasting systems, with a success unparalleled in the history of communications in modern democratic societies. Their switch of line was remarkable: as soon as Colonel Ojuwu's forces were pressed back out of the western areas, and indeed out of Enugu and other Ibo heartland areas, the cry was 'genocide'. Should Biafra fall there would be mass extermination, so they said.[10]

He was clearly hurt by the accusations levelled at the British government: 'The nonconformists all, bar a few, condemned us, and placed the guilt for the prolongation of the war, and for every single death through military action or starvation, at our door.'[11]

By the summer of 1968 public protest about Biafra was growing across Europe: pressure for political action was particularly high in the Scandinavian countries, West Germany, and France, but also in countries such as Ireland and Italy, where reports from Catholic missionaries in Biafra fuelled public alarm.[12] In June 1968, France and the Netherlands announced an arms embargo on both sides of the civil war; Belgium followed suit in July.

In July 1968, the French position shifted towards more overt support for Biafra. On 31 July, the French Secretary of State for Information declared that the Biafrans had demonstrated their will to assert themselves as a people.[13] John Stremlau argues that French President de Gaulle's public show of support for Biafra was mostly a response to domestic pressures: 'A public opinion poll taken in the summer of 1968

[10] Harold Wilson, *The Labour Government 1964–1970: A Personal Record* (London: Weidenfeld and Nicolson, and Michael Joseph Ltd, 1971), p. 557.

[11] Wilson, *The Labour Government*, p. 558.

[12] See Stremlau, *International Politics*, pp. 294–7; Staunton, 'The Case of Biafra, Ireland and the Nigerian Civil War'. An FCO background note for the Prime Minister's visit to Bonn in February 1969 rather presumptuously speculated, 'It seems possible that many Germans find a psychological compensation in protesting against allegations of genocide in Nigeria for their failure to make similar protests in Germany under Hitler.' Document PMVB (69) of 16 January 1969 in UKNA file FCO 65/179.

[13] Cronje, *The World and Nigeria*, p. 194.

had revealed that Biafra ranked number one, ahead of Vietnam, as the international issue of greatest concern to the French people. Sentiment was overwhelmingly pro-Biafran, and was led by the French left that, not incidentally, had been at the vanguard of the student and workers' protest in May.'[14] In August 1968, the head of the Secretariat of African Affairs at the Quai d'Orsay, Jacques Foccart, informed Biafra that France would ensure that necessary military equipment would continue to reach the enclave, though it was only after Biafra survived the FMG's offensive later that month that substantial deliveries of arms began arriving.[15] The open secret that France was supplying arms to Biafra then helped to justify the UK's continued supply of arms to Nigeria. For Stremlau, however, 'French military assistance, whether valued at five million dollars or twice that figure, was tiny when compared to the financial contribution that France made to the Federal Government by continuing to import Nigerian goods.' During 1969 alone, Nigeria had a trade surplus with France that amounted to more than $66 million.[16]

The only other European country to show material support for Biafra was Portugal – then under an authoritarian regime clinging onto its African colonies. But not even France and Portugal went so far as to recognise the Biafran republic. For John Stremlau, 'the question of Biafra's survival probably was never more than of marginal interest to de Gaulle, and his equivocation reflected this.' France may have wanted to see the Nigerian federation weakened, but it wasn't insensitive to the majority of African states, which supported the FMG.[17] Furthermore, neither France nor Portugal repeated the genocide allegations.

Other European countries did not respond to public pressure to support Biafra. None would support Biafra openly; all publicly declared their support for Nigerian unity. The East European countries were vociferous in their opposition to secessionism.[18]

[14] Stremlau, *International Politics*, p. 227.

[15] The French always claimed that they didn't supply arms or equipment to Biafra. But Ivory Coast and Gabon provided French-backed loans to Biafra, with which it could buy arms. Stremlau, *International Politics*, p. 230

[16] Stremlau, *International Politics*, p. 233.

[17] Stremlau, *International Politics*, p. 228.

[18] The Soviet Union supplied arms to the Federal Military Government. And Poland was very supportive of the FMG – and their Observers reflected this. In an interview, one of the Polish Observers, Col Alfons Olkiewiz, stated, 'The charge of genocide was purposely made by the chief of secessionists,

No government was prepared to jeopardise good relations with the Nigerian government, most of Africa, and the British government. The Irish government, for example, sent a circular to all Irish embassies in September 1967 reiterating that the government recognised the Federal Republic of Nigeria, and it never shifted from that stance.[19] Furthermore, no government used the term genocide, though MPs, journalists, NGOs, and political activists in many countries did do so.[20]

Public pressure was quite strong across Europe. The UK came in for much criticism, because of its support for the FMG.[21] The UK's policy reflected a mixture of economic interests (particularly investments by Shell-BP) and geopolitics. Arms sales were justified because it 'was undoubtedly right to help an ex-colony and fellow Commonwealth country when it faced secession ... to change our policy now when both sides have reached virtually irreconcilable positions, would have a catastrophic effect on our relations with the Federal Government and would put our interests in Nigeria in jeopardy.' Nigeria was potentially a major power in Africa; a breakup of the federation would reduce such power – and allow France and its francophone allies in the region to exercise more influence. France, with its overt support for Biafra would also benefit from oil concessions granted by an independent Biafran state. The UK also needed to counter Soviet support for the FMG (the Soviets were also selling arms to it). Furthermore,

Col Ojuwku – supported by imperialist propaganda centres – in order to move world public opinion and spurt [sic] on benevolent institutions to collect money which the secessionists needed for the purchase of arms.' Myths and Facts, Interview with Col Olkiewicz, Poland's Representative in the International Group of Observers in Nigeria, Trybuna Ludu no. 254, of September 13, 1969, in UKNA file FCO 65/174.

19 Staunton, 'The Case of Biafra', 516.

20 US presidential candidate Richard Nixon stated, in September 1968, that genocide was taking place – 'and starvation is the grim reaper', and called for strong action. But after he entered office, US policy followed the British line. Joseph E. Thompson, *American Policy and African Famine: The Nigeria-Biafra War, 1966–1970* (New York: Greenwood Press, 1990), quote on p. 74.

21 The UK government steadfastly maintained that it was merely continuing its traditional supplies of arms to Nigeria, and that it supplied no more than 15 per cent of Nigeria's arms imports. But figures published by the Nigerian government at the same time showed that the British proportion of arms imports was 47.84 per cent in 1967, 79.19 per cent in 1968 and an astonishing 97.36 per cent in 1969. Cronje, *The World and Nigeria*, pp. 38–65.

'if the principle of secession on a tribal basis were once accepted there would be chaos on the [African] continent'.[22]

On 12 June 1968, the first major debate on British policy took place in the House of Commons, during which numerous calls for a cessation of British arms exports were made. At the end of that debate, the Foreign Secretary, Michael Stewart, declared that:

> If we make the supposition that it were the intention of the Federal Government not merely to preserve the unity of Nigeria but to proceed without mercy either with the slaughter or the starvation of the Ibo people, or if we were to make the supposition that it were the intention of the Federal Government to take advantage of a military situation in order to throw aside with contempt any terms of reasonable settlement, then the arguments which justified the policy we have so far pursued would fall, and we would have to reconsider, and more than reconsider, the action we have so far taken.[23]

The continuation of British government policy, and therefore the preservation and promotion of what were perceived to be important British interests, was thus indelibly linked to proving that the FMG was not conducting a genocide.

In August 1968, the Nigerian government was overtly preparing a 'final push' to defeat Biafra; public alarm accordingly grew. An emergency – and very heated – debate was held in the UK House of Commons on 27 August 1968, with extraordinary scenes of protest, from both MPs and the gallery.[24] As Harold Wilson described later events: a demonstration in Trafalgar Square that evening was followed by a 'large group of Biafran students ... converging on Downing Street, where they lit an enormous bonfire which was kept going by petrol. It could easily have caused damage, but they then suddenly rushed the door of No. 10, surprising the custodians and almost succeeding in

[22] Confidential (not for public use), Nigeria: a background note on British interests and the government's approach to the civil war (no date, but in file from November 1968 to March 1969), in UKNA file FCO 65/179. Such reasons were actually frequently cited by the government, as in debates in the Houses of Parliament.

[23] Hansard, vol. 766, col. 293.

[24] Hugh Noyes, 'Protests by MPs over Arms for Nigeria', *The Times* (28 August 1968); Hansard, House of Commons debate (27 August 1968), vol. 769, cols. 1433–1534.

entering in strength.'[25] The British government was under quite severe pressure – also because ministers had not admitted (or known) that the 'final push' was under way, even though Gowon had announced it publicly.[26] This then led to the establishment of the International Observer Team, announced by the Nigerian government on 30 August, just days after the debate in the House of Commons.

The origins of the International Observer Team lie in discussions regarding the possible setting up of a Commonwealth peacekeeping or peace force. The Commonwealth Secretary-General, Arnold Smith, had pushed the idea during his various mediation attempts from late 1967. In November 1967, the Commonwealth Office asked the Ministry of Defence for estimates of the sort of force required to act as a buffer between the two sides or 'to act as reassuring presence in the Ibo areas after an Ibo surrender'.[27] As the two sides refused to negotiate, the idea for a peace force went nowhere. But the possibility still existed that peace talks could start, 'in which case the proposal for the Commonwealth force could assume great importance as the most effective means of guaranteeing the Ibos against massacres by Federal troops after a surrender.'[28] On 18 June 1968, ministers agreed that the UK should be prepared to provide part of a peacekeeping force in Nigeria – as long as the Federal Government gave consent, there was a ceasefire and Canada agreed to bear an equal share of the cost.[29] Canadian and UK officials met in London in late May, to discuss problems involved in providing a peace force for Nigeria. Canada was lukewarm about the idea, and insisted that a substantial part of the force be non-white; other contributing countries could include India and Ethiopia.[30] But India was not so interested, and UK

[25] Wilson, *The Labour Government*, p. 561.

[26] The UK had been urging the FMG not to embark on military activities until a peace conference in Addis Ababa had concluded. Confidential minute from Lord Shepherd (Minister of State for Commonwealth) to Prime Minister, on 6 August 1968 (UKNA file FCO 25/242).

[27] Minute to Williams from Norris, 24 November 1967, in UKNA file, FCO 38/293.

[28] Cabinet Defence and Oversea Policy Committee, Peacekeeping Force for Nigeria, memorandum by the Secretary of State for Commonwealth Affairs, OPD (68) 20, 18 March 1968, in FCO 38/293.

[29] Letter to E.G. Willan in the UK Embassy in Lagos, from D.C. Tebbit in the Commonwealth Office, 1 April 1968, in UKNA file FCO 38/293.

[30] Telegram 602 from Commonwealth Office to Kampala (where peace talks were ongoing), 30 May 1968, in UKNA file FCO 38/294.

ministries were even scrambling to figure out how to pay the proposed £2 million cost of the force.[31]

In the various international negotiations (held under the auspices of the OAU) and in meetings with the UK, Nigeria accepted that the Igbos needed reassurances of their safety if they were to surrender, but it was hostile to the idea of a peacekeeping force. During the summer of 1968, the UK pressed Nigeria to try to counter Biafran propaganda more seriously, and, as part of such an attempt, to accept observers, which could ensure a better press for the Federal Government. The UK reminded the Nigerians that if they were embarking on a policy of genocide or massacre, the British government would be obliged to reconsider their policy of supplying arms.[32] But the Nigerians were not yet convinced. The Commonwealth Office even prepared a paper, entitled 'Observers', which suggested that the Federal Government might find it 'helpful to have a small number of outside observers attached to their own forces at this stage in the campaign … The main purpose of such observers would be to demonstrate that the Federal authorities were not seeking to conceal the truth and to provide a degree of objective and authoritative checking on future propaganda stories about misconduct by Federal troops, so that world opinion could be quickly reassured about the true facts in a supposed incident.' The International Red Cross would be the most suitable organisation to arrange for such observers.[33]

Just after the stormy debate in the House of Commons on 27 August, the Commonwealth Secretary, George Thomson, and Lord Shepherd, the Minister of State in the Commonwealth Office, held a meeting with Chief Enahoro, in which it was clear that they were quite angry. Thomson stated that 'if a final offensive was unavoidable and

[31] Confidential brief for D.O.P.C.[Defence and Oversea Policy Committee] Meeting on 17 September on Nigeria: Commonwealth Observer Force, by the West and General Africa Department, 16 September 1968, in UKNA file FCO 38/296.

[32] Confidential record of a meeting between the Prime Minister and the Federal Nigerian Commissioner for Information and Labour, in the Prime Minister's Room at the House of Commons on Wednesday June 12 at 7 p.m., in UKNA file FCO 25/242. See the record of another attempt to push for observers, in Telegram 1365 from Commonwealth Office to Lagos, 20 August 1968, in UKNA file PREM 13/2259. And of yet another attempt: Record of meeting between the Commonwealth Secretary and Chief Enahoro on Monday, 26 August 1968, in UKNA file FCO 25/243.

[33] 'Observers', in UKNA file FCO 38/225.

at the same time the British Government was to continue its present policy, it was imperative that the offensive should be accompanied by measures', including 'an invitation to outside observers to accompany the troops and to testify that there were no massacres. If the Federal Government could not make these policies effective, he was bound to say as a convinced friend of Nigeria that no British Government could continue its present policies of support for the Federal Government.' Lord Shepherd then handed Enahoro the paper on Observers.[34]

Two days later, the Nigerian government announced the creation of an International Observer Team. Very rapidly, the UK agreed to take part, even though it would have preferred the Nigerians to have asked the International Red Cross to arrange for observation.[35] The formal invitation from the Nigerian Ministry of External Affairs was directed to Canada, Poland, Sweden, the UK, the OAU, and the UN Secretary-General. 'The Federal Government's reason for establishing this Observer Team is in pursuance of its desire to satisfy the world opinion, contrary to the malicious propaganda of the rebels, that there is no intentional or planned systematic and wanton destruction of civilian lives or their property in the war zone.' It invited one observer from each country or organisation, who would 'visit all war affected areas and newly liberated areas, on the Federal-controlled side, to witness the conduct of Federal troops – re charges of genocide, etc.' The FMG would provide transport, and board and accommodation, for the Observers. The Team was to serve for two months.[36]

The FMG allowed each observer to have an assistant, but did not bow to pressure from the UK government to permit the further

[34] Record of meeting between the Commonwealth Secretary and Chief Enahoro at 8 p.m. on Tuesday, 27th August, 1968, in UKNA file FCO 25/243.

[35] See letter from Commonwealth Secretary George Thomson to the Prime Minister, 29 August 1968, in UKNA FCO 25/254. The Canadian government was not happy to have been asked, 'because it has been our belief that peacekeeping forces and truce observation groups should normally be constituted under the aegis of an international organization, whether it be the UN or some other body'. But they felt it their duty to participate. Statement by the Secretary of State for External Affairs on 'Nigeria – International Observers', Ottawa, 13 September 1968, in UKNA file FCO 38/226.

[36] Letter from A.A. Baba-Gana, Permanent Secretary, Ministry of External Affairs, Federal Military Government of Nigeria, to Sir David Hunt, British High Commissioner, Lagos, 6 September 1968, in UKNA file FCO 38/225.

expansion of the Observer Team. The FMG also, eventually, agreed to allow the Team to remain in Nigeria 'until such time as may be determined by the Federal Military Government unilaterally or by mutual consultation with the respective governments or organisations'[37] – though only after prodding by the British government, which reminded Nigeria of the usefulness of the Observers in 'taking the sting out of Biafran claims of genocide'.[38] The Nigerian government would not agree, however, to allow the Observer Team to operate in Biafra (assuming the Biafrans would allow them to do so), even though many MPs and officials in the Foreign and Commonwealth Office tried to push for this.[39] Allowing the Observers to operate in Biafra would confer status on the rebels.[40]

Over the course of seventeen months, from September 1968 to January 1970, the observers periodically issued reports on their activities, which included visits to displaced persons camps, prisoner of war camps, and villages that had been retaken by Nigerian Federal forces. The OAU and UN representatives reported to their own organisations; the representatives of the four participating countries issued joint reports. Those reports invariably found no evidence of genocide. The first report, of 2 October 1968, concluded that 'There is no evidence of any intent by the Federal troops to destroy the Ibo people or their property, and the use of the term genocide is in no way justified.'[41] Every subsequent report repeated that message.[42]

[37] Telegram from British High Commission in Lagos to the FCO, 9 December 1968 in UKNA file FCO 65/168.

[38] Confidential minute dated 18 November 1968 on 'Observers', in UKNA file FCO 65/167.

[39] Poland was not in favour of such a move. And Prime Minister Wilson was unenthusiastic about the idea – as the safety of the observers could not be guaranteed. Brief by the Foreign and Commonwealth Office on Observers, for the Prime Minister's visit to Nigeria, March–April 1969, PMN (69) B.3, 20 March 1969, in UKNA file FCO 65/172.

[40] Telegram 556 from UK High Commission in Lagos to FCO, 12 March 1969, on the question of observers visiting rebel held areas, reporting a meeting with Gowon and Arikpo (Minister for External Affairs) in UKNA file FCO 65/171.

[41] Report dated 2 October 1968 on International Observer Team's visit to 1st Nigerian Division (UKNA file FCO 65/178).

[42] The other reports are: Second report of the Observer Team to Nigeria, 15 October 1968, published in Keesing's Contemporary Archives, 25 January–1 February 1969; Third interim report, visit to Second Nigerian Division, 22 October 1968 (UKNA file FCO 65/166); Report on activities during the

The International Observer Team appears to have been successful in dampening down the accusations of genocide, and therefore helping the UK to continue its support for the Nigerian government.[43] Biafran propaganda shifted away from the genocide theme to one that stressed Biafran self-reliance.[44] Public opinion in Sweden even seems to have been affected by reports from one of the returning Swedish observers that there was no genocide in Nigeria, which made headlines in the Swedish press in April 1969.[45]

Towards the end of the war, however, concerns about genocide resurfaced. The French Foreign Minister, Maurice Schumann, called for protection of Igbo civilians; there were demonstrations across Europe demanding that an international peacekeeping force be sent

period 24 Sep–23 Nov 1968, Lagos, Nigeria, 25 November 1968 (UKNA file FCO 65/168); Report on activities of the Representatives of Canada, Poland, Sweden and the United Kingdom during the period 24 November 1968–13 January 1969, Lagos, Nigeria, 20 January 1969 (UKNA file FCO 65/169); Report on activities of the Representatives of Canada, Poland, Sweden and the United Kingdom during the period 14 January 1969–6 March 1969, Lagos, Nigeria, 7 March 1969 (UKNA file FCO 65/171); Report on activities of the Representatives of Canada, Poland, Sweden and the United Kingdom during the period 7 March–30 April, 1969, Lagos, Nigeria, 5 May, 1969 (UKNA file FCO 65/172); Report on activities of the Representatives of Canada, Poland, Sweden and the United Kingdom during the period from 1 May 1969–27 June 1969, Lagos, Nigeria, 27 June 1969 (UKNA file FCO 65/173); Report on activities of the Representatives of Canada, Poland, Sweden and the United Kingdom during the period 28 June to 30 September 1969, Lagos, Nigeria, 3 October 1969 (UKNA file FCO 65/174). The UN representative concurred: 'During the period under review the Observer has found no evidence of genocide according to the accepted definition [in the Genocide Convention].' United Nations, Fourth interim report by Representative of Secretary-General to Nigeria on Humanitarian Activities, Press Release SG/1725, 17 January 1969, in UKNA file FCO 65/169.

43 Confidential Diplomatic Report no. 211/70, from the British High Commissioner in Nigeria to the Secretary of State for Foreign and Commonwealth Affairs, 11 March 1970, on 'Nigeria: International Team of Observers', in UKNA file FCO 65/782. In fact, the Observer Team appears to have been so successful that the UK government decided to stop publishing its reports. It was even feared that if the government kept publishing them, 'we may find that we are taking on an indefinite commitment, possibly extending into the activities of some form of ceasefire observe force.' Minute to Mr Moberly, from A. J. Collins, 18 July 1969, with signed agreement from Moberly; in UKNA file FCO 65/163.

44 Stremlau, *International Politics*, pp. 320–8.

45 As reported in a letter from the British embassy in Stockholm to the Foreign Office in London, on 9 April 1969. Letter in UKNA file FCO 65/287.

to Biafra; the Pope even referred to the possibility of genocide.[46] The Save the Children charity was alarmed by 'the continuing slaughter of IBO villagers, – men, women and children – by Federal soldiers since July of last year'.[47] And even the International Observer Team noted a 'breakdown of law and order' at the end of the war, which was actually hampering the relief effort. But their report was confidential.[48] The final report of the International Observer Team, of 12 February 1970, reiterated that 'There was no evidence of genocide – intentional or planned systematic and wanton destruction of civilian lives or property – in the war zone. Continued accusations of intended genocide can only be interpreted as malicious disregard of the authenticated facts.'[49] And it is the case that Biafra and the Igbos were for the most part reintegrated into the Nigerian federation – no mass murder took place after their surrender. The extent to which the presence of observers – or world attention – helped to avert atrocities is an open question, and one worth investigating further.

The International Observer Team was criticised. As was to be expected, the Biafran side claimed it was 'nothing but a shameless conspiracy', aimed at preventing the UN and OAU 'from taking a positive stand or positive action against the genocide being practiced'.[50] Ojukwu claimed that the observer exercise would 'hardly achieve anything that can be presented to the world as original, accurate and impartial' so long as there are so few of them and their movements are restricted on the Federal side.[51]

The Biafran objections cannot be dismissed out of hand. As Suzanne Cronje notes, the International Observer Team was not neutral; it was not instructed on what genocide is nor how to identify it; it was

[46] Stremlau, *International Politics*, pp. 367–8.

[47] Letter from Andrew Gray, Save the Children Fund in Nigeria, to Save the Children Fund in London, 1 January 1970, in UKNA file FCO 65/784.

[48] Confidential report of observer team on effect of breakdown of law and order on relief effort, sent in telegram no. 539 to the FCO, 25 January 1970, in UKNA file FCO 65/784.

[49] Observer Team to Nigeria Report on activities of the Representatives of Canada, Poland, Sweden and the United Kingdom for the period 1 October 1969 to 31 January 1970, Lagos, Nigeria, 12 February 1970 (UKNA file FCO 65/784).

[50] Markpress News Feature Service, '"Observers" in Nigeria Would be Absurd, Says Biafra', in UKNA file FCO 38/225.

[51] In a radio broadcast on 4 October 1968; referred to in minute of 28 February 1969 by A.N.R. Millington, in UKNA file FCO 65/171.

dependent on the FMG for transport and accommodation; it never investigated the 1966 massacres of Igbos.[52] The lack of instruction regarding genocide is apparent in the various government files now open to public view: at no point did the UK government ever provide its Observers with the definition of genocide (and at the time, the UK had not yet acceded to the Genocide Convention), nor provide guidance on how one might determine whether or not a genocide was taking place or had taken place.

The Observer Team did refer to the Genocide Convention definition in one of its reports,[53] but as Cronje notes, all the members of the Observer Team except for the UN representative were military men (often retired): 'they had no means of judging in legal terms what constituted genocide, and it was within their terms of reference to pronounce on this issue. At the very least the team should have included international jurists and professionals experienced in the investigation of crime and the recording of evidence, not to speak of social workers, medical men and people capable of telling an Ibo from a non-Ibo.'[54] Furthermore, 'the team accepted the U.N. definition of genocide, but told a visiting international jurist that they were not lawyers and therefore not interested in any legal definitions. Looking closely at the work of the team and the approach of its members to the conflict, it is difficult to understand why the world was so ready to accept its findings.'[55] Yet it certainly suited European governments

[52] Cronje, *The World and Nigeria*, pp. 83–92. One (partial?) observer argues that 'There can be little doubt that the massacres of East Nigerians in the north of Nigeria in 1966 provide a classic example of genocide.' George Knapp, 'Aspects of the Biafran Affairs: A Study of British Attitudes and Policy towards the Nigerian-Biafran Conflict', British-Biafra Association (December 1968), 22. In 'Nigerian Civil War Collection', SOAS, MS 321463, vol. 69.

[53] Report on activities during the period 24 Sep–23 Nov 1968, in UKNA file FCO 65/168.

[54] Cronje, *The World and Nigeria*, p. 84.

[55] Cronje, *The World and Nigeria*, p. 83. The British government did consider other non-military men, but ended up selecting a retired army officer, Major General H. T. Alexander, as its first Observer (a pattern which continued). The directive appointing Alexander repeated the terms of reference of the Nigerian letter, and did not elaborate on the definition of genocide nor on how to identify genocide. Directive for Major-General Alexander, from George Thomson, Commonwealth Secretary, in UKNA file FCO 38/225.

to accept the findings, because they could use them to resist public pressure to change their policies – which would have created far more problems for them.

The Biafra case illustrates several aspects of European discourses on and policy responses to allegations of genocide that will appear again during and after the Cold War. The most obvious is that 'genocide' is an extremely emotive term and suspicions that it is ongoing can generate public concern. For governments this creates dilemmas, as they feel under pressure to act in ways that might go against important material interests. As a result, they avoid the use of the term altogether – and in the Biafra case, even participate in or accept the findings of an International Observer Team whose purpose was to prove that no genocide was taking place by Nigerian military forces.

East Pakistan/Bangladesh

After the 1947 partition between India and Pakistan, Pakistani territory comprised two geographically separate (and distant) Muslim-majority areas. But shortly thereafter, a Bangladesh nationalist movement emerged in East Pakistan, to defend Bengali language and culture against perceived discriminatory practices of West Pakistan. In 1970, the Awami League, the Bengali nationalist party, won the first free national elections and could have formed the Federal Government. But in early March 1971, the military ruler General Ayub Khan postponed the first meeting of parliament, prompting a general strike and demonstrations in East Pakistan. On 25 March 1971, he launched military operations in East Pakistan. Pakistani troops engaged in a brutal repression, with deliberate targeting of civilians. Estimates of the dead vary from 1 million to 3 million; 200,000 girls and women were raped; over 10 million people fled to India.[56] The Indian parliament described the repression as genocide just a few days after the Pakistani military operations began. On 3 December, following military clashes between India and Pakistani troops, India

[56] Samantha Power cites between one and two million dead (*'A Problem from Hell'*, p. 82); Rounaq Jahan cites three million (Rounaq Jahan, 'Genocide in Bangladesh', in Samuel Totten, William S. Parsons and Israel W. Charney, eds., *Century of Genocide*, 2nd edition, London: Routledge, 2004, p. 295); Nicholas Wheeler cites one million (*Saving Strangers*, p. 55); Leo Kuper cites an upper number of 3,000,000 (Kuper, *Genocide*, Harmondsworth: Penguin, 1981), p.79.

invaded East Pakistan (Bangladesh), and on 16 December Pakistani forces surrendered.[57]

India's principal justification for using force was 'refugee aggression', as well as other humanitarian grounds: the Indian ambassador to the UN said the military repression was so grave as to 'shock the conscience of mankind'. Further he asked, 'what... has happened to our conventions on genocide, human rights, self-determination, and so on?'[58] The defeat of the Pakistani forces in December, though, put an end to discussions at the UN. Although the majority of states recognised the new state of Bangladesh in the next few months, Wheeler maintains that 'there was no support for a doctrine of unilateral humanitarian intervention'[59] – even where genocide was alleged to be taking place.

The reactions of European governments, and principally the UK, the former colonial power, were similar. Pakistan's right to sovereignty and the norm of non-interference were reaffirmed – as maintained by both France and the UK at the UN.[60] Sweden did highlight inhuman conditions in East Pakistan (Bangladesh), but nonetheless emphasised that the UN Charter prohibits the use of force except in self-defence.[61] Civil society and the media in Western Europe were more supportive of Bangladesh, but governments were not under significant pressure to take action against Pakistan.[62] India – though formally non-aligned, was supported by the Soviet Union and its allies, while Pakistan was aligned with the USA and China, so Cold War

[57] About 92,000 Pakistani troops were detained by India. Bangladesh later tried to prosecute these Pakistani prisoners for genocide. But when India signalled that it was willing to extradite them to Bangladesh, Pakistan launched a case against India at the International Court of Justice in 1973. It argued that under article 6 of the Genocide Convention, only Pakistan had jurisdiction to try persons charged with genocide, because at the time the offences were said to have been committed, East Pakistan was part of Pakistan. The case was settled out of court when India agreed to repatriate the prisoners to Pakistan. No one was prosecuted for genocide in Bangladesh. Schabas, *Genocide in International Law*, 2nd edition, p. 417 and pp. 499–502.

[58] Both quotes in Wheeler, *Saving Strangers*, pp. 62–3.

[59] Wheeler, *Saving Strangers*, p. 74.

[60] Wheeler, *Saving Strangers*, p. 58. Of course, 'non-interference' here really means 'in the cause of human rights'; as just noted, France and the UK interfered in the Nigerian Civil War by sending arms to the warring parties.

[61] Wheeler, *Saving Strangers*, p. 68.

[62] Jahan, 'Genocide in Bangladesh', pp. 304–5.

politics inevitably coloured the official reactions. No European state made an allegation of genocide against Pakistan – in fact, quite the opposite. In June 1971, the Dutch government, for example, 'concluded' that events in Pakistan did not constitute genocide.[63]

However, the UK's analysis – kept confidential – was not as dismissive of the genocide charge. The UK was more informed of events than other European countries because it had a relatively extensive diplomatic presence in East Pakistan. Yet the Foreign Office nonetheless concluded that nothing could be done under the Genocide Convention – and as a result, it did not publicly declare that the situation was genocide. Its grounds for concluding that any potential action would be limited by the terms of the Convention were, however, based on quite a narrow reading of the Convention.

Within days of the start of Pakistani army actions in East Pakistan, massacres were being reported by the British High Commission in Dacca (now Dhaka). India was loudly claiming there was a genocide ongoing. On 31 March, the Indian High Commissioner in London pressed the UK Foreign Office for its view on UN action 'in view of the genocide', but the response was that the situation was an internal Pakistan affair, and that 'we had no evidence of genocide'. There is, however, a hand-written note in the margins of the report on the UK-India meeting to the effect that the UK interlocutor (Mr Anthony Royle) 'did not have the recent tels [telexes] from Pakistan at this time'.[64]

Those telexes repeatedly declared that the Pakistani army was using 'terror tactics' or waging a 'reign of terror', with 'widespread killing of unarmed civilians', mostly Hindus, in East Pakistan.[65] The Deputy High Commissioner in Dacca, Frank Sargeant, reported that the army was 'killing indiscriminately' in a 'campaign of ruthless terror'. Resistance was blamed on Indian aggression, which helped to justify the killing of Hindus. Armed Bihari irregulars also do the

[63] 'Prime Minister de Jong answers questions: No known proof of genocide in East Pakistan', *De Leeuwarder Courant* on 18 June 1971 (translation TvC).

[64] Record of conversation between Mr Royle and the Indian High Commissioner on 31 March 1971 at the Foreign and Commonwealth Office, in UKNA file FCO 37/881.

[65] For example, in telex from Islamabad to the FCO on 29 March 1971, in UKNA file FCO 37/879, or from Dacca on 31 March 1971 in file FCO 37/880, or from Dacca on 30 April in file FCO 37/885, or from Dacca on 12 May in file FCO 37/887.

work of the Army, 'slaughtering the Hindus'. 'As I write this despatch, reports reach me daily of continued killings on a large scale, of wanton destruction of villages and of widespread looting.'[66] A later despatch reported that 'a policy of extermination of Hindus is still being ruthlessly pursued in area south of Dacca'. Such reports are 'consistent with the pattern of punitive killing and destruction, aimed mainly but not exclusively at Hindus, which has been experienced throughout the greater part of the province since March.'[67] The despatches do not use the term genocide, though arguably they are in fact describing it.

What the UK could do about this was considered to be limited. For understandable reasons it did not wish to get too involved in disputes between its former colonies in the sub-continent. And with the USA supporting the Pakistani government, there would have been little desire to counter publicly US policy. The UK was also resistant to the idea that the UN Security Council should be involved, unless either Pakistan or India raised the matter there. The UN was only involved in organising relief efforts for the millions of refugees in India.

In confidential messages to the Pakistani President, Prime Minister Edward Heath did urge an end to the bloodshed and use of force, and a resumption of the process of resuming civilian rule in the country.[68] But these were kept confidential, and the government was keen to reiterate publicly that it did not wish to interfere in the internal affairs of Pakistan. The UK was not a principal arms supplier to Pakistan anyway, and had decided that it would not deliver any new aid to the country until there was a political settlement. It encouraged other members of the Pakistan Aid Consortium to follow suit, though France and West Germany were uneasy about setting conditions for aid.[69]

[66] Letter from Sargeant to R.A. Burrows, the Acting British High Commissioner in Islamabad, 5 June 1971, in UKNA file FO 37/888.

[67] Telex from Sargeant in Dacca to Islamabad on 14 June 1971 on conditions in East Pakistan, in UKNA file FCO 37/887.

[68] On 7 April 1971 (UKNA file FCO 37/884), and 11 June 1971 (UKNA file FCO 37/887). Furthermore, at a meeting of European and US ambassadors in Delhi on 20 April, it was agreed that they should continue, on a bilateral and private basis, to urge moderation in Islamabad. Report of meeting in UKNA file FCO 37/884.

[69] Telex from British embassy in Paris, 13 July 1971, in UKNA file FCO 37/898. Sweden, however, apparently felt strongly that aid should be withheld to force the Pakistani government to end the military action and find a political solution to the problem. Letter from Miss M. Ramsay in British embassy in Stockholm to R. G. M. Manning in the Overseas Development Administration, 16 June 1971, in UKNA file FCO 37/898.

The former Prime Minister, Harold Wilson, actually pressed the current Prime Minister, Edward Heath, to consider the same sort of policy he had towards Nigeria:

[W]e at least used our influence with the Nigerian Government together with others, to persuade them to invite observers into the areas concerned to provide some guarantee that there was no genocide and that there was no truth in some of the allegations being made internationally about what was going on, and what would go on, in the so-called Biafran territory. That was totally successful, and the reports showed that there was no genocide. Has the Prime Minister made such a proposal, either separately or with Commonwealth colleagues, that there should be international observers – one from this country, perhaps, one from Asia, one from the United Nations, and so on – to report to the world outside about conditions in East Pakistan and about the very grave accusations of murder of civilian populations?

Wilson almost seems to be implying here that allegations of genocide in East Pakistan equally had 'no truth' in them, and thus needed to be proved as such. In any event, Heath answered that he would not reveal the content of the exchanges he was having with the Pakistani president.[70] The idea of observers then went nowhere: the norm of non-interference was felt strongly.

The events in East Pakistan/Bangladesh were discussed extensively in the UK parliament throughout 1971. Numerous MPs cited allegations of atrocities by Pakistani troops – and genocide. In early June 1971, an early day motion was proposed by John Stonehouse MP, and signed by almost 200 MPs:

That this House believes that the widespread murder of civilians and the atrocities on a massive scale by the Pakistan Army in East Bengal, contrary to the United Nations Convention on Genocide, signed by Pakistan itself, confirms that the military Government of Pakistan has forfeited all rights to rule East Bengal ... therefore believes that the United Nations Security Council must be called urgently to consider the situation both

[70] Hansard, House of Commons debate (20 April 1971), vol. 815, cols. 944–6. This came up again: on 4 May 1971, for example, Heath was asked if he had raised the matter with the Pakistani president (and gave the same reply). Hansard, House of Commons debate (4 May 1971), vol. 816, col. 1171.

> as a threat to international peace and as a contravention of the Genocide Convention.[71]

The government never found the time for a debate on the motion. In July, the same motion was put forward again, and over 200 MPs signed it. Again, the Conservative government never found the time for a debate on it.[72]

The early day motion forced the Foreign Office to consider the question of genocide more explicitly. In the notes for supplementaries prepared on the situation in East Pakistan, the Foreign Office suggested that the relevant minister state: 'We cannot, from direct evidence available to me, confirm allegations of army brutality against Hindus in East Pakistan'[73] – quite an extraordinary statement in light of the information coming from the High Commission in Dacca. On genocide, the suggested argument was:

> It would serve no useful purpose to raise the matter under the Genocide Convention. Under Article VI of the Convention, persons charged with genocide are in the first instance to be tried either by a competent tribunal of the state in the territory of which the act was committed or by an international penal tribunal. There is as yet no international penal tribunal. (We have pointed out that the effective implementation of the Convention is dependent upon the establishment of such a tribunal).[74]

This line of argument had been suggested by the UN (Economic and Social) Department, in a note on the Genocide Convention and Pakistan. That note repeats the definition of genocide in article 1 of the Convention, and observes that Pakistan ratified the Convention in 1957, and the UK in 1970. It further remarks that article 9 states that disputes between contracting parties regarding to 'the interpretation, application or fulfilment of the Convention' can be submitted

[71] Hansard, House of Commons (17 June 1971), vol. 819, col. 651. Somewhat confusingly, East Pakistan was also referred to in this period as East Bengal (as well as Bangladesh).

[72] Hansard, House of Commons (15 July 1971), vol. 821, cols. 723–4.

[73] Notes for supplementaries, in UKNA file FCO 37/888. This was not repeated in parliament; the government's line there was often that both sides had engaged in acts of brutality.

[74] Notes for supplementaries, in UKNA file FCO 37/888.

to the ICJ. Pakistan did not make a reservation to this article (and nor did the UK), though India did. The note continues:

It could be held that the events in East Pakistan show that the Government of Pakistan are in breach of the Genocide Convention; it would certainly be difficult to argue that they are not. But the question is academic since the other Government most closely involved, India, will not really be able to bring the matter to the International Court for the reasons explained above – and it is highly unlikely that any other Government will attempt to do so.

The note then continues with the argument – outlined above – regarding the trial of persons charged with genocide. The UK's view is that 'the effective implementation of the Genocide Convention and of the four Geneva Conventions of 1949 depended upon the establishment of an international penal tribunal. No-one has ever been tried by a Government specifically for a breach of the Conventions.' It also repeated the traditional view of the UK – stated during the negotiations on the Convention – that

genocide was not a crime which an individual could commit, or indeed a small group of individuals. It was a crime which could only be committed with the resources available to Governments and if genocide was committed within the state of a Contracting Party it was, therefore, nonsense to suppose (as Article VI lays down) that there would be a trial 'by a competent tribunal of the state in the territory of which the act was committed'.[75]

There are several important points to make about this evidence from the Foreign Office. First of all, despite the public pronouncements, which ignore the question of genocide altogether, it is privately acknowledged that 'it would be difficult to argue' that the Pakistani government was *not* in breach of the Genocide Convention. Second, there is nonetheless nothing the UK government can do about that – an astonishing argument to make. It is not clear why the UK could not submit a dispute with Pakistan over the fulfilment of the Convention to the ICJ, as neither of them had made a reservation to article 9. And article 8 of the Convention appears to have been ignored. Under

[75] K.G. MacInnes, UN (E&S) Department, 'Pakistan: The Genocide Convention' (17 June 1971), in UKNA file FCO 37/888.

that article, contracting parties can call upon the UN to take action appropriate for the prevention and suppression of acts of genocide. Furthermore, there is also no mention of the obligation in article 1, under which the contracting parties 'undertake to prevent and to punish' genocide.[76]

The Bangladesh case illustrates that even relying on the definition of genocide in the legal norm, the Foreign Office felt Pakistan was in breach of the Convention. But its interpretation of what the Convention required in such a situation was quite narrow – leading to no action taken and no declaration using the term 'genocide' to describe events. This reflects the broader zeitgeist, in which the norm of non-interference in the internal affairs of other countries (at least in the name of human rights) was considered to be an imperative, obligations under the Genocide Convention notwithstanding.

Cambodia

The suffering that Cambodians endured during the tortured decade of the 1970s is hard to fathom. In 1969, the USA took its fight against Vietnamese communists onto Cambodian soil, launching massive bombing raids and eventually a ground invasion. Following its withdrawal from Vietnam and a Congressional ban on the bombing of Cambodia in 1973, the USA continued to prop up an anti-communist but highly corrupt government in Phnom Penh. But the Lon Nol government was incapable of countering the communist revolutionary group the Khmer Rouge, which captured the entire country in April 1975.

The Khmer Rouge regime proceeded to isolate the newly renamed 'Democratic Kampuchea' – only a very few foreigners were allowed in, and then only on carefully controlled visits. Over the next four

[76] A narrow and incomplete reading of the Genocide Convention is apparent also in a later document from the Foreign Office. A supplementary background brief prepared for the UK delegation at the Inter-Parliamentary Conference in Paris, 2–10 September 1971, stated that an allegation of genocide 'has not been made at the United Nations, since such an accusation would have to be dealt with first in the courts in the country and then at an international tribunal under the auspices of the United Nations: as yet no such tribunal has ever been set up.' The Convention does not stipulate such a route, nor is action limited to just these two options. Brief is in UKNA file FCO 37/890.

and a half years, in a mixture of executions, starvation and forced labour, 1.5 to 1.7 million Cambodians were killed by the Khmer Rouge.[77] Ben Kiernan has shown that not a single member of the ethnic Vietnamese community survived; 50 per cent of ethnic Chinese and 40 per cent of other ethnic groups perished; and overall an estimated 21 per cent of Cambodia's population died under Khmer Rouge rule.[78]

There is a debate in the genocide studies literature about whether the Khmer Rouge can be accused of engaging in genocide against the Cambodian people in general: they may constitute a 'national group' but hardly a minority one (seemingly an intention of the Genocide Convention was to protect minority groups from extermination), and can one engage in genocide against one's own people? This has even resulted in the bizarre term 'auto-genocide' to try to describe the atrocities. If the negotiations on the Genocide Convention had not ended up excluding 'political groups' from the definition of genocide, then the Cambodian case would have been easier to identify as one of genocide. What is interesting from our perspective is that during the negotiations on the Genocide Convention, most European governments had supported the inclusion of political groups in the definition, and one, France, later included it in its implementing legislation (but only in 1994). None of them, however, used a more expansive understanding of genocide to describe the Cambodian case.

As the Khmer Rouge steadily approached Phnom Penh, the US government issued warnings of a looming 'bloodbath'. But these were dismissed by many observers as anti-communist hysteria; similar warnings had circulated before the communist takeover of South Vietnam, which did not result in the feared 'bloodbath'. While numerous foreigners had witnessed the forced (and brutal) evacuation of Phnom Penh in April 1975, this was not generally considered to be proof of an impending bloodbath. For the next couple of years,

77 UN General Assembly and Security Council, Report of the Group of Experts for Cambodia established pursuant to General Assembly Resolution 52/135, document no. A/53/850 and S/1999/231 (16 March 1999), 13.

78 Ben Kiernan, 'The Cambodian Genocide – 1975–1979', in Totten, Parsons and Charney, eds., *Century of Genocide*, 2nd edition (London: Routledge, 2004), pp. 344–9.

reports of high death tolls were often rejected as misinformation spread by right-wing anti-communist hardliners.[79]

Furthermore, it was very difficult to obtain information about what was going on in Cambodia – particularly because initially the stories of refugees who made it out of Cambodia were not considered 'sufficient evidence', or were dismissed as the exaggerations of loyalists of the former regime, or were blasted as 'contradictory', or, if they were believed, were in and of themselves not gory enough to merit much attention (because those refugees had managed to survive).[80] Thus, on 15 July 1975, the Dutch Minister of Foreign Affairs could easily tell parliament that because the government could not verify reports coming from Cambodia, it could not classify the situation in Cambodia as genocide.[81] And in April 1976, the French Foreign Minister Jean Sauvagnargues declared in the National Assembly that 'preliminary investigation has resulted in finding that there is not absolute concordance between that which is reported by different people'.[82]

Visits to the country did not necessarily confirm human rights violations. The Danish, Swedish and Finnish ambassadors in Peking visited Cambodia in January 1978, and 'friendship delegations' from Sweden and Belgium visited in August. The Swedish delegates published articles in various newspapers praising the Cambodian regime and condemning Vietnam for its interference in Cambodia. The Belgian party reported that they saw no sign of massacres, forced labour or famine.[83]

In addition, 'Vietnam fatigue' was widespread – above all in the USA, without whom it was inconceivable for any other western country to do much regarding Cambodia. For a start, any military option was so far off the table as to merit not even a passing thought; but in addition, given the recent history, western (and especially US) influence in the region was at a nadir. In any event, public interest in events in Indochina was low.

But by early 1977, it was becoming harder to ignore information coming out of Cambodia on the extent of the atrocities. Occasional

[79] See Power, *'A Problem from Hell'*, pp. 102–4 and pp. 108–113; Jamie Frederic Metzl, *Western Responses to Human Rights Abuses in Cambodia, 1975–80* (Houndmills: Palgrave, 1996), pp. 10–15, 21–9

[80] Metzl, *Western Responses*, pp. 50–9.

[81] Parliamentary question no. 1600 on the situation in Cambodia, 15 July 1975. Translation by TvC.

[82] Cited in Metzl, *Western Responses*, p. 60.

[83] Metzl, *Western Reponses*, p. 105.

news stories on the subject sparked more and more concern among politicians and the interested public. In the General Assembly plenary session of September 1977, French Foreign Minister Louis de Guiringaud declared that 'In spite of our commitment to the principle of non-interference in the affairs of states, we can not remain silent in the face of the news reaching us from Kampuchea ... I express the hope that [it] will respect the fundamental rights of the human being as set forth in our charter.'[84] After a robust response from the Democratic Kampuchean delegate, the French dropped their criticism.

Even if states had felt more of an imperative to speak out on human rights abuses in Cambodia thus chipping away at the norm of non-interference (and not many did), it was not clear what more could actually be done. Cambodia was isolated, and seemed to care little about what the rest of the world thought of it. Economic and diplomatic sanctions were therefore irrelevant (and western countries were at this time still reluctant to make linkages between economic and diplomatic relations and human rights anyway). Military intervention was out of the question. Even discussion at the UN was questionable, as it would be considered interference in Cambodia's domestic affairs, and Cambodia's internal tragedy was not considered to be a threat to international peace and security. Such limited policy options were debated in the UK House of Commons in March 1977, when several MPs pressed the Under-Secretary of State for Foreign and Commonwealth Affairs, Evan Luard, to 'take some positive action about the genocide of these people', and particularly to 'take an initiative on this matter in the United Nations'. Luard – an expert on the UN – rejected the idea of interfering in the internal affairs of another country, but did state that 'If anything, this is a question for the United Nations Commission on Human Rights, and I would be glad to see that body discuss the matter.'[85] In November 1977, Luard informed the House of Commons that the government was considering raising the issue at the next meeting of the UN Commission on Human Rights, in February-March 1978.[86] This even though everyone knew that any action by the CHR was likely to be of a symbolic nature, and that 'naming and shaming' in that body (presuming a majority of the

[84] Cited in Metzl, *Western Responses*, p. 88.
[85] Hansard, House of Commons (30 March 1977), vol. 929, cols. 379–80.
[86] Hansard, House of Commons (9 November 1977), vol. 938, cols. 650–2.

states serving on the CHR could even be convinced to do this) was highly unlikely to influence the Cambodian government.

The Foreign and Commonwealth Office then prepared a resolution for the 1978 CHR. It asked several countries for support, including their partners in the European Community and the Scandinavian states.[87] In Europe, only Sweden and Austria agreed to co-sponsor the resolution. France told the UK that while they were concerned about the human rights situation in Cambodia, 'they doubted whether this was a good moment to take up the issue in the Human Rights Commission. Their concern stemmed principally from their view that our initiative would be interpreted as taking sides in the Vietnam-Cambodia border dispute.'[88] As Vietnam was increasingly backed by the Soviet Union and Cambodia was on the anti-Soviet side, Cambodia should not be demonised.

The proposed resolution recommended that the CHR appoint a special rapporteur to investigate the human rights situation in Democratic Kampuchea. Luard told the CHR that there appeared to be numerous violations of various articles on the UN Declaration on Human Rights, but genocide was not mentioned at all.[89] In the CHR itself, outspoken criticism of the UK resolution came from the Soviet bloc and Third World countries. The compromise resolution that resulted was that the Cambodians should respond to the criticisms made of their human rights record, and that this response and other information should be considered by the CHR's Sub-Commission on Prevention of Discrimination and Protection of Minorities.

Only the UK, Norway, the USA, and Canada, along with Amnesty International and the International Commission of Jurists, then submitted information on Cambodian human rights violations to the

[87] Minute to Mr Smith from Miss S. M. Bull, on 'Cambodia: Human Rights Commission' (9 February 1978), in UKNA file FCO 15/2342.

[88] Letter to M. K. O. Simpson-Orlebar in the UN Department of the FCO, from Lord Gordon Lennox in the British Embassy in Paris (1 February 1978), in UKNA file FCO 15/2343.

[89] Nor do internal FCO documents on Cambodia in this period mention genocide at all. See a report on Democratic Kampuchea prepared by the South East Asian Department for an FCO seminar on human rights (22 June 1978), in UKNA file FCO 15/2345, and the brief prepared by the same department in preparation for the CHR meeting; document IOC (78) 2 (27 January 1978), in UKNA file FCO 15/2341.

Sub-Commission.[90] Much of the information they submitted was based on interviews with refugees. The chair of the Sub-Commission summarised the information submitted in a January 1979 report, which includes the response of the government of Democratic Kampuchea, rejecting the allegations as 'the slander and calumny of hoodlums, traitors and stateless persons'. He presented the document 'with the recommendation that the Commission [on Human Rights] give this matter highest priority at its thirty-fifth session'.[91] By this time, however, Vietnam had invaded Cambodia (see below).

UK Foreign and Commonwealth Office files from 1978 – only recently released – reveal that another way of pressuring Cambodia had been considered by both the USA and the UK. In September 1978, the Deputy Legal Adviser in the US State Department, Stephen Schwebel, wrote to the Foreign Office about the possibility of instituting proceedings against Cambodia before the International Court of Justice. One of the bases for such proceedings, Schwebel suggested, would be the Genocide Convention, even though such a case might not be well grounded because the gross violations 'apparently have been aimed not at destroying, in whole or in part, a "national, ethnical, racial or religious group" but rather at those whom Cambodian authorities deem to be politically unsympathetic'.[92]

[90] France did not, despite British pressure to do so. 'British Embassy officials in Washington told the State Department that the French had demurred, noting that they had already referred to the Cambodian human rights situation in the General Assembly.' Metzl, *Western Responses*, p. 117. Metzl surmises that this was because of France's perceived special relationship with its former colony, Cambodia, in view of which the French might possibly act as a mediator. In addition, French president Giscard d'Estaing was continuing a Gaullist foreign policy, trying to distinguish French foreign policy from that of the USA. Nor was it under much domestic pressure to take action against Cambodia.

[91] United Nations Economic and Social Council, 'Analysis prepared on behalf of the Sub-Commission by its Chairman of materials submitted to it and the Commission on Human Rights under decision 9 (XXXIV) of the Commission on Human Rights', document E/CN.4/1335 (30 January 1979).

[92] Other grounds for a case included the Slavery Convention and the ILO Forced Labour Convention. US Department of State, memorandum from Stephen Schwebel. Subject: should the U.K. – or the United States – charge Cambodia or Uganda before the World Court?, September 27, 1978, in UKNA file FCO 15/2348. Samantha Power's assertion that the USA 'could have urged its allies to file genocide charges at the International Court of Justice', but did not do so (*'A Problem from Hell'*, p. 124), thus needs to be amended in light of this recently-released information. The USA did ask; one European ally said no. It should be noted that the Schwebel memorandum

The UK reply, which came on 28 December 1978, was that 'the arguments against instituting proceedings are too strong for the UK to wish to consider such a course of action'. On the specific question of using the Genocide Convention as the basis of a case, the reply was negative:

> Much obviously depends upon the facts of what has happened in Cambodia, but it is not clear that we can point to any particular national, ethnical, racial or religious group which has *as such* been killed, etc. The criterion for executions appears to have been political attitude (or assumed attitude) vis-à-vis the Cambodian government. It may therefore be difficult to establish that genocide has been committed.

Other grounds were also considered as weak. However, the real reasons for not proceeding with a case against Cambodia 'are mainly concerned with the broader issues involved'. First of all, the UK felt that it would be ineffective in changing Cambodia's behaviour, and as it was likely Cambodia would simply refuse to appear before the ICJ, the court's standing would be harmed. But secondly:

> We also agree that the worst Cambodian atrocities may now be in the past. International concern about Cambodian actions appears to be diminishing. Many countries, including Western ones, are instead increasingly worried about the dangers of isolating Cambodia in case she falls prey to Vietnam.

Instead, the best forum to address Cambodian human rights violations was the CHR, which was to consider the Sub-Commission's report in February 1979.[93]

does not dwell for long on the question of Uganda, and the UK's reply does not even mention it.

[93] Letter to Schwebel from Ian Sinclair, Legal Adviser, Foreign and Commonwealth Office, 28 December 1978, in UKNA file FCO 15/2348. A minute from the FCO's legal counsellor, A.D. Watts, was less adamant in dismissing the possibility of genocide. He asked 'Can we point to any particular national, ethnical, racial or religious group which has, *as such*, been killed, etc? Or is it primarily the case that people of all kinds have been killed, etc, the criterion for doing so not being their membership of any such group but rather their political attitude (or assumed attitude) vis-à-vis the Cambodian Government? I rather suspect that it is the latter, and if that is so, it might make it difficult to establish that genocide had been committed.'

In the meantime, Vietnam invaded Cambodia, completing its takeover of the country on 7 January 1979. Because Vietnam was backed by the USSR, and Cambodia by China, and because Chinese-US relations were (relatively) warm, the question of human rights violations in Cambodia became wrapped up in Cold War politics. Immediately after the invasion, Vietnam (and the USSR) loudly accused the Khmer Rouge of genocide. In Phnom Penh, the Tuol Sleng torture centre was opened as a genocide museum, and Khmer leaders Pol Pot and Ieng Sary were tried in absentia and found guilty of genocide – but these trials were dismissed as show trials by western governments.[94]

The Vietnamese invasion put European governments in an uncomfortable position. The widespread response was to declare that human rights violations in a country could not justify foreign intervention. Thus the Norwegians stated at the UN:

> The Norwegian Government and public opinion in Norway have expressed strong objections to the serious violations of human rights committed by the Pol Pot Government. However, the domestic policies of that government cannot – we repeat, cannot, – justify the actions of Vietnam over the last days and weeks.[95]

And in the UN Security Council, the French declared

> The notion that because a regime is detestable foreign intervention is justified and forcible overthrow is legitimate is extremely dangerous. That could ultimately jeopardize the very maintenance of international law and make the continued existence of various regimes dependent on the judgements of their neighbours.[96]

In the Commission on Human Rights in February 1979, consideration of the Sub-Commission's report on human rights violations in Cambodia was postponed for a year – although France, the UK, the USA and other western states opposed this move. But Metzl argues that their opposition was quite low-key, and they made no public

Minute to Miss Elliot in the UN Department from Watts, 11 December 1978, in UKNA file FCO 15/2348.

[94] Metzl, *Western Responses*, pp. 140–1.

[95] Cited in Metzl, *Western Responses*, p. 133.

[96] Cited in Metzl, *Western Responses*, p. 133.

statements on the matter in the Security Council or General Assembly. 'While bringing the issue of human rights abuses in Democratic Kampuchea to the attention of the Commission on Human Rights in 1978, when there had been little political cost for doing so, had been a relatively straightforward matter, pushing the issue of the abuses of the Pol Pot regime now ran counter to the flow of policies of Western governments regarding Cambodia.'[97]

The Vietnamese-backed regime in Phnom Penh and the Khmer Rouge both claimed that they should represent Cambodia at the UN. A majority of the Credentials Committee supported the Khmer Rouge claim, and this was then voted on in the General Assembly in September 1979. Again, most western states expressed their revulsion at Khmer Rouge human rights violations, but their even greater disapproval of the Vietnamese invasion, and voted in favour of the Khmer Rouge claim. But five European states abstained: Austria, France, the Netherlands, Spain, and Sweden. They justified their abstention because they could not support a government (the Khmer Rouge) that had so systematically abused human rights.[98] That France took such a strong stance at this stage is surprising, given that it had been fairly passive regarding human rights violations in Cambodia before this. A year later, European countries were still divided. But most voted to allow the Khmer Rouge regime to take the Cambodian seat, with Belgium justifying its position by arguing that the Vietnamese-backed regime could not be considered legitimate since it had been imposed on the Cambodian people.[99] For over a decade, the Khmer Rouge continued to assume the UN seat, though from 1982, they were in a formal coalition with non-communist forces.[100]

[97] Metzl, *Western Responses*, p. 143.

[98] Metzl, *Western Responses*, p. 154.

[99] Christian Franck, 'Belgium: committed multilateralism', in Christopher Hill, ed., *National Foreign Policies and European Political Cooperation* (London: George Allen & Unwin, 1983), p. 100.

[100] And that coalition received western help, including military help. According to Kiernan, in the 1980s the UK's SAS trained forces allied to the Khmer Rouge. Ben Kiernan, 'The Inclusion of the Khmer Rouge in the Cambodian Peace Process: Causes and Consequences', in Ben Kiernan, ed., *Genocide and Democracy in Cambodia: The Khmer Rouge, the United Nations, and the International Community* (New Haven: Yale University South East Asian Studies, 1993), p. 230.

The European Community member states issued numerous declarations about Cambodia from 1979 to 1981, papering over their disagreements on the UN seat. They persistently denounced the invasion of Cambodia and called for the withdrawal of Vietnamese forces from the country.[101] On only a few occasions did they mention the 'atrocities of the barbarous Pol Pot regime'; the most extensive condemnation came from the British presidency before the General Assembly in October 1981: 'we abhor that odious regime, whose human rights violations were more flagrant than those of any other in recent history'. However, 'the history and record of that regime is no justification for invasion and occupation'.[102]

The Commission on Human Rights resumed its discussion of Cambodia in 1980, but the resolution – co-sponsored by the UK – principally condemned the Vietnamese invasion (a violation of Cambodia's right to self-determination) and said little about Khmer Rouge atrocities. But in 1985, the report by the Special Rapporteur on genocide, Benjamin Whitaker, listed the Khmer Rouge massacres between 1975 and 1979 as an example of genocide, 'even under the most restricted definition'.[103]

European governments were under some pressure to take more decisive action against the Khmer Rouge. There were protests over the votes and abstentions on the credentials issue at the UN. In March 1988, under pressure from several Dutch MPs to take action in the International Court of Justice against the Khmer Rouge for violating the Genocide Convention, the Dutch Minister of Foreign Affairs, Hans van den Broek, stated that no such action would be taken.

[101] As in European Council, 'Statement on Iran and Cambodia', Dublin (30 November 1979), or 'Joint statement by the nine on Cambodia at the 35th General Assembly of the UN', New York (15 October 1980), both documents in Press and Information Office, Federal Government Bonn, *European Political Co-operation (EPC)*, 1982.

[102] 'Statement by the Presidency on behalf of the ten on Cambodia at the 36th session of the United Nations General Assembly', New York (19 October 1981); 'Joint statement by the nine on Cambodia at the 35th General Assembly of the UN', New York (15 October 1980), in Press and Information Office, Federal Government Bonn, *European Political Co-operation (EPC)*, 1982.

[103] United Nations Economic and Social Council, Commission on Human Rights, 'Revised and updated report on the question of the prevention and punishment of the crime of genocide prepared by Mr B. Whitaker', document E/CN.4/Sub.2/1986/6 (2 July 1985), 10.

The question of Cambodia had been discussed at the CHR, and the peace process in Cambodia was too fragile to bring a case before the ICJ.[104]

In 1989, Vietnam withdrew from Cambodia; a peace agreement was signed in 1991, which led to a UN-supervised democratisation process and elections in 1993. The new government outlawed the Khmer Rouge and in 1998 all remaining Khmer Rouge leaders surrendered to the government. Official discussion about genocide in Cambodia could thus take place. The CHR resolution on Cambodia in 1991 finally mentioned the word genocide, and the need to prevent its recurrence in Cambodia. In 1997, the Cambodian government asked the UN to set up an international tribunal on Khmer Rouge crimes. UN Secretary-General Kofi Annan then set up a Group of Experts to evaluate the proposal, and it found sufficient evidence to justify holding the Khmer Rouge to account for numerous crimes, including genocide. With respect to genocide, the Group of Experts justified the need to investigate the 'commission of genocide against the Cham, Vietnamese and other minority groups and the Buddhist monkhood.' And

> the Khmer people of Cambodia do constitute a national group within the meaning of the Convention. However, whether the Khmer Rouge committed genocide with respect to part of the Khmer national group turns on complex interpretive issues, especially concerning the Khmer Rouge's intent with respect to its non-minority-group victims. The Group does not take a position on this issue, but believes that any tribunal will have to address this question should Khmer Rouge officials be charged with genocide against the Khmer national group.[105]

After lengthy negotiations, the Cambodian government finally agreed that the tribunal set up to try the Khmer Rouge should be a joint UN/Cambodian one. The Extraordinary Chambers in the Courts of Cambodia (ECCC) was created in 2001. European states (especially France and the UK) and the European Commission are among the

[104] Second chamber debate on human rights (14 March 1988). Translation by TvC.

[105] UN General Assembly and Security Council, Report of the Group of Experts for Cambodia.

top financial contributors to the ECCC (though Japan is by far the largest contributor).[106] On 18 July 2007, the Co-Prosecutors found evidence of 'crimes against humanity, genocide, grave breaches of the Geneva Conventions, homicide, torture and religious persecution.' They requested the co-investigating judges to charge those responsible for those crimes.[107]

Elsewhere

The cases above are not the only ones in which accusations of genocide were made during the Cold War, but they are the most serious and the ones in which European states did take some sort of stand. In fact, genocide was frequently alleged to be taking place somewhere in the world, often by opposition or backbench members of various parliaments around Western Europe. Journalists and editorial writers, and civil society and human rights organisations also made allegations. But in virtually every such case either governments ignored the term altogether, or they specifically rejected its applicability. Sometimes this appears to be due to Cold War or other geopolitical considerations.

From the late 1950s, China was accused of genocide against Tibetans, and in 1960 the International Commission of Jurists issued a finding that the Chinese had committed genocide against the Buddhist religious group in Tibet, on the grounds that Buddhism could not be practiced in Tibet, religious figures had been killed, and large numbers of Tibetan children had been transferred to a Chinese 'materialistic environment' to prevent them from having a religious

[106] See the finances section on the ECCC website. European states give to both the Cambodian side and the UN side (but more to the latter): www.eccc.gov.kh/english/finances.aspx [last accessed 13 April 2010]. The ECCC have been plagued by accusations of corruption and political interference. 'The Court on Trial', *The Economist* (4 April 2009).

[107] Extraordinary Chambers in the Courts of Cambodia, 'Statement of the co-prosecutors', Phnom Penh (18 July 2007); available at www.yale.edu/cgp/downloads/Statement_of_Co-Prosecutors18-July-2007.pdf [last accessed 14 April 2010]. There has been much academic debate over whether there was a genocide in Cambodia. See the contrasting views of Jason Abrams and William Schabas in a symposium, 'Were the Atrocities in Cambodia and Kosovo Genocide?', *New England Law Review*, vol. 35, no. 2 (Winter 2000).

upbringing.[108] But these accusations were not echoed by European *governments* (as opposed to Tibetan exiles and some NGOs who have made accusations – particularly of 'cultural genocide' – ever since).

In 1964, the Rwandan government was alleged to be engaging in a genocide against members of the Tutsi minority.[109] This is one of the rare cases where a government admitted that a genocide had occurred. In the UK House of Commons on 10 February 1964, the Minister of State for Foreign Affairs, Peter Thomas, stated:

> Although the reports received have been far from clear I agree that it appears that these deplorable acts are acts of genocide, but it is not clear what the circumstances are. I believe that the Ruanda Government are taking steps to prevent any further indiscriminate killing, and Her Majesty's Ambassador reports that the great majority of these events took place a month ago. Apparently, these events seem to have occurred in the panic which was caused among the general population by Tutsi raids from neighbouring country.[110]

No further action was taken.

Almost a decade later, in the troubled Great Lakes region another genocide was alleged to have taken place. The Tutsi-led government of Burundi killed tens of thousands of Hutus in May to July 1972. Two years later, the Minority Rights Group (a think tank) argued that it was a genocide.[111] As *The Times* noted in 1977, 'Hardly a voice was raised in protest.' The OAU, UN, UK and USA said little. 'As for Belgium ... there were mutterings in Brussels about sanctions, but no one in Bujumbura took them seriously, knowing that the French would be only too happy to step in should the Belgians drop out.'[112] In May 1972, the Belgian Prime Minister had told his cabinet that

[108] 'Chinese Acts of Genocide in Tibet', *The Times* (20 June 1960).

[109] The reaction of 'UN officials' was that the matter was the internal affair of the government. 'Rwanda Policy of Genocide Alleged', *The Times* (3 February 1964).

[110] Hansard, House of Commons (10 February 1964), vol. 689, col. 16.

[111] As is often the case, the number of dead cited varies from source to source: 80–100,000 in 'The Massacre the World Ignored', *The Times* (15 July 1974). But René Lemarchand argues that the death toll was between 200,000 and 300,000. Lemarchand, 'The Burundi Genocide', in Totten, Parsons and Charney, eds., *Century of Genocide*, 2nd edition, (London: Routledge, 2004), p. 321.

[112] 'Even in Africa's Scarred History, Never Genocide on this Scale', *The Times* (15 July 1977); see also Lemarchand, 'The Burundi Genocide', pp. 328–9.

the evidence he had indicated there was a genocide in Burundi; the Belgian ambassador in Burundi was instructed to express Belgium's concern. But France supported the Burundi government, as did the OAU; the CHR postponed discussion of the case.[113]

Idi Amin's dictatorship in Uganda, 1971–9, was often accused of mass atrocities – but only rarely of genocide. An editorial in *The Times* argued against permitting the Ugandan President Idi Amin attending a Commonwealth conference in the UK, and asserted that he was responsible not only for murder, but 'so far as Acholi is concerned, genocide'.[114] In the event, Amin did not attend the conference. UK MPs did not make many accusations that the Amin government was engaging in genocide, though there were a few. MP Jeremy Thorpe said that the pattern of oppression in Uganda had 'led to acts of genocide against members of the Langi and Acholi'.[115] But these accusations were never repeated by government officials. A 1977 UK-Canadian attempt to have the CHR investigate the human rights situation in Uganda was defeated.[116]

Periodically there were concerns that native Indians were being exterminated in various Latin American countries. Again, allegations of genocide were usually dismissed out of hand by European governments. On 9 July 1974, the British embassy in Asuncion, Paraguay, reported that the allegation that the Paraguayan government had engaged in earlier genocide against native Indians was false; instead the situation was just one of problematic assimilation. It further reported that such allegations come from foreigners, ill disposed to 'use terms like "genocide" scrupulously.'[117] In response to a parliamentary question in October 1983, the Dutch ministers of foreign affairs and of development argued that there were no indications of genocide in Colombia and 'therefore no further intervention on the part of the Dutch government was necessary'.[118] This was a glimmer

[113] Kuper, *Genocide*, pp. 163–4.
[114] 'No Welcome for Murder', *The Times* (18 February 1977).
[115] Hansard, House of Commons debate (1 March 1977), vol. 927, col. 235. Even when Tanzania toppled Amin in 1979, no other state legitimised Tanzania's use of force on humanitarian grounds. Wheeler, *Saving Strangers*, p. 134.
[116] Kuper, *Genocide*, p. 168. [117] UKNA file FCO 7/2718.
[118] Second Chamber Appendix, written questions and answers (182) on the human rights situation in Colombia (Q: 27 October 1983; A: 22 November 1983). Translation by TvC.

of an indication of how at least one European government interpreted obligations that might arise ('further intervention') in the event of a proven genocide.

In the Dutch parliament, in the late 1970s and early 1980s Indonesia was often accused of engaging in genocide in East Timor and in West Papua. In 1982, the Minister of Foreign Affairs argued that it had sufficient information to establish that genocide was not occurring in West Papua; in December 1983, the Minister of Foreign Affairs again denied that genocide was occurring there. Further, on that latter occasion, the Minister stated that if regular reports indicated a change in the situation, 'the government would be prepared, in accordance with the UN, to verify concrete reports of the human rights situation in West Papua and to take necessary action.'[119]

Accusations that Iraq was engaging in genocide against the Kurds surfaced, particularly in the late 1980s.[120] Again, these garnered little attention. In a debate in the House of Lords in June 1989, the government was pressed as to whether it considered the Iraqi persecution as 'genocide' under the Genocide Convention, and if so, what action it would take under the Convention. The Minister of State, Foreign and Commonwealth Office, Lord Glenarthur replied, 'on the evidence we have, we do not believe that the alleged actions of the Iraqi authorities towards the Kurds, about which we have forcefully expressed our concern, constitute genocide as defined under the Convention on the Prevention and Punishment of the Crime of Genocide.' But at least in this case, the Minister expanded on exactly why it did not consider the case to be one of genocide:

> But it is a fact also that the crime of genocide comprises two elements: the intent to destroy and one or more of the acts as listed in the convention...

[119] Second Chamber Report 17100V, no. 139, on the parliamentary debate on human rights situation in Malaysia, Taiwan, West Papua and South Africa (9 September 1982); written answers from the Minister and State Secretary of Foreign Affairs to questions on the budget for foreign affairs for 1984, 18100V (15 December 1983). Translation by TvC.

[120] Much earlier, on 11 July 1963, the British (and US) governments voted against a Soviet attempt to add an item to the UN ECOSOC agenda on 'the policy of genocide which is being pursued by the Government of the Republic of Iraq against the Kurdish people'. The British argued that it was a political matter, outside ECOSOC's competence. 'Russian Charge of Genocide', *The Times* (12 July 1963).

Under the convention, conspiracy to commit genocide is punishable as well as the act itself. Of course we condemn Iraq's human rights record, but the evidence we possess does not back up genocide under the UN convention.

He later admitted that it is difficult to prove intent, 'and it is made even more difficult when the crime must be supported not only by intent but also by the actions to which I referred.'[121] The use of the term became more acceptable after Iraq invaded Kuwait in August 1990 (see chapter 4), but especially after the USA and UK invaded Iraq in 2003. In June 2003, the then Prime Minister Tony Blair stated: 'We have always believed that those who have been responsible for genocide, crimes against humanity and war crimes in Iraq should be brought to justice. No decisions have yet been taken on how this should be pursued.'[122] And in December 2003, a Dutch court ruled that the Iraqi government did commit genocide against the Kurds in 1988.[123]

Conclusion

In almost all of the cases discussed in this chapter, European governments did not publicly use the word 'genocide' to describe atrocities and massacres, despite domestic pressure to use the term and act accordingly. Most often they simply did not use the term – with no explanation provided; sometimes they dismissed genocide as the right descriptive term; and occasionally they dismissed use of the word as the work of clever propagandists. Only rarely, though, is the rejection of the term publicly linked to the definition in the Genocide Convention. Further, European governments appeared to be little inclined to investigate seriously whether genocide was taking place at all, as in the case of Biafra. This non-use of the term did not change during the Cold War. But after it ended, the term was used by governments to describe some of the events in the previous decades. In

121 Hansard, House of Lords (27 June 1989), vol. 509, cols. 575–8.

122 Hansard, House of Commons (10 June 2003), vol. 406, col. 718.

123 'Killing of Iraq Kurds "Genocide"', *BBC News online* (23 December 2003). The court made this ruling in the case against a Dutch trader, who was convicted of complicity in war crimes for selling the ingredients for poison gas to the Iraqi regime in the 1980s; he was acquitted on the grounds that the trader was not aware of Iraq's genocidal intentions.

the case of Cambodia, European governments admitted well after the fact that it had been a genocide – in their acquiescence to UN resolutions that mentioned it and in their support for the Extraordinary Chambers in the Courts of Cambodia. The case of Iraq and the Kurds is similar: once Iraq had demonstrated itself an 'outlaw' the term became widespread even among governments.

Governments' non-use of the word is related to their understanding that if genocide was proven they would have to do *something*. In the case of Bangladesh, in private the UK did consider Pakistan to be in breach of the Genocide Convention, but was not prepared to take any action in response – and so it did not label events as genocide in public. Governments dismissed allegations of genocide because to admit it would create a need to take some sort of action. The norm of non-interference was certainly dominant in their discourse – governments apparently feared that a finding of genocide would force them to 'interfere'. Interference would certainly not include 'humanitarian intervention' – this sort of response was generally considered beyond the pale during the Cold War.[124] But other responses (demanded by public pressure) might endanger security and economic interests: it could entail cutting off lucrative arms supplies or damaging alliances and ties with friendly states. It could entail 'taking the wrong side' in the Cold War. It could threaten the very basis of the international system by encouraging the break-up of states, as in Nigeria (the only case of legitimate 'secession' during the Cold War was that of Bangladesh). Therefore it is clearly better to avoid use of the term altogether. The next four chapters consider the extent to which this continued to be the prevalent attitude after the end of the Cold War.

[124] As Nicholas Wheeler has argued in *Saving Strangers*, while humanitarian justifications for the interventions of Tanzania in Uganda, India in East Pakistan, and Vietnam in Cambodia may have been given in public, these cannot be said to have been accepted or legitimised by the international community.

4 *Bosnia and Herzegovina*

One norm of the international order that seemed to be in flux at the end of the Cold War was 'non-interference'. As seen in the previous chapter, European governments cited this to justify not taking action in several cases of alleged genocide. At the end of the Cold War, however, there appeared to be a new liberal consensus in favour of fostering the protection of human rights and the spread of democracy, including through such interfering means as requiring aid recipients to meet political conditions, sending observers to monitor elections, and even, more controversially, using military force to protect civilians from their own government. UN peacekeeping missions – required more than ever to 'clean up' the mess left by superpower competition in southern Africa, south-east Asia, Central America, and so on – were given wide mandates to engage in peace-building, democracy building, and state building. The USA led a coalition under a UN flag to clear Iraqi occupying forces out of Kuwait in early 1991; even more strikingly, when the Saddam Hussein regime quashed uprisings against his rule by Kurds in the north of Iraq, the UN Security Council 'demanded' the end of repression (in Resolution 688, 5 April 1991). Western countries interpreted this resolution as allowing the deployment of military forces to protect a 'safe haven' in the Kurdish region.

In calling for this action, the French government cited a 'duty of intervention' to protect people from massive human rights violations, which reflected the influence of Bernard Kouchner, founder of Médecins sans Frontières after the Biafra war, and between 1988 and 1992 a French minister for humanitarian affairs.[1] Allegations that the

[1] See the chapter on 'Safe Havens and No-Fly Zones in Iraq' in Wheeler, *Saving Strangers*. Kouchner believed the 'right' to intervene flowed from the duty to do so. See Tim Allen and David Styan, 'A Right to Interfere? Bernard Kouchner and the New Humanitarianism', *Journal of International Development*, vol. 12, no. 6 (2000).

Iraqi government was engaging in genocide were made: the German Chancellor Helmut Kohl, the German Foreign Minister Hans-Dietrich Genscher, and the Luxembourg Foreign Minister Jacques Poos all used the term to describe Iraqi actions against the Kurds, and Genscher also repeatedly called for the prosecution of Saddam Hussein.[2] On 19 April 1991 the European Parliament called on the EC governments to bring action against Saddam Hussein at the International Court of Justice, for violating the Genocide Convention.[3] In the UK, the opposition pressed the government to request a UN investigation into the specific charge of genocide. On 16 April 1991 Prime Minister John Major told the Commons that he had asked for legal advice on the subject of genocide,[4] but this advice must have pointed out the limits of the Convention. Foreign Secretary Douglas Hurd noted that individuals accused of genocide had to be tried before national courts, and that it had to be proved that those individuals intended to destroy in whole or in part one of the groups defined in the convention; he also noted that Saddam Hussein was not within 'our power'.[5] In the House of Lords the government stated that it would be difficult to set up an international tribunal to try Hussein against his will.[6]

What is striking about the European response to the specific issue of genocide against the Kurds, is that it concentrated on the legal front, on the measures suggested in the Genocide Convention to punish the crime. The British and French justification for the safe havens policy was never *specifically* that of preventing or suppressing genocide. Just over a year later, when allegations of genocide were made regarding Bosnia and Herzegovina, neither the French nor the British government cited a 'duty of intervention' to protect civilians, and the specific issue of genocide was generally ignored by both governments.

[2] Power, *'A Problem from Hell'*, p. 481.

[3] European Parliament resolution of 18 April 1991 (see *Bulletin of the European Communities*, no. 4 (1991), part 1.3.17). Michael Knipe, 'Foreign Office Reluctant to Use "Genocide" Label', *The Times* (6 April 1991); Ian Murray, 'Bonn to Join Aid Effort', *The Times* (21 April 1991); 'Charge Saddam', *The Independent* (19 April 1991); Colin Brown, 'UN Genocide Convention May Allow Military Help for Kurds', *The Independent* (17 April 1991).

[4] Hansard, House of Commons debate (16 April 1991), vol. 189, col. 158.

[5] Hansard, House of Commons debate (15 April 1991), vol. 189, col. 23; House of Commons debate (17 April 1991), vol. 189, col. 421.

[6] Hansard, House of Lords debate (19 April 1991), vol. 527, cols. 1659–60.

An international tribunal to try individuals for, among other crimes, genocide, was, however, one of the outcomes of the international response to the war in Bosnia and Herzegovina. So here too, the overall response to allegations of genocide centred on the legal front, on measures to punish the crime. Governments did not use the norms against genocide to enable or require intervention.

Any optimism that a new world order would spring from the stultifying Cold War proved distinctly premature when war broke out in Yugoslavia. Here the new fashion for elections provided an easy route to power for ethnic nationalists, above all Slobodan Milošević, the president of Serbia between 1989 and 1997. His plotting for a 'greater Serbia' alarmed the other constituent republics in the Yugoslav federation, and in June 1991 Croatia and Slovenia declared their independence. In response, the Federal Army of Yugoslavia – increasingly acting at Serbia's behest – launched military action to defeat 'separatists' in both republics. After ten days it abandoned the attempt to do so in Slovenia, but war raged in Croatia, in which the Yugoslav/Serbian army supported action by ethnic Serb militias to seize control of territory in which ethnic Serbs constituted a substantial part of the population. The European Community responded to the outbreak of war with a variety of means, from mediation to sending ceasefire observers. When, however, it became clear that the EC on its own could not bring about a peaceful resolution of the conflict, European states brought in the UN. In February 1992, the UN Security Council launched a peacekeeping operation (UN Protection Force, or UNPROFOR) to patrol a ceasefire between ethnic Serbs and Croatian forces in Croatia. In the meantime, the European Community – pushed by Germany – recognised the independence of Croatia and Slovenia, and held out the prospect of recognition to two other republics, Bosnia and Herzegovina, and Macedonia, if they met certain conditions. Bosnia and Herzegovina was particularly vulnerable to further fragmentation – as three main ethnic groups made up most of its population, Croats (17 per cent), Serbs (31 per cent), and Muslims (44 per cent).

On 29 February and 1 March 1992 Bosnia-Herzegovina held a referendum on independence; 64.4 per cent of the population participated, of which almost 100 per cent voted in favour. But most Bosnian Serbs did not vote, as the Serbian Democratic Party led by Radovan Karadžić had called for a boycott. On 6 April the European

Community and its member states recognised the independence of Bosnia and Herzegovina; on 7 April, the USA did likewise. Within days, Serb paramilitaries and Yugoslav/Serbian army units were 'cleansing' the north-eastern town of Zvornik of its Muslim inhabitants; by the end of the summer of 1992, Serb forces had 'cleansed' much of northern and eastern Bosnia and were in control of about two-thirds of the territory of Bosnia and Herzegovina.[7] Over the course of the next three and a half years, approximately 100,000 people were killed (about half of whom were civilians), and two million forced to flee their homes.[8] While the fighting was not always a straightforward Serb vs. Muslim/Croat affair (between 1993 and 1994, for example, Muslims and Croats fought each other), and while all fighting forces committed atrocities, Muslims were the principal victims. At least 7000 Bosnian Muslim men were massacred by Serb forces in the eastern town of Srebrenica in July 1995 – the single worst massacre of the war, for which Karadžić and the Bosnian Serb military commander Ratko Mladić, among others, have been indicted for genocide.

The response of the 'international community' – principally the UN and the major western governments – to the war was a humanitarian and not a coercive one. After much hesitation, UNPROFOR's mandate was extended to Bosnia and Herzegovina, first to ensure the security of the Sarajevo airport (June 1992) and then to protect the delivery of humanitarian aid; a no-fly zone over Bosnia and Herzegovina was

[7] See Laura Silber and Allan Little, *The Death of Yugoslavia*, revised edition (London: Penguin Books, 1996), chapters 16 and 18 for the history of this part of the war.

[8] The number of deaths has been the subject of controversy for many years. Two detailed studies have been done recently. Two researchers from the Demographic Unit of the International Criminal Tribunal for the former Yugoslavia estimated that 102,622 individuals died as a result of the war, of which 55,261 (54 per cent) were civilians; the war created over two million refugees. Ewa Tabeau and Jakub Bijak, 'War-related Deaths in the 1992–1995 Armed Conflicts in Bosnia and Hezegovina: A Critique of Previous Estimates and Recent Results', *European Journal of Population*, vol. 21, nos. 2–3 (2005). The Sarajevo-based Research and Documentation Center has been compiling a list of the names of the dead, and concluded that 97,207 were killed or are missing, of which 39,684 were civilians (40.82 per cent), and of which 64,036 (65.88 per cent) were 'Bosniaks' (Muslims). See www.idc.org.ba/aboutus.html [last accessed 23 April 2009]. The ICTY indictment of the Bosnian Serb leader Radovan Karadžić states that over 7000 Muslim men and boys from Srebrenica were killed by Bosnian Serb forces in July 1995.

declared, and then enforced by NATO planes; the EU and UN, and then the Contact Group (UK, France, Germany, USA and Russia), tried to negotiate a solution; an arms embargo was imposed on the entire former Yugoslavia; sanctions were imposed on Serbia and Montenegro, considered to be responsible for supporting the war and for preventing a peaceful solution to the conflict; six cities besieged by Bosnian Serb forces were declared 'safe areas' (Srebrenica, Tuzla, Zepa, Gorazde, Bihac and Sarajevo) and UNPROFOR was given the job of ensuring free access of humanitarian aid to the safe areas (but not the protection of people inside the safe areas). But no real military action (other than occasional pin-prick air strikes against specific military targets) was taken against any of the fighting forces. In September 1995 came the endgame. After the Srebrenica massacre, after the fall of Zepa, after another shell had killed numerous civilians in Sarajevo, and, crucially, after the Croatian army drove out Serb forces (and civilians) from Croatian territory and Bosnian government forces recaptured territory from Serb forces, the UN and NATO engaged in two weeks of air strikes against the Bosnian Serbs. The USA brokered a peace agreement in Dayton, Ohio, which was signed in December 1995 and created a state made up of two component parts, the Republika Srpska (in control of 49 per cent of territory) and the Bosnian-Croat federation (in control of 51 per cent).

As the then UN Secretary-General, Kofi Annan, stated in 1999, 'The community of nations decided to respond to the war in Bosnia and Herzegovina with an arms embargo, with humanitarian aid and with the deployment of a peacekeeping force. It must be clearly stated that these measures were poor substitutes for more decisive and forceful action to prevent the unfolding horror.'[9] International actors viewed the war through a 'prism of "moral equivalency"', and failed to grasp the Bosnian Serb war aims, namely the creation of a greater Serbia through ethnic cleansing.[10] They tried to negotiate with 'an unscrupulous and murderous regime', but 'these Bosnian Serb war aims were ultimately repulsed on the battlefield, and not at the negotiating table.'[11]

[9] United Nations General Assembly, Report of the Secretary-General pursuant to General Assembly Resolution 53/35: the fall of Srebrenica (hereinafter 'The fall of Srebrenica'), A/54/549 (15 November 1999), p. 105.

[10] 'The fall of Srebrenica', quote on p. 104.

[11] 'The fall of Srebrenica', pp. 107–8.

The emphasis in this chapter is on the issue of genocide: did European governments say a genocide was taking place in Bosnia and Herzegovina, and what action did they take as a result? There has been some academic and legal debate about whether or not a genocide did occur, and more specifically, on whether 'ethnic cleansing' is genocide.[12] This chapter does not enter directly into that debate, but instead analyses the discourse and actions of the three principal European governments (France, Germany and the UK), and the Netherlands, whose troops were serving in Srebrenica in 1995.

There are two periods during the Bosnian war when genocide is particularly an issue: after journalists revealed the existence of 'detention camps' in northern Bosnia in July and August 1992, and after the fall of the Srebrenica 'safe area' in July 1995. This chapter thus covers the 1992 and 1995 events respectively, and then the creation and operation of the International Criminal Tribunal for the former Yugoslavia (ICTY) – the first such tribunal to be created since Nuremberg, and the first international tribunal to include genocide within its remit.

Bosnia, 1992: ethnic cleansing and genocide?

From 19 July 1992, *Newsday* published a series of articles by its journalist, Roy Gutman, exposing brutal conditions inside 'detention camps' run by Bosnian Serbs in northern Bosnia.[13] Here were corralled the civilian victims of the Serbs' 'ethnic cleansing', not just prisoners of war. On 6 August, Independent Television News broadcast film from the Trnopolje camp, which showed emaciated Bosnian

[12] For clear views that a genocide did take place, see (among others): Norman Cigar, *Genocide in Bosnia: The Policy of 'Ethnic Cleansing'* (College Station: Texas A&M University Press, 1995); Roy Gutman, *A Witness to Genocide: The First Inside Account of the Horrors of 'Ethnic Cleansing' in Bosnia* (Shaftesbury: Element, 1993); David Rieff, *Slaughterhouse; Bosnia and the Failure of the West* (New York: Touchstone, 1996); Bruun, 'Beyond the 1948 Convention'. Others have their doubts that 'ethnic cleansing' is genocide, including Martin Mennecke in Martin Mennecke and Eric Markusen, 'Genocide in Bosnia and Herzegovina', in Totten, Parsons and Charny, eds., *Century of Genocide*, and Schabas, in *Genocide in International Law*, 2nd edition, p. 234.

[13] Gutman was awarded the Pulitzer Prize in 1993 for his reporting from Bosnia. Gutman, *A Witness to Genocide*.

Muslim men behind barbed wire. The images – coming on top of images of burning villages, corpses and refugees – had an electric effect on public opinion in many European countries, and their governments came under pressure to respond appropriately, to 'do something'. Numerous commentators, including Gutman himself, had no problem in describing ethnic cleansing as a euphemism for genocide. And many others drew parallels with Auschwitz or Belsen; Medécins du Monde, a humanitarian NGO, began a campaign in France comparing Milošević with Hitler.[14]

Information about the camps and the brutality of 'ethnic cleansing' had been passed to governments before the news hit the headlines. Mohamed Sacirbey, the ambassador of Bosnia and Herzegovina to the UN, told Secretary-General Boutros Boutros-Ghali about the existence of the camps on 15 May; in mid June, Médecins du Monde reported that there could be camps in the vicinity of Prijedor; on 3 July the UN High Commissioner for Refugees circulated a report to the International Committee of the Red Cross, UNPROFOR and the EU about abuses at four camps.[15] On 10 July, the President of Bosnia and Herzegovina, Alija Izetbegovic, told a CSCE summit that there were widespread atrocities and genocide against civilians ongoing, and twenty-seven concentration camps, in Serb-occupied territory.[16]

And during French President Mitterrand's rather theatrical visit to besieged Sarajevo on 28 June 1992, Izetbegovic told Mitterrand about the camps and reports of massacres of civilians and pleaded for a commission of inquiry to investigate. Mitterrand asked for no further information and only inquired about how the Bosnian Serbs were reacting.[17] In comments to the press during the visit, Izetbegovic

[14] Thierry Tardy, *La France et la gestion des conflits yougoslaves (1991–1995): Enjeux et leçons d'une opération de maintien de la paix de l'ONU* (Brussels: Bruylant, 1999), p. 159.

[15] Silber and Little, *The Death of Yugoslavia*, pp. 251–2; Matheiu Braunstein, *François Mitterrand à Sarajevo, 28 Juin 1992: Le rendez-vouz manqué* (Paris: L'Harmattan, 2001), pp. 128–9.

[16] Michael Binyon, 'Bosnia Makes Plea for Military Help', *The Times* (10 July 1992).

[17] Georges-Marie Chenu, 'Postface' in Braunstein, *François Mitterrand à Sarajevo*, pp. 181–3. Chenu was the French Ambassador to Croatia. Until the Lisbon European Council of 26–27 June 1992, Mitterrand had famously refused to label the Serbs as the aggressors in either Croatia or Bosnia. He was widely considered to be pro-Serb – which some

reported that he had told Mitterrand 'about murders and massacres and that nobody can know the number of people in concentration camps' – this was repeated, as far as I have been able to find out, in only one major English-language newspaper on the following day, nor was it covered in the French press.[18] But the reports alarmed the French ambassador to Croatia enough that when he returned to Zagreb, he launched an investigation to gather information on the camps and on ethnic cleansing in Serb-occupied Croatia and Bosnia and Herzegovina. He sent nineteen despatches to the Foreign Affairs Ministry and the Elysée about the numerous expulsions of civilians and their detention in concentration camps, and even about widespread rapes; the Foreign Affairs Ministry never requested further details or evidence.[19]

It was only in late July and early August – as Gutman's reports hit headlines and in particular as the televised images were replayed – that governments felt pressured to respond. The first question, then, is whether the three major European governments used the term 'genocide' to describe the atrocities in Bosnia-Herzegovina.

Naming genocide?

Uniquely, German politicians – from almost all the major parties – did use the term genocide to describe events in Bosnia-Herzegovina in 1992 (and beyond). Chancellor Helmut Kohl (Christian Democratic Union) and Foreign Minister Klaus Kinkel (Free Democrat Party) frequently charged that what was happening in Bosnia and Herzegovina was genocide perpetrated by the Serbs. In August 1992, Kohl referred to the concentration camps as genocide.[20] Kinkel was particularly insistent

commentators linked to geopolitical manoeuvering against Germany (seen to be a supporter of Croatia) or harking back to traditional alliances. See also Joseph Kurlic, 'La France et la crise yougoslave jusqu'au traité de l'Elysée (1991–1995)', *Journal of European Integration History*, vol. 10, no. 1 (2004).

[18] 'Mitterrand visits Sarajevo; Gunbattles Delay Departure', *St Petersburg Times* (Florida), 29 June 1992; the report was compiled from Associated Press and Reuters wire reports. Mattheiu Braunstein reports that the French media did not pass on Izetbegovic's comments (*François Mitterrand à Sarajevo*, p. 134).

[19] Chenu, 'Postface', pp. 185–6.

[20] 'Bush Hedges on Force', *The Advertiser* (Australia), 13 August 1992. Later in February 1993 Kohl spoke of 'genocide' in Bosnia in general. Steve Crawshaw, 'Kinkel Backtracks as Bonn Policy Wavers', *The Independent* (3

on the issue, repeatedly using the term genocide that August: on 19 August, he stated, 'The attempt by the Serbian aggressors to carry out an ethnic cleansing action aimed at other population groups in order to achieve their national goals in Bosnia-Herzegovina is genocide'.[21] At the London conference later that month (see below), he directly accused the Serbs of genocide.[22] The former Foreign Minister, Hans-Dietrich Genscher (Free Democrat Party) also described the events as genocide.[23]

A few other European governments did use the term genocide in this period. In June 1992, the Portuguese Prime Minister (and then the president of the EC), Cavaco Silva, declared that 'if the genocide continues then we cannot exclude a military solution'.[24] At the first ever special session of the UN Commission on Human Rights, held on 13 and 14 August 1992, Austria declared:

> The odious policy of ethnic cleansing must cease immediately. It is in fact genocide, in the sense of the UN Convention for the Prevention and Punishment of the Crime of Genocide. Such events should be the object of severe condemnation by the international community and it should put pressure on those responsible to put an end to it.[25]

But almost all the West European governments (bar Austria, which voted in favour) abstained on UN General Assembly Resolution 47/121 of 18 December 1992, which explicitly stated that ethnic cleansing was a form of genocide. However, the few explanations of vote given

February 1993); 'Ex-Yugoslavia: Peacemongers', *The Economist* (6 February 1993).

21 David Gow, 'Germany to Call for War Crimes Trials', *The Guardian* (20 August 1992).

22 Barbara Crosette, 'Balkans Session is Long on Talk, Short on Action', *New York Times* (27 August 1992). See also BBC Summary of World Broadcasts, 'FRG Foreign Minister Presents Ten Policy Points at Conference' (28 August 1992); Leonard Doyle, 'UN Urged to Act on Bosnia Rights Abuses', *The Independent* (24 September 1992).

23 *Agence France Presse*, 'M. Genscher demande un "bloccus total" contre la Serbie et crique la communauté internationale' (8 August 1992).

24 Hella Pick, 'British Troops Stay Out', *The Guardian* (3 June 1992).

25 Austria's was the only European government to call it genocide at this meeting; some members of the Organisation of the Islamic Conference did so as well. United Nations Commission on Human Rights, first special session, summary record of the second meeting (first part), E/CN.4/1992/S-1/SR.2 (22 October 1992) paragraph 80.

indicated that the problem with the resolution was the fact that it called for the use of military force to restore the sovereignty and territorial integrity of Bosnia-Herzegovina, and for lifting the arms embargo on the country; no-one addressed the issue of genocide directly.[26] At the second special session of the Commission on Human Rights, held 30 November–1 December 1992, the resolution debated and approved specifically called upon 'all States to consider the extent to which the acts committed in Bosnia and Herzegovina and in Croatia constitute genocide'. But despite urging by the Turkish ambassador to address this specific issue in the debate, few states present did so – other than Iran and Bosnia and Herzegovina. The European states – including Germany and Austria – condemned human rights violations and 'ethnic cleansing', but did not mention genocide.[27]

France and the UK steadfastly avoided the term, and resisted the comparisons with Nazi practices, thought they did condemn the camps. In an interview with *Le Figaro* on 7 August 1993, a French Foreign Ministry official, Georges Kiejman, stated:

> We are not in a situation comparable to that of the 1930s... this concept [of ethnic cleansing] is in part a marginal means of propaganda which the extremists on all sides throw in your face. The reality is that this is a civil war between states and their national components. The overlapping of the various communities on the ground makes military action difficult.[28]

In the UK, the revelations about ethnic cleansing and the camps did not shake the government – or much of the opposition, press, or civil society – into reconsidering the widespread discourse of 'moral

[26] United Nations General Assembly, provisional verbatim record of the 92nd meeting, held on 18 December 1992, A/47/PV.92 (22 January 1993). The USA voted in favour of the resolution.

[27] The special session had been requested by Turkey, to discuss the first report of the Special Rapporteur on human rights in the former Yugoslavia. The resolution passed with only one negative vote (that of Yugoslavia) and one abstention (that of Cuba). United Nations Commission on Human Rights, report on the second special session (30 November – 1 December 1992), E/1992/22/Add.2 and E/CN.4/1992/84/Add.2; United Nations Commission on Human Rights, second special session, summary record of the first meeting (30 November 1992), E/CN.4/1992/S-2/SR.1.

[28] 'Interview accordée par le ministre délégué auprès du ministre des Affaires étrangères, M. Kiejman au Figaro' (7 August 1992), in *La Politique Étrangère de la France: Textes et Documents*, July-August 1992 (Paris: Ministère des Affaires Étrangères), p. 77 (my translation).

equivalency': all sides were guilty. Thus, in the House of Lords, the Minister of State for the Foreign and Commonwealth Office, Baroness Chalker, stated:

> It is important that we are absolutely clear about the work that is being done by various different groups in Yugoslavia. It is quite clear that the Bosnian Serbs, encouraged by the Serbian leadership in Belgrade, precipitated the conflict. That is why we in the international community have condemned the Bosnian Serb air attacks, the existence of the detention camps and the abhorrent policy of ethnic cleansing. *The Bosnian Moslems and the Croats must also bear a measure of responsibility for the tragedy in Bosnia. All three parties have had detention camps and have carried out forcible expulsions.*[29]

In contrast with France, there was also much less pressure on the British government to use the term genocide or to draw comparisons with Auschwitz or Belsen – although a few people did, including Lord Owen (later to become the EU's negotiator and converted to the moral equivalency thesis),[30] and former Prime Minister Margaret Thatcher.[31] But these critics were easily and summarily dismissed. Gregory Kent notes that the term genocide 'was almost never used as a descriptor

[29] Hansard, House of Lords debate (25 September 1992), cols. 591–2 (my emphasis). The Bosnian government and Bosnian Croat forces also had detention camps, but in the case of the first a UN Commission of Experts found that it could not detect a particular pattern of wrongdoing, and that allegations of human rights violations were in any event limited; there were more reports of killings in the Croat-run camps, but again the Commission reported no particular pattern of wrongdoing. In the camps run by Bosnian Serbs, however, 'grave breaches of the Geneva Conventions and other violations of international humanitarian law' were committed over a long period of time and on a large scale. UN Security Council, final report of the commission of experts established pursuant to Security Council Resolution 80 (1992), S/1994/674 (27 May 1994), 52–5.

[30] On 30 July, Owen wrote a letter to the *Evening Standard* (London), arguing that we were 'witnessing, 50 years on, scenes in Europe that mirror the early stages of the Nazi holocaust under the dreadful description of "ethnic cleansing"'. Brendan Simms, *Unfinest Hour: Britain and the Destruction of Bosnia* (London: Penguin Books, 2002), p. 135.

[31] Throughout the war, Thatcher repeatedly called for intervention against the Serbs. In December 1992, she said, 'There is still time to save the intended victims of this second Holocaust.' Anthony Bevins and Stephen Goodwin, 'Thatcher Warns of "Holocaust" Risk in Bosnia Appeal', *The Independent* (17 December 1992). See also Simms, *Unfinest Hour*, pp. 49–51.

of events in Bosnia' in 1992: 'neither TV nor press editors nor correspondents made use of a wealth of evidence of genocide to draw appropriate conclusions about it.'[32] And he argues that the 'apparent failure to report systematic massacres of the Bosnian people and to label this action "genocide" can be seen, in part, as an indirect consequence of the framing of the war as one of moral equivalence. If differences were minimal between the Balkan "tribes" – aside from the initial "support" for "the Serbs" from Belgrade and admitted Serbian "pre-emptive" aggression – then wasn't the notion of genocide a little farfetched?'[33] Brendan Simms' *Unfinest Hour* meticulously dissects the prevailing British attitude that there was moral equivalence between all the 'warring factions' in Bosnia and Herzegovina. He notes that in contrast to France or the USA, in the UK 'there was no revolt of "civil society", no revolution of the elites. Instead, parliamentary and public discussion tended to reinforce existing historical preconceptions, to perpetuate the notion of moral equivalence, to express ill-considered polemics against the Americans, to defer to "the men on the ground", and generally – as the late Lord Richard put it – to "emulsify the whole affair".'[34]

Governments' response

The UK held the presidency of the European Community in the second half of 1992, and did thus feel under some obligation to respond to the revelations from Bosnia and Herzegovina – but the response needed to 'defuse the pressure for military intervention'.[35] The UK convened a conference in London on 26–27 August, to which various international actors and the warring parties (including the Bosnian Serbs) were invited. It was at this conference that Germany made the explicit denunciation of genocide. The London Conference merged the EC and UN mediation efforts, and declared a series of principles,

[32] Gregory Kent, *Framing War and Genocide: British Policy and News Media Reaction to the War in Bosnia* (Cresskill, NJ: Hampton Press, 2006), p. 281.

[33] Kent, *Framing War and Genocide*, p. 388.

[34] Simms, *Unfinest Hour*, p. 313. See also Daniele Conversi, 'Moral Relativism and Equidistance in British Attitudes to the War in the Former Yugoslavia', in Thomas Cushman and Stjepan G. Meštrović, eds., *This Time We Knew: Western Responses to Genocide in Bosnia* (New York: New York University Press, 1996).

[35] Simms, *Unfinest Hour*, p. 20.

including the imperative of respecting ceasefires, cooperating in the delivery of humanitarian aid, cooperating with peacekeeping operations, and respecting human rights. But what the EC or UN would do if such principles were violated was not made clear – there was clearly no will to use coercion to enforce compliance, nor to liberate the camps or stop ethnic cleansing.[36] This was perfectly in tune with French and British preferences.

At the UN level there was some response to the revelations. The UN Security Council met on 13 August and demanded that the International Red Cross and other humanitarian organisations be granted 'unimpeded and continuous access to all camps, prison and detention centres'.[37] As discussed further below, moves began to set up an international criminal tribunal to prosecute individuals for violations against international humanitarian law committed in the former Yugoslavia. Furthermore, on 13–14 August 1992, the Commission on Human Rights held its first ever 'special session', on violations of human rights in the former Yugoslavia (requested by the USA), and it unanimously agreed a resolution to send a special rapporteur (Tadeusz Mazowiecki) to the region to investigate the human rights situation there.[38] On 6 October 1992, the Security Council asked the Secretary-General to create a 'Commission of Experts' to issue conclusions on the evidence of violations of international humanitarian law in the former Yugoslavia. The Commission's remit explicitly included considerations of whether genocide had occurred, and its first report argued that acts committed during 'ethnic cleansing' 'could also fall within the meaning of the Genocide Convention.'[39] But the Commission was starved of funds, and its first Chairman admitted to being 'overwhelmed by the job'. The UK allegedly opposed the Commission because it thought that pursuing individuals for war crimes would endanger the peace process.[40] The UK refused to allow

[36] See James Gow, *Triumph of the Lack of Will: International Diplomacy and the Yugoslav War* (London: Hurst & Company, 1997), pp. 224–32.

[37] UN Security Council Resolution 770 (1992), 13 August 1992.

[38] Commission on Human Rights Resolution 1992/S-1/1, in Economic and Social Council, Report of the Commission on Human Rights on its first special session (Geneva, 13 and 14 August 1992), E/CN.4/1992/S-1/8.

[39] United Nations Security Council, Interim report of the Commission of Experts established pursuant to Security Council Resolution 780 (1992), S/25274 (10 February 1993), p. 16.

[40] Gutman, *A Witness to Genocide*, p. 153.

the commission to be called a 'war crimes commission', and would not supply it with evidence.[41]

The overall international response regarding the conflict did not deviate from the course set upon in April 1992, when war broke out in Bosnia and Herzegovina. The 'peacekeeping force', UNPROFOR, was primarily charged with protecting humanitarian aid convoys, not civilians. It was not going to be mandated to take coercive action against the Serbs. No military action was going to be taken to liberate the camps, or to stop ethnic cleansing. On the diplomatic side, efforts continued to find a peaceful solution to the conflict, through the combined mediation of the EC and UN.

What was the position of the three European governments on these moves? What the German government could do about what it considered to be genocide in Bosnia and Herzegovina was limited, considering that almost no other western government shared this view. Unilateral action was unthinkable for a country in which the multilateral instinct was so deeply ingrained, but also because sensitivities about a newly united Germany throwing its weight around were particularly widespread in the early 1990s. Even participation in multilateral military action was controversial, as discussed further below. Nor indeed could Germany take much of a leading role in the wider debates: it is not just that Germany was wildly accused of seeking the 'annihilation of the Serbian people' by Mladić and others but that there was great suspicion in general of Germany's intentions within the former Yugoslavia (where echoes of Nazi brutality continued to reverberate in the discourse) and Western Europe, above all, in the UK.[42] Germany's assertive stance on recognition had led many in Western Europe (and beyond) to blame it for having sparked the war in Bosnia and Herzegovina – an erroneous position[43] – and for much of the rest of the war it played quite a low-key role.

In the immediate aftermath of the discovery of the camps, the German government pressed for the establishment of an international

[41] Simms, *Unfinest Hour*, p. 62. Neither the Commission's interim report (published in February 1993) nor its final report (published in May 1994) list the UK among the suppliers of information or evidence.

[42] Quote by Mladić, in Cigar, *Genocide in Bosnia*, p. 78; and pp. 75–8 for the more general view that Germany was a threat to Serbia. On the UK's 'issues' with Germany, see Simms, *Unfinest Hour*, generally.

[43] See in particular Richard Caplan, *Europe and the Recognition of New States in Yugoslavia* (Cambridge: Cambridge University Press, 2005), pp. 120–33.

court to prosecute Serbs for crimes against humanity and genocide.[44] The explicit inclusion of genocide is important: a few days before Germany's declaration, the UN Commission on Human Rights created the post of Special Rapporteur on the human rights situation in the former Yugoslavia. Among other tasks, the Special Rapporteur was to collect 'information on possible human rights violations, including those which may constitute war crimes ... [which] could be of possible future use in prosecuting violators of international humanitarian law'.[45] Genocide was not mentioned. Arguably Kinkel's insistence that genocide was ongoing in Bosnia and Herzegovina put the issue on the agenda with respect to the remit of any future international tribunal.

Otherwise, the German government called for stronger measures against Serbia and the Bosnian Serbs. Kohl called for a 'total international and sea blockade against Serbia and Montenegro' and for 'much stronger sanctions'.[46] At the London Conference, Kinkel also called for a lasting cease-fire, international control of heavy weapons, and the immediate closure of all camps.[47] But encouraging stronger military action against the Serbs was controversial – and there was certainly little domestic support for Germany itself to be involved in such action: there was deep attachment to the sentiment, 'never again war'.[48] In July 1992, the parliamentary leader of the Social

44 David Gow, 'Germany to Call for War Crimes Trials', *The Guardian* (20 August 1992); Leonard Doyle, 'UN Urged to Act on Bosnia Rights Abuses', *The Independent* (24 September 1992).

45 Commission on Human Rights Resolution 1992/S-1/1, paragraph 16; in Economic and Social Council, Report of the Commission on Human Rights on its first special session (Geneva, 13 and 14 August 1992), E/CN.4/1992/S-1/8. Only in the preamble it is 'recalled' that Yugoslavia had been a party to the Genocide Convention. The resolution was adopted without a vote (by consensus). See also Payam Akhavan, 'Punishing War Crimes in the Former Yugoslavia: A Critical Juncture for the New World Order', *Human Rights Quarterly*, vol. 15, no. 2 (May 1993).

46 'Bush Hedges on Force', *The Advertiser* (Australia), 13 August 1992.

47 BBC Summary of World Broadcasts, 'FRG Foreign Minister Presents Ten Policy Points at Conference' (28 August 1992). In Germany there was tremendous support for the Bosnians, which enabled it to accept hundreds of thousands of refugees from the conflict – many of whom were even hosted by Germans in their own homes. Marc Fisher, 'In Germany, Welcome Mat for Refugees: Outpouring of Sympathy for Displaced Bosnians', *Washington Post* (30 July 1992).

48 See Karin Johnston, 'German Public Opinion and the Crisis in Bosnia', in Richard Sobel and Eric Shiraev, eds., *International Public Opinion and the Bosnia Crisis* (Lanham, MD: Lexington Books, 2003).

Democratic Party (SPD) (then in opposition), Hans-Ulrich Klose, 'stressed that Serbia was embarking on genocide in the Balkans', but argued that military intervention would cause an 'even greater bloodbath' and Germany certainly could not intervene militarily.[49] A few months later, in December, the chairman of the Bundestag's foreign affairs committee, Hans Strecken (CDU), stated that the 'present peace-making policy is just encouraging genocide' and called for 'actions against Serbia on every possible front'. Such actions did not, however, include military action: 'this would only complicate the situation since nobody can be successful against a Serbian partisan army'.[50] In December 1992, the military inaction caused a member of Kohl's cabinet, Christian Schwarz-Schilling, to resign in protest.[51]

In mid 1992, the German government began to participate in some of the various international missions in Bosnia and Herzegovina (but not UNPROFOR): the German air force helped to airlift humanitarian goods to Sarajevo from July 1992 (and drop supplies over eastern Bosnia from March 1993); the German navy participated in the NATO/WEU patrols in the Adriatic monitoring the embargos from July 1992; and German military personnel formed part of the crews of AWACS radar aircraft patrolling Bosnian airspace from October 1992. The last two missions in particular were controversial, and the Free Democratic Party (FDP) and SDP asked the Federal Constitutional Court to rule on their legality. The German constitution forbids use of the armed forces except in self-defence and in participation in NATO missions within NATO territory. In July 1994, the Constitutional Court ruled that Germany could participate in the operations of multilateral security organisations such as NATO or the UN, provided a simple majority of the parliament approved participation. In July 1994, the Bundestag voted overwhelmingly in favour of continuing participation in the missions in the former Yugoslavia.

[49] David Gow, 'Germany Ready to Widen Military Row', *The Guardian* (23 July 1992).

[50] BBC Summary of World Broadcasts, 'Leading Bundestag Politician in Hungary Speaks of Destabilisation in the Region' (3 December 1992).

[51] David Gow, 'Long-Serving Minister Quits Kohl's "Do Nothing" Cabinet', *The Guardian* (15 December 1992). Schwarz-Schilling became a mediator in Bosnia and Herzegovina under the 1994 Washington Agreement, and served as High Representative in Bosnia and Herzegovina from January 2006 to June 2007.

But doing more than that was controversial: as Marie-Janine Calic notes, 'Notwithstanding vehement criticism of European policy in Yugoslavia, the majority of Germans seemed to prefer non-military solutions. Opinion polls continued to show a public unwilling to commit ground forces.'[52]

While Kinkel and Kohl supported lifting the arms embargo on the Bosnian government, Kinkel was still keen to stress that Germany would not take unilateral action to lift it. And when the Defence Minister, Volker Ruhe, argued in February 1993 that 'Concentration camps in Germany were stopped by soldiers, and not by demonstrations in another country', Kinkel backed away. He thought Germany could not call for military action because according to the German constitution, German troops would not be allowed to take part.[53] Even after the Constitutional Court ruling, the government was reluctant to take a larger part in the UN and NATO missions in Bosnia-Herzegovina. The 'German government was thoroughly convinced that the presence of German soldiers in the former Yugoslavia would intensify the conflict.'[54]

In any event, the nature of any mission in Bosnia and Herzegovina depended fundamentally on two countries only, France and the UK. And both countries were committed to a limited role: the mission was 'humanitarian', not military. Of the two countries, the UK had the most conservative position. As Brendan Simms argues, 'Her political leaders became afflicted by a particularly disabling form of conservative pessimism which disposed them not only to reject military intervention themselves, but to prevent anybody else, particularly the Americans, from intervening either.'[55] The predominant view in the UK was that this was a civil war, and therefore not amenable to outside intervention to end it (Northern Ireland providing the most relevant example of this). There was little public pressure to intervene: a

[52] Marie-Janine Calic, 'German Perspectives', in Alex Danchev and Thomas Halverson, eds., *International Perspectives on the Yugoslav Conflict* (Houndmills: Macmillan, 1996), p. 64.

[53] Steve Crawshaw, 'Kinkel Backtracks as Bonn Policy Wavers', *The Independent* (3 February 1993).

[54] Calic, 'German Perspectives', p. 67.

[55] Simms, *Unfinest Hour*, p. xvii. Bosnia and Herzegovina was so frustrated with Britain that in late 1993, it threatened (rather foolhardily) to launch a case at the ICJ charging the UK with complicity to genocide, but dropped its threat shortly thereafter.

public opinion poll in mid August 1992 found that 60 per cent of Britons expressed no particular sympathy with any party to the conflict, and 51 per cent agreed that the situation did not justify putting British lives at risk through military action. Instead, 86 per cent thought troops should protect aid convoys – and over the next few years, support for this use of British troops remained high.[56]

French politicians and officials often referred to the British refusal to use force against the Serbs.[57] But until mid 1995, the French were not willing to use force either. As Thierry Tardy has argued, 'France systemically rejected the possibility of using force on the Bosnian territory, a mission whose feasibility and effectiveness were judged to be very uncertain and for which France was not prepared to assume the costs.'[58] Instead, France would concentrate on ensuring the delivery of humanitarian aid. For Tardy, the humanitarian response reflects in part Kouchner's influence on policy-making.[59]

The French position was not shifted by the revelations about the camps. In early August, a French Foreign Ministry official was repeatedly asked by journalists whether the option of using force to close the camps was under consideration: he repeatedly rejected this as potentially leading to 'carnage'; instead, the emphasis would be on demanding that the camps be closed and allowing humanitarian aid to be delivered.[60] 'For France in effect, the idea of using force to liberate the camps is from the beginning systematically and clearly discarded; straight away French officials were prone to appeasement and sought to avoid a military escalation, in perfect agreement with the British.'[61] The non-interventionist policy was

[56] Peter Kellner and Donald MacIntyre, 'Don't Risk UK Troops in Bosnia, Says Poll', *The Independent* (16 August 1992). See also Robert J. Wybrow, 'British Attitudes toward the Bosnian Situation', in Sobel and Shiraev, eds., *International Public Opinion*, pp. 38–41, p. 66.

[57] See for example the views of General Jean Cot (who was the overall commander of UNPROFOR between June 1993 and March 1994): 'no European head of state wished to go to war against the Serbs, the British least of all. In this context, France took refuge – along with its European partners – behind the humanitarian option.' Jean Cot, 'La France e le conflit de Bosnie-Herzégovine', *Défense Nationale*, vol. 55, part 11 (1999), 15 (my translation).

[58] Tardy, *La France et la gestion des conflits yougoslaves*, p. 147 (my translation).

[59] Tardy, *La France et la gestion des conflits yougoslaves*, p. 186.

[60] See *La Politique Étrangère de la France: Textes et Documents*, July-August 1992 (Paris: Ministère des Affaires Étrangères), pp. 77–81.

[61] Tardy, *La France et la gestion des conflits yougoslaves*, p. 163 (my translation).

virulently criticised by the opposition, media and certain intellectuals (including Pierre Hassner and Alain Finkielkraut). The discovery of the camps led the opposition to underline the insufficiency of a strictly humanitarian action, and the leaders of the Union des Démocrates pour la République (UDF) and Rassemblement pour la République (RPR), Jacques Chirac and Alain Juppé, declared themselves in favour of military action to end the crimes committed in Bosnia.[62] Public opinion was generally in favour of military intervention, throughout the conflict.[63] But this did not shift the policy.

France and the UK were the largest troop contributors to UNPROFOR; in November 1994, there were 4500 French and 3400 British troops serving with UNPROFOR.[64] This led them to be even firmer in their opposition to more coercive action, such as air strikes against the Serbs (particularly because such proposals came from the USA, which had no troops on the ground). Their argument was that they could not engage in coercion against one party and continue to deliver humanitarian aid throughout the country. This would endanger their troops, who would be exposed to retaliatory action. The humanitarian operation became a '*pallatif utile*', in Thierry Tardy's words: European governments were under domestic and/or international pressure to 'do something', but did not want to take coercive action. A humanitarian operation was the most they would agree to do – and this was not only difficult to criticise, but justified preventing the taking of even more forceful action.[65]

Srebrenica, 1995

Between 6 and 16 July 1995, the Bosnian Serb army captured the safe area of Srebrenica, expelled all of the Muslim women and children there, and executed at least 7000 men – most of whom were civilians. The Dutch battalion (around 370 peace-keepers) stationed in Srebrenica did not – and could not – prevent the Serbs from capturing the town, and although the Dutch commander in Srebrenica

[62] Tardy, *La France et la gestion des conflits yougoslaves*, p. 214.
[63] Marc Morjé Howard and Lise Morjé Howard, 'Raison d'état or Raison populaire? The Influence of Public Opinion on France's Bosnia Policy', in Sobel and Shiraev, eds., *International Public Opinion*, p. 117.
[64] See the UN website on the background of UNPROFOR: www.un.org/Depts/dpko/dpko/co_mission/unprof_b.htm [last accessed 21 April 2009].
[65] Tardy, *La France et la gestion des conflits yougoslaves*, p. 182.

requested NATO air strikes on several occasions, most of his requests were rejected higher up the chain of command. After authority was finally given to launch limited airstrikes, only two Serb tanks were struck, in the afternoon of 11 July, but the air strikes were immediately suspended when the Serb forces threatened to kill captured Dutch soldiers. Once Srebrenica had been captured, about 25,000 terrified Muslim refugees flooded inside and around the Dutch compound in Potocari, north of the town. The Bosnian Serb commander, Ratko Mladić, then sought to remove all refugees, and began to do so on 12 July. However, only women and young children were allowed to leave, and were transported to territory held by the Bosnian government; the men were separated out and taken elsewhere to be executed, for the most part between 13 and 15 July. In addition, during the night of 11–12 July, approximately 15,000 men tried to break out of Srebrenica and head for Bosnian government-held territory, initially walking in a long column. Over the next six days, Bosnian Serb soldiers repeatedly attacked the column; some of the men in the column also died after stepping on mines or by their own hand (to avoid capture) or from exhaustion. In November 1995, the ICTY indicted Karadžić and Mladić for genocide with respect to the atrocities carried out at Srebrenica; the judge who confirmed the indictment stated that 'These are truly scenes from hell, written on the darkest pages of human history.'[66]

It took some time for the news about the executions to reach the outside world. On 24 July, the UN Special Rapporteur on human rights in the former Yugoslavia, Mazowiecki, reported that thousands of Srebrenica residents were missing. On 10 August, the US Ambassador to the UN Madeline Albright showed satellite photographs to the UN Security Council, which she argued provided evidence of mass graves near Srebrenica.[67] In the meantime, the safe area of Zepa, also in eastern Bosnia, was overrun by the Bosnian Serb army – but large scale massacres did not ensue.

The immediate reaction of the UN and Contact Group governments concerned the fact that the safe area Srebrenica had fallen: the possibility that a genocide had taken place did not play a major role in

[66] Cited in 'The Fall of Srebrenica', p. 6. For a detailed account, see also Jan Willem Honig and Norbert Both, *Srebrenica: Record of a War Crime* (London: Penguin, 1996).

[67] Power, *'A Problem from Hell'*, pp. 416–20.

discussions – in fact, very few politicians used this term in the following months. Only one Dutch politician, the Minister for Development Cooperation, Jan Pronk, used the word 'genocide' (on 18 July); the Foreign Minister Hans van Mierlo and the Defence Minister Joris Voorhoeve expressed concern in 'rather more guarded terms'.[68] On 16 July, the new French President Jacques Chirac (elected in May) stated that 'ethnic cleansing' was comparable to the Nazi Holocaust, and called for military action to stop the Bosnian Serbs.[69] In the UK, the 'Srebrenica massacre provoked public horror, political mortification, and important operational changes, but no fundamental change in government policy.'[70] And no mention of genocide by ministers.

On 12 July, the UN Security Council (in Resolution 1004 (1995)) demanded that the Bosnian Serbs withdraw from the safe area, but only called on the *Secretary-General* to use all means available to restore the status of the safe area. On 21 July, members of the Contact Group, UN and NATO met in London for an emergency meeting. The participants demanded that the UNHCR and the International Red Cross be granted immediate access to male detainees from Srebrenica, but the emphasis of the meeting lay not in responding to the fall of Srebrenica but in warning that any attack on the safe area of Gorazde, also in eastern Bosnia, would be met with a decisive response. Nothing was said about Zepa, which was under attack at the time.[71] Brendan Simms describes the British strategy at the London conference as simply allowing the USA to let off steam: 'London was going to have to be dragged kicking and screaming into enforcement action'.[72] The

[68] Netherlands Institute for War Documentation, 'Srebrenica, A "Safe" Area: Reconstruction, Background, Consequences and Analyses of the Fall of a Safe Area', (Amsterdam 2002), Epilogue, section 13.

[69] Alex Duval Smith, 'Chirac Rhetoric on "New Holocaust" Plays To Neo-Gaullist Patriots', *The Guardian* (17 July 1995). The journalist argued that this was 'another inflammatory historical analogy'.

[70] Simms, *Unfinest Hour*, p. 317.

[71] 'The Fall of Srebrenica', pp. 89–90

[72] Simms, *Unfinest Hour*, p. 319. But James Gow argues that by this stage, the UK was already convinced of the need to strengthen UNPROFOR (perhaps before deciding to withdraw it): the British government backed General Rupert Smith's approach (which included withdrawing UNPROFOR troops from exposed and vulnerable positions so they could not be taken hostage, which would enable tougher action to be taken against the Bosnian Serbs) as well as the reinforcement of UNPROFOR with the Rapid Reaction Force. Gow, *Triumph of the Lack of Will*, pp. 267–71.

acceptance of the fall of Srebrenica and Zepa led Mazowiecki to resign his post as UN Special Rapporteur on 27 July, stating that he could not 'continue to participate in the pretence of the protection of human rights'.[73]

The reaction to the fall of Srebrenica was nonetheless one of the indications that the endgame was approaching. In late May 1995 after Bosnian Serb shelling of Sarajevo, NATO launched air strikes on Serb positions around Sarajevo. The following day, on 27 May, Bosnian Serb forces captured over 400 UN personnel and kept them hostage – using some as 'human shields' to deter attacks on military targets; the hostages were all freed by 18 June. The hostage crisis prompted a distinct hardening of attitudes among key actors. The new UNRPOFOR commander in Bosnia-Herzegovina, General Rupert Smith, and French President Chirac were both more willing to envisage the use of force against the Serbs. In June, France and the UK announced the formation of a 'rapid reaction force', which could engage in more robust action – such as opening corridors around Sarajevo. The German government agreed to send fighter planes to support the force, and the Netherlands pledged troops as well.[74] After the fall of Srebrenica, the US position hardened considerably, and the USA began to push for enforcement action. It also supported – if not encouraged and directly supplied – the combined Croatian/Bosnian government military push against Serb forces in August, which led to a massive exodus of Serbs from Krajina and Slavonia in Croatia (and thus somewhat clouded the picture for a time; all sides again looked guilty of war crimes). After another Serb shell killed 37 people in Sarajevo on 28 August, NATO planes bombed Serb targets over the next two weeks. The Dayton accord followed shortly thereafter.

Given the wider context, the horror of Srebrenica sank in only gradually. It certainly cannot be argued that the military actions launched against the Bosnian Serbs from late August were a reaction to the genocide; at most, the fall of the Srebrenica safe area contributed to a hardening of attitudes among the key international actors, which eventually led to the end of the war.

[73] Mazowiecki's resignation letter is attached to his final report, which mostly covered Srebrenica, in UN Security Council/General Assembly document no. A/50/441 and S/1995/801 (18 September 1995).

[74] Katherina von Waldersee, 'Kohl Backs Role for Germany in Bosnia Misison', *The Guardian* (27 June 1995).

It did, though, lead to intense debate within the German Green Party – a debate which would have implications for Germany's policy on Kosovo in 1998–9. The parliamentary leader of the German Green Party, Joschka Fischer, sparked a debate within his party regarding the use of force. In early August 1995, he called for the defence of the remaining UN 'safe areas' by force, though he opposed German military intervention to that end. This was controversial as the Greens rejected the use of military force in general.[75] Several months later, following the Dayton agreement, Fischer again led a debate in support of the use of military force. Fischer argued that 'force was the only answer to prevent genocide' – and that the international community should have used force to stop the massacre of Bosnian Muslims at Srebrenica. The Green Party in the end only agreed that 'lightly-armed' troops could use force to defend themselves in extremis.[76] Just a few days later, the Bundestag overwhelmingly approved sending 4000 German troops to participate in the NATO Implementation Force (IFOR) enforcing the peace agreement. The SPD voted with the government. The Green Party was split, with Fischer voicing approval of the deployment while others were still opposed.[77] As we will see in chapter 6, Fischer – by then the German Foreign Minister – played a major role in determining the NATO response to the Kosovo crisis, using similar arguments to justify coercive action.

'Srebrenica' has since sparked a considerable amount of soul-searching in the UN, the Netherlands and France – but not, notably, the UK. Combined with the failure to prevent genocide in Rwanda, the Srebrenica experience prompted much critical analysis of the UN, with one observer charging it with 'complicity with evil'.[78] In November 1999, the then UN Secretary-General Kofi Annan (who had been serving as the Under-Secretary-General for Peacekeeping Operations at the time) issued a remarkably frank report on 'The Fall of Srebrenica', in which the failings of the UN and its member states were laid bare. The principal conclusions of that report were cited at the start of this chapter.

[75] Denis Staunton, 'Greens Urged to Rethink Total Pacifism', *The Irish Times* (3 August 1995).

[76] *Deutsche Presse-Agentur*, 'Greens Drop Pure Pacifism, Voting for "Lightly-Armed" Troops' (3 December 1995).

[77] *Deutsche Presse-Agentur*, 'Bonn Parliament Approves Sending 4,000 Troops to Ex-Yugoslavia' (6 December 1995).

[78] Adam Lebor, *'Complicity with Evil' The United Nations in the Age of Modern Genocide* (New Haven: Yale University Press, 2006).

The Dutch government ordered a report on the Srebrenica case in 1996; the Netherlands Institute for War Documentation (NIOD) issued its report in April 2002.[79] In response to this highly critical report, the entire Dutch government resigned on 16 April, and the army chief of staff resigned a day later. In January 2003, the Dutch parliament published its own critical findings.[80] And in November 2001, the French National Assembly issued the report of a parliamentary mission analysing France's role in the failure to defend Srebrenica.[81] The mission found that the French commander of UNPROFOR, General Bernard Janvier – like the French government and other members of the Security Council – gave priority to the lives of soldiers, not to those of the civilian population (a doctrine of 'zéro mort').[82]

The NIOD report criticised the Dutch government's decision to send peacekeepers in the first place. Dutchbat was sent:

- on a mission with a very unclear mandate
- to a location that was described as a Safe Area but where there was no clear definition of what that actually meant
- to keep the peace where no peace existed ...
- with an unfounded trust in the willingness of the upper echelons of the UN leadership to deploy air power in the event of difficulties
- without any clear exit strategy.[83]

[79] Netherlands Institute for War Documentation, 'Srebrenica, A 'Safe' Area: Reconstruction, Background, Consequences and Analyses of the Fall of a Safe Area' (Amsterdam 2002) (www.niod.nl [last accessed 23 April 2009]).

[80] Toby Sterling, 'Parliamentary Commission Assigns Blame for Dutch Failure to Prevent Srebrenica Massacre', *Associated Press Worldstream* (27 January 2003).

[81] Assemblée Nationale, Mission d'information commune sur les événements de Srebrenica, Rapport d'Information no. 3413 (22 November 2001). The NGO Médecins sans Frontières had asked for a parliamentary inquiry commission to be set up to investigate French responsibilities. The French mission had no judiciary powers, and the Ministries of Defence and Foreign Affairs were not always cooperative in terms of providing documents and notes. Yves Beigbeder, *Judging War Crimes and Torture: French Justice and International Criminal Tribunals and Commissions (1940–2005)* (Leiden: Martinus Nijhoff, 2006), p. 322 and p. 311.

[82] Assemblée Nationale, Mission d'information commune sur les événements de Srebrenica, p. 191.

[83] Netherlands Institute for War Documentation, 'Srebrenica, A 'Safe' Area', Epilogue, point 3.

It argued that the decision to send Dutch troops was taken principally on moral grounds – and that the events of the summer of 1992 played a major role in building support for intervention. The Dutch parliament met several times during that summer to discuss the humanitarian crisis, and to call for intervention, prompting the government to consider sending forces. Thus, almost a year later, in June 1993 the Dutch government informed the UN and NATO that it would contribute about 400 soldiers for the safe areas.[84]

What is more interesting from the perspective of this book is that the term 'genocide' was *not* used in the reports on Srebrenica. One member of the French parliamentary mission had argued that it should be used, but the majority of the mission felt only the courts could decide whether genocide had taken place.[85] The NIOD report justifies not using the term as such:

> As 'genocide', 'war crimes' and 'crimes against humanity' have a specific meaning in international law, these words demand the utmost caution. The brutal murder of thousands of Bosnian Muslims is therefore described as 'mass murder'. No misunderstandings can arise as to what this in fact refers to. The seriousness of the event is not being trivialised, but any intermingling with international criminal justice is avoided.[86]

The UN report refers to 'attempted genocide' a handful of times, presumably for similar reasons. The International Criminal Tribunal for the former Yugoslavia was to decide whether genocide had taken place, not governments or the UN. Once the court had its say, and *if* it convicted individuals for genocide, then governments *could* use the term more freely.

[84] Bob de Graaff, 'Activist and Catalyst: Dutch Moralistic Decision-making Regarding (former) Yugoslavia, 1991–1994', *Journal of European Integration History*, vol. 10, no. 1 (2004), 158–64. By the end of 1992, public opinion in the Netherlands had become very favourable to military intervention in the conflict – though most people favoured intervention for humanitarian purposes only. Philip Everts, 'Innocence Lost: The Netherlands and the Yugoslav Conflict', in Sobel and Shiraev, eds., *International Public Opinion*, p. 227. See also Honig and Both, *Srebrenica*, pp. 118–26.

[85] Beigbeder, *Judging War Crimes and Torture*, p. 327.

[86] Netherlands Institute for War Documentation, 'Srebrenica, A 'Safe' Area', Introduction, section 2.

ICTY and the ICJ

The war in Bosnia and Herzegovina, and the question of whether genocide took place there, led to two landmark developments in international law. The first was the creation of an ad hoc international tribunal; the second was the *Bosnia and Herzegovina v. Serbia and Montenegro* case before the International Court of Justice on the application of the Genocide Convention.

The idea of setting up an international tribunal to try individuals in the former Yugoslavia for violations of war crimes, crimes against humanity, and, even, genocide, began floating around in mid 1992, following the Bosnian Serbs' 'ethnic cleansing' operations in northern and eastern Bosnia-Herzegovina, and around the time of confirmation of the existence of horrific 'detention camps' run by the Bosnian Serbs. Samantha Power suggests that the 'coincidence of imagery between the Bosnian war and the Holocaust' helped to trigger the creation of the tribunal: just as at Nuremberg the Nazis were held to account for the Holocaust, so there needed to be a tribunal to hold individuals to account for atrocities in Bosnia.[87] Certainly states turned to the Genocide Convention and the legal norm for guidance on what to do; to an extent though, this was a substitute for taking more robust action.

According to Yves Beigbeder, the French Foreign Minister, Roland Dumas, suggested to Mitterrand that an ad hoc criminal tribunal be created, 'on the grounds that it would calm French public opinion and that it would be a political assurance against possible later charges of French complicity with the Serb nationalists.'[88] Then came the Kinkel proposal (backed by France), made at the London conference in August 1992 – which explicitly included genocide alongside other international humanitarian law violations in the remit of the tribunal. In October 1992, three Conference on Security and Cooperation in Europe (CSCE) rapporteurs suggested drawing up a convention for an international tribunal to deal with war crimes and crimes against humanity committed in the former Yugoslavia.[89] In addition, the UN

[87] Power, *'A Problem from Hell'*, p. 483.

[88] Yves Beigbeder, *Judging Criminal Leaders: The Slow Erosion of Impunity* (The Hague: Martinus Nijhoff Publishers, 2002), p. 51.

[89] UN Security Council, Letter dated 18 February 1993 from the Permanent Representative of Sweden to the United Nations addressed to the Secretary-General, S/ 25307 (18 February 1993), Annex III.

Commission of Experts in its first report of February 1993 noted that a decision to set up an international tribunal 'would be consistent with the direction of its work'.[90]

Around that time, several proposals for a tribunal were circulated, including those by France, Italy, and the CSCE. Apparently the USA had been planning to propose to the UN Commission on Human Rights in Geneva in February 1993 that an expert group prepare a statute for an ad hoc tribunal, but had the 'rug pulled out from under them' by the French, who in the meantime circulated a draft statute at the Security Council in New York.[91] The French and Italian governments had separately set up committees of legal experts to draw up draft statutes for an international tribunal.[92]

On 22 February, the UN Security Council unanimously decided that an international tribunal should be set up to prosecute individuals for violating international humanitarian law in the former Yugoslavia, and asked the Secretary-General to submit specific proposals to that end (Resolution 808 (1993)). Several countries then sent in their views, including the USA, Russia, Canada and the Netherlands.[93]

The three proposals from France, Italy and the Netherlands (and those of non-European states, including members of the Organisation of the Islamic Conference, Russia, the USA and Canada), all included genocide within the remit of the proposed tribunal; the CSCE draft mentioned that the court should have jurisdiction over war crimes and crimes against humanity. The Dutch 'observations' included genocide but grouped under 'crimes against humanity'.[94]

[90] UN Security Council, Interim report of the Commission of Experts established pursuant to Security Council Resolution 780 (1992), S/25274 (10 February 1993), p. 20.

[91] Michael P. Scharf, *Balkan Justice: The Story Behind the First International War Crimes Trial Since Nuremberg* (Durham: Carolina Academic Press, 1997), p. 52.

[92] UN Security Council, Letter dated 10 February 1993 from the Permanent Representative of France to the United Nations addressed to the Secretary-General, S/ 25266 (10 February 1993); UN Security Council, Letter dated 16 February 1993 from the Permanent Representative of Italy to the United Nations addressed to the Secretary-General, S/25300 (17 February 1993).

[93] Schabas, *Genocide in International Law*, 2nd edition, pp. 112–14.

[94] UN Security Council, Note verbale dated 30 April 1993 from the Permanent Representative of the Netherlands to the United Nations addressed to the Secretary-General, S/25716 (4 May 1993), pp. 3–4.

The French decision to propose a tribunal to try genocide, among other crimes, indicates the extent to which the government was under pressure to respond to the revelations about Serbian atrocities. The French government was unenthusiastic about creating a tribunal and, along with the UK, 'believed that the prosecution of war criminals would damage prospects for a peace settlement'.[95] But it also recognised that the tribunal was a useful response to the revelations of the summer of 1992 – a 'foil' for public opinion. In the context of this book, however, what is interesting is that while the French proposal explicitly included genocide, the French Foreign Minister, Roland Dumas, did not refer to genocide when discussing the proposals for a tribunal – including at the press conferences where the tribunal was discussed. He referred to violations of humanitarian law, ethnic cleansing, war crimes, crimes against humanity, and, once, to international conventions on massacres of populations on the basis of their racial or religious origins, but did not use the term genocide.[96]

William Schabas suggests that the creation of ICTY 'implicitly' meant that the Security Council 'was taking action to prevent genocide'. But he further notes that it had never declared that genocide had been committed.[97] (And it must be noted that the setting up of ICTY did not prevent the genocide at Srebrenica.) For one of the two European permanent members of the Security Council,

95 Yves Beigbeder, *Judging War Crimes and Torture*, p. 306. The French proposal begins with a curious phrase – in light of French policy: 'An end was put to Hitler's atrocities by force of arms, not arguments'. Yet the French, like the British, had no intention of putting an end to atrocities in Bosnia and Herzegovina by force of arms.

96 See for example, 'Yougoslavie – Conférence de Londres – Intervention du ministre d'Etat, ministre des Affaires étrangères, M. Roland Dumas' (26 August 1992), in *La Politique Étrangère de la France: Textes et Documents*, July-August 1992 (Paris: Ministère des Affaires Étrangères), p. 123; 'Ex-Yougoslavie – Comité national de réflexion pour la mise en place d'un tribunal pénal international – Conférence de press du ministre d'Etat, ministre des Affaires étrangères' (8 February 1993), and 'Intervention prononcée par le représentant permanent de la France aux Nations unies à la suite de l'adoption de la resolution 808' (22 February 1993), both in *La Politique Étrangère de la France: Textes et Documents*, January-February 1993 (Paris: Ministère des Affaires Étrangères). At the 8 February press conference he referred to 'Conventions internationals qui prévoint des massacres de populations pour des raisons qui tiennent à leur origine raciale, religieuse, etc.' (p. 89).

97 Schabas, *Genocide in International Law*, 2nd edition, p. 546.

France, it certainly appears that the creation of ICTY was a more convenient (and cheap) way of responding to public opinion pushing for more 'to be done' about the war. Because neither France nor the UK used the term genocide, it is difficult to interpret their actions on the Security Council as seeking to prevent genocide. Furthermore, the UK's attitude was distinctly hostile; it apparently prepared a 'non-paper' in March 1993, which suggested that the tribunal could only be set up on the basis of an international treaty (rather than a UN Security Council decision, as happened), and that heads of state should be immune from prosecution (to ensure they engaged in peace negotiations). It later sought to block the appointment of an activist prosecutor.[98] Arguably the most that can be said is that the two principal European governments agreed to take action (eventually) to *punish* genocide – but even that seemed to be without much conviction.

Their attitudes towards ICTY after the war were lukewarm, at best. IFOR, which policed the Dayton agreement in the immediate aftermath of the war, did not arrest a single indictee during the first eighteen months of its deployment.[99] France 'adopted unofficially a policy of non-cooperation with the Tribunal, initiated and carried out by its Ministry of Foreign Affairs with the full support of its senior military leaders.'[100] In December 1997, the tribunal's chief prosecutor, Louise Arbour, stated that 'the vast majority of the indicted, including the most important ones, are in the French sector. We have an opportunity to take sizeable actions in the French sector. Yet, we are in the face of total inertia.'[101] Apparently a French military officer had also prevented the arrest of Karadžić. The French 'policy' of non-cooperation was reversed in March 1998 – and several arrests of indictees were made by French troops thereafter.[102] British policy after the election of Tony Blair as prime minister in May 1997 also changed, becoming much more supportive of ICTY: the first arrest by NATO of an indictee came in July 1997, on Blair's initiative.[103]

98 Simms, *Unfinest Hour*, pp. 62–4.
99 Power, *'A Problem from Hell'*, p. 492.
100 Beigbeder, *Judging War Crimes and Torture*, p. 310.
101 Beigbeder, *Judging War Crimes and Torture*, p. 311.
102 Beigbeder, *Judging War Crimes and Torture*, p. 312
103 Power, *'A Problem from Hell'*, p. 493. See also Simms, *Unfinest Hour*, p. 344.

In the wake of the Dayton agreement, the European Union began to flesh out a common policy towards south-eastern Europe, which culminated in a package of agreements offered in 1999 (the Stabilisation and Association process) and the promise of eventual accession to the Union. These 'benefits', however, are all conditional on the south-east European countries meeting certain conditions – including 'full' cooperation with ICTY, which means all possible efforts to arrest and transfer indictees. But applying conditionality strictly is not cost-free for the EU: if a country is making progress (in the EU's eyes) in most areas but not, say, cooperation with ICTY, then withholding benefits may be too hard a decision to take. And cooperation with ICTY has been a contentious issue in the EU's relations with Croatia and Serbia.

Negotiations on a Stabilisation and Association agreement (SAA) with Serbia were suspended in May 2006 over its lack of cooperation with ICTY, but were resumed a year later, in June 2007, as the risks of continuing to isolate Serbia became more apparent: a decision on Kosovo's final status was due to be taken in 2007 and Serbia's opposition needed to be overcome. The fact that the most important ICTY indictee, Ratko Mladić, had still not been captured was put aside, because Serbia pledged to cooperate 'fully' with the ICTY. In May 2008, important parliamentary elections were held in Serbia – the EU sought to boost the chances that 'reformers' would win, and isolate the more extreme nationalist voices in domestic politics. It was seen as particularly important to strengthen relations with Serbia because just a few months earlier, twenty-two of the twenty-seven EU member states had recognized the independence of Kosovo. To that end, in February 2008, the EU offered Serbia a 'European partnership' (a framework for aid) and in April 2008, the EU and Serbia signed the SAA. This last move was, however, controversial within the EU; the Netherlands was quite opposed to signing the SAA given that, at the time, neither Karadžić nor Mladić had been arrested and transferred to The Hague. After Karadžić was arrested and transferred, some EU member states wished to proceed with ratifying the SAA and implementing an interim trade agreement – but the Netherlands blocked this. The arrest of Mladić – the 'butcher of Srebrenica' – is an extremely sensitive an issue in the Netherlands.[104] But the Netherlands has been

[104] In July 2007, relatives of the victims of the Srebrenica genocide sued the Dutch government for compensation, over its failure to protect the safe area.

rather isolated on this point, with even Germany indicating the SAA should be ratified quickly.[105] In March 2008, Bernard Kouchner and Carl Bildt, the foreign ministers of France and Sweden – two men generally regarded as serious about the protection of human rights, and both with considerable direct experience of the wars in the Balkans – called publicly for Serbia to be given EU membership candidate status as soon as possible, without mentioning ICTY conditionality, much less Mladić and Karadžić.[106] European commitment to impunity for the crime of genocide can evidently make way for higher political considerations when it is deemed necessary to do so.

In any event, the experience of ICTY thus far illustrates how constricting the Genocide Convention can be: in only one case, General Krstic, has ICTY convicted a defendant of aiding and abetting genocide (in Srebrenica); 'otherwise, the tribunal has consistently acquitted persons charged with genocide with respect to "ethnic cleansing" and the atrocities perpetrated in concentration camps during the conflict'.[107] As a result, the Office of the Prosecutor has declined to charge genocide or withdrawn genocide indictments in several cases. In contrast, German courts have convicted two Bosnian Serbs of genocide (Nicolai Jorgić, in 1997, and Maksim Sokolovic, in 1999). The German Federal Constitutional Court has tended to equate ethnic cleansing with genocide.[108] This mirrors the German government's willingness to use the term genocide to describe ethnic cleansing and the concentration camps in the summer of 1992.

Their case was rejected the following year – as was a case by two relatives of other victims. The courts essentially ruled that the Dutch government was not responsible because Dutch soldiers had been operating under UN command and the UN could not be sued for compensation (as it enjoys immunity from prosecution). In December 2006, the government of Bosnia and Herzegovina – and Srebrenica survivors and relatives of victims – reacted negatively when the Dutch government gave insignia to the battalion which had served in Srebrenica.

105 'Dutch Block EU-Serbia Trade Deal', *BBC News online* (16 September 2008); Toby Vogel, 'Dutch Face Calls to Halt Resistance to Serbia', *European Voice* (19 November 2009).

106 Bernard Kouchner and Carl Bildt, 'Why Serbia Will Join the EU', *The Times* (12 March 2008). Bildt took over from Lord Owen as EU negotiator in June 1995 and served as High Representative in Bosnia and Herzegovina from December 1995 to June 1997. Kouchner was the UN's representative in Kosovo after the war there.

107 Schabas, 'Genocide and the International Court of Justice', 112.

108 Schabas, *Genocide in International Law*, 2nd edition, pp. 437–8.

The first ever defendant to appear at ICTY was Dusko Tadic. Tadic had been arrested in Munich, Germany in February 1994, on suspicion of murder, aiding and abetting genocide and causing grievous bodily harm.[109] ICTY, however, also wanted to try him, and in February 1995, he was indicted, charged with numerous counts of human rights violations (but not genocide); in April 1995, Germany handed Tadic over to the tribunal. Germany's charge of genocide had 'amazed' ICTY officials: Germany had no specific evidence, and planned to prove intent only on the basis of expert witness testimony. But while the ICTY prosecutor Richard Goldstone 'felt he could make a strong case that Tadic committed the alleged rape, murders, and acts of torture, it was not at all clear that his actions were intended to further the Serb policy of ethnic cleansing rather than merely a by-product of it'.[110]

However, it should also be noted that ICTY has not ruled on the 'big fish'. Slobodan Milošević was indicted for genocide in Bosnia and Herzegovina, but because he died in prison in The Hague in March 2006, no further action was taken on the case. But in a rule 98bis proceeding on 16 June 2004,[111] the Trial Chamber found, with respect to the specific charges regarding genocide, that:

> (3) the Accused was a participant in a joint criminal enterprise, which included members of the Bosnian Serb leadership, to commit other crimes than genocide and it was reasonably foreseeable to him that, as a consequence of the commission of those crimes, genocide of a part of the Bosnian Muslims as a group would be committed by other participants in the joint criminal enterprise, and it was committed;
>
> (4) the Accused aided and abetted or was complicit in the commission of the crime of genocide in that he had knowledge of the joint criminal enterprise, and that he gave its participants substantial assistance, being aware that its aim and intention was the destruction of a part of the Bosnian Muslims as group;
>
> (5) the Accused was a superior to certain persons whom he knew or had reason to know were about to commit or had committed genocide of a part of the Bosnian Muslims as a group, and he failed to take the necessary

109 Scharf, *Balkan Justice*, p. 97.

110 Scharf, *Balkan Justice*, p. 101.

111 Under rule 98bis, after the prosecution has presented its evidence, the defence can ask for dismissal of the case because the prosecution did not present sufficient evidence to prove the charges.

measures to prevent the commission of genocide, or punish the perpetrators thereof.[112]

Because Milošević died in prison, while the defence was still presenting its case, the trial was terminated – thus leaving open very important questions regarding whether genocide was committed or not in Bosnia and Herzegovina, and who was responsible for it.

Ratko Mladić remains on the run. Radovan Karadžić was arrested in Serbia in July 2008 and extradited to stand trial at ICTY in The Hague. Both Karadžić and Mladić have been indicted for genocide. On 25 July 1995, Radovan Karadžić and Ratko Mladić were indicted by the ICTY for crimes including that of genocide, committed from April 1992 in the territory of Bosnia-Herzegovina; in November 1995, both were indicted also for the crime of genocide specifically with respect to Srebrenica. The latest version of the indictment against Karadzic, of 27 February 2009 is more specific about the charge of genocide between 31 March and 31 December 1992: in some municipalities, the 'campaign of persecutions included or escalated to include conduct that manifested an intent to destroy in part the national, ethnical and/or religious groups of Bosnian Muslims and/or Bosnian Croats as such. In such municipalities, a significant section of the Bosnian Muslim and/or Bosnian Croat groups, namely their leaderships, as well as a substantial number of members of these groups were targeted for destruction. The most extreme manifestations of an intent to partially destroy these groups took place in Bratunac, Brćko, Foća, Ključ, Kotor Varoš, Prijedor, Sanski Most, Višegrad, Vlasenica and Zvornik.'[113] Karadžić and Mladić (should he be captured and transferred to The Hague) will be among the last trials at ICTY, as the goal is to complete all proceedings by 2012 (though this date may slip if Mladić is not captured soon).

[112] Case No. IT-02–54-T, *Prosecutor* v. *Slobodan Milosevic*, decision on motion for acquittal, 16 June 2004. Bob de Graaf argues that this ruling did not sufficiently take into account the fact the Milošević had a 'fluctuating power relationship' with Bosnian Serb leaders, and that from early 1993 to summer 1995, he had 'hardly any control over' them, including at the time of the Srebrenica murders. Bob de Graaf, 'The Difference between Legal Proof and Historical Evidence: The Trial of Slobodan Milosevic and the Case of Srebrenica', *European Review*, vol. 14, no. 4 (2006), 505–6.

[113] Case No. IT-95–5/18-PT, The Prosecutor of the Tribunal against Radovan Karadzic, Third Amended Indictment (27 February 2009).

The paltry record of convictions for genocide at the ICTY influenced the International Court of Justice in its ruling *Bosnia and Herzegovina* v. *Serbia and Montenegro*. Bosnia and Herzegovina filed the case in March 1993, alleging that Serbia and Montenegro (then known as the Federal Republic of Yugoslavia) had breached articles 1–5 of the Genocide Convention. It also requested that the ICJ issue a provisional measure ordering Serbia and Montenegro to cease from genocide against the people and state of Bosnia-Herzegovina. Such provisional rulings were issued in April and July 1993.

The case was not decided until February 2007. Significant aspects of the ruling include:

(1) The ICJ concluded that states (and not just individuals) can commit the crime of genocide, and that there is also an obligation on states to prevent genocide.
(2) Genocide was not committed in Bosnia and Herzegovina except in the specific case of Srebrenica. 'Ethnic cleansing' cannot be designated as genocide as such, and the ICJ was 'not convinced, on the basis of the evidence before it, that it has been conclusively established that the massive killings of members of the protected group were committed with the specific intent (*dolus specialis*) on the part of the perpetrators to destroy, in whole or in part, the group as such'.
(3) The Federal Republic of Yugoslavia was found not to have been responsible for events at Srebrenica.
(4) However, it did have influence on Bosnian Serb authorities and should have made efforts to try to prevent genocide at Srebrenica; it also has the obligation to punish genocide, which means extraditing indictees to the ICTY. But because the ICJ found that the causal nexus between the violation of the obligation to prevent and the genocide at Srebrenica had not been proven, it was not appropriate to order financial compensation.[114]

[114] See the International Court of Justice, summary of the judgment of 26 February 2007, application of the Convention on the prevention and punishment of the crime of genocide (*Bosnia and Herzegovina* v. *Serbia and Montenegro*). There was some debate about whether the ICJ had been under political pressure to appease Serbia, given its likely loss of Kosovo. It was also quite controversial that Serbia was allowed not to hand over some transcripts to the ICJ – it gave them to the ICTY but only on condition that they be kept out of the public sphere. 'Where the Past is Another Country', *The Economist* (3 March 2007).

But, as David Scheffer argues, there could have been a different outcome of this case if there had been an ICTY judgment in the Milošević case, or if evidence provided by the Serbian government in that case had been turned over to the ICJ.[115] It remains to be seen, however, whether ICTY does indeed convict Karadžić and/or Mladić for genocide during 1992, in addition to genocide at Srebrenica. If it does, then the ICJ ruling on whether genocide was committed in Bosnia before the Srebrenica massacre should arguably be disregarded.

Conclusion

The term 'genocide' was widely used in European public debates (though more so outside the UK) about events in Bosnia and Herzegovina in 1992, and with respect to Srebrenica in 1995. Again, the general understanding of the term reflects the wider definition of the social norm – and 'ethnic cleansing' is often defined *as* genocide, rather than as a practice that is not quite genocide. Commentators thus seem to agree with Martin Shaw that 'cleansing language invariably oozes genocidal intent, resonating with the idea of destroying, if not murdering, the groups to whom it is applied.'[116]

But, as was the case during the Cold War, the term genocide was hardly used by European governments. There is a notable exception here: the German government did use the term quite freely. What is also notable is that 'genocide' was not often used even with respect to Srebrenica – even though the ICTY and ICJ have 'ruled' that it was a genocide. It would appear that any debate – at the level of governments – about naming genocide has been transferred to the legal system, which can only make a 'definitive ruling' well after the fact.

If the reluctance to use the term with respect to Srebrenica is a reluctance to pronounce on such issues before the international tribunals do, there is still the question of why most European governments were reluctant to use the word in 1992, before a tribunal was established. France and the UK did not want to suggest publicly that genocide might be ongoing, and the UK even objected to investigating seriously such claims (seen in its opposition to the UN Commission of

[115] David Scheffer, 'The World Court's Fractured Ruling on Genocide', *Genocide Studies and Prevention*, vol. 2, no. 2 (2007).

[116] Shaw, *What is Genocide?*, p. 58.

Experts). France did (unenthusiastically) support setting up a tribunal to try individuals for crimes, including genocide, which the UK was much less keen on. The legal norm guided state action on this, but also served as a shield from domestic pressure to do more: 'Bosnia has been in the media spotlights, yet the information supplied by the media on genocide in Bosnia has not moved the West to put a decisive stop to it.'[117]

But why were France and the UK not moved to take coercive action? Firstly, policy-makers may have been genuinely convinced that this was a civil war, in which one side may have been nastier than the others, but in which no side was angelic. In 1993 and 1994, it is the case that this became a more accurate representation of what was going on. A lingering attachment to Serbia – or, more probably, a belief that a strong Serbia was necessary for stability in the region – played a role too. As Brendan Simms argues, 'If British statesmen and diplomats clung tenaciously to a policy of non-intervention, it was because they were intellectually convinced.'[118] What Lene Hansen calls the 'Balkan discourse', and others refer to as the 'moral equivalence' thesis, prevailed in much of their discourse about the conflict.[119] The extent to which this was a really deeply held conviction, or a useful way to deflect pressure to act against Serbia, may have to wait until the archives are opened.

Secondly, shifting policy from the 'humanitarian course' would have entailed difficult decisions – aid deliveries could not have continued throughout the territory of Bosnia and Herzegovina (though they surely could have continued in areas controlled by the Bosnian government), and UNPROFOR would have had to withdraw from 'hostile' territory (as eventually happened after the fall of Srebrenica). French politicians continually argued they did not want to 'add war to war'. Certainly the US experiences in Somalia illustrated the sort of catastrophe that could fall upon those that tried to mix 'impartiality' with coercive action against one of the parties to a conflict. But it is nonetheless striking that neither France nor the UK considered it to be in their interests to stop aggression and ethnic cleansing/genocide

117 Thomas Cushman and Stjepan G. Meštrović, 'Introduction', in Cushman and Meštrović, eds., *This Time We Knew*, p. 10.

118 Simms, *Unfinest Hour*, p. 2.

119 Hansen, *Security as Practice*.

in a country so geographically close.[120] Here the social norm against genocide may have played a role. France and the UK did not want to intervene with strong measures against the Serbs; accusing them of genocide would imply that such action was necessary. They could have been be wary that, 'If there really were a Belsen in Bosnia, if the many accusations of genocide were true, the moral imperative to intervene might indeed sweep all else before it.'[121] In Germany, where the government used the term genocide and argued for stronger measures, 'never again Auschwitz' was still not stronger than 'never again war'. Eventually, in summer 1995, the main European governments did come round to the idea of taking sides. But it cannot be said that this was specifically or solely in reaction to 'genocide' – the drip-drip of events in that summer, combined with American pressure, prompted the actions that stopped the war. The next three chapters discuss whether these findings apply in other cases.

[120] As Simms notes, such a definition of the security interest occurred to few British MPs, and 'even then only to be rejected'. Simms, *Unfinest Hour*, p. 278.

[121] 'Into Yugoslavia', *The Economist* (15 August 1992); the article argued, however, 'the balance of the evidence so far does not suffice'.

5 *Rwanda*

Of all the cases in this book, Rwanda is the most shocking – for two reasons. The first is the sheer mind-numbing scale and speed of the bloodshed: perhaps 800,000 Rwandans, mostly Tutsi, were slaughtered in about 100 days.[1] The brutality of those killings is sickening. Rwanda 1994 is widely considered to be an unambiguous case of genocide, fitting the legal definition of the Genocide Convention. It also sparked an horrendous cycle of violence in the region, including 'Africa's world war' in the Democratic Republic of Congo, which at one point involved the armies of seven states (including Rwanda) and assorted militias, and in which it is estimated that at least three million people died between 1998 and 2003. The cycle has still not come to an end, sixteen years later.

The second reason that the Rwanda case shocks is the role that the rest of the world played before, during and after the genocide. Numerous countries and the UN ignored various warning signs before the genocide; the UN and its member states were largely indifferent to the genocide while it was ongoing (and moreover, spent weeks avoiding the use of the term 'genocide' to describe events); and most aid after the genocide was sent to sustain Rwandan refugees, including many *genocidaires*, in what was then Zaire (now the Democratic Republic of Congo) rather than to Rwanda itself. In addition, the extent to which France supported the Rwandan government before and during the genocide, and its attitude since the genocide, have generated

[1] As is usual for cases of mass murder, the exact numbers of those killed will never be known, and estimates can vary widely; 800,000 is a widely cited figure (including by Gérard Prunier, a leading expert on the genocide), but some sources also cite 1,000,000 while others maintain the number killed was 500,000. Among the latter are Alison des Forges, *Leave None to Tell the Story: Genocide in Rwanda* (New York: Human Rights Watch and Fédération Internationale des Ligues de Droits de l'Homme, 1999), and Alan J. Kuperman, *The Limits of Humanitarian Intervention: Genocide in Rwanda* (Washington, DC: Brookings Institution Press, 2001), p. 20.

considerable controversy – and led to very tense relations between the current Rwandan government and France.

Much has been written on the genocide, by academics, human rights experts, foreign witnesses (including members of the UN peacekeeping mission in Rwanda), survivors and journalists.[2] Some of this work focuses on explaining why the genocide occurred; a large share of it analyses the role of the international community before and during the genocide. Much of this latter work is highly critical of what was done by outsiders (and especially the French) and what was not done (especially by the USA and UN). The UN and the Organisation of African Unity published reports on the genocide, and the Belgian and French parliaments conducted investigations into the role of their governments in the genocide.

This chapter looks primarily at the public record – at what European governments said in public, to their parliaments, in international organisations, to journalists. It seeks to answer the two core questions of the book: firstly, at what point (if at all) did European governments use the term genocide to describe events in Rwanda and what justifications (if any) did they give for using or not using the term; and secondly, what were the policy responses of European governments after the term genocide was used, and to what extent do these responses reflect an understanding of what they should do under the Genocide Convention? First, however, the chapter summarises the history of the genocide, highlighting in particular the role of France, Belgium and the UN.

The genocide in Rwanda

Rwanda, the 'land of a thousand hills', was a German colony from 1885 (when the Berlin conference divvied bits of Africa out to various European colonial powers) until 1918, when it was 'assigned' to Belgium under a League of Nations mandate. There is considerable debate in the literature about the extent to which there were 'really existing' ethnic groups – namely Hutus and Tutsis – before colonisation, as opposed to ethnic categories invented or exacerbated by the Belgian colonial administration. A convincing argument is that

[2] For a review of the already extensive literature, see Peter Uvin, 'Reading the Rwandan Genocide', *International Studies Review*, vol. 3, no. 3 (2001).

the differences between the groups were not invented 'from nothing' by Belgium, but that 'during the colonial period, these distinctions became more rigid'.[3] Identity cards specified Rwandans' ethnic group. Moreover, ethnic identity was linked to power structures: for most of the period of Belgian rule, the Tutsis were privileged power holders. But before independence (in 1962), the Belgians switched sides and favoured Hutu 'majority rule'. According to the 1991 census (whose accuracy is contested), Tutsis constituted just over eight per cent, Twa (pygmies) less than one per cent, and Hutus over 90 per cent of the population.

Hutu-Tutsi violence had already broken out before independence, but in 1963 and 1964 perhaps 10,000 Tutsis were slaughtered in a planned and organised attack. The killings sparked a mass exodus of hundreds of thousands (the exact number is contested) of Tutsi into neighbouring countries. In 1973, a coup d'etat brought to power President Juvenal Habyarimana. Habyarimana's Hutu regime was rigidly authoritarian; Tutsi were marginalised and discriminated against, but there were no more mass killings of Tutsi until the early 1990s.

In October 1990, the Rwandan Patriotic Front (RPF), a relatively small group of Rwandans (mostly Tutsi) who had served in the Ugandan army, invaded Rwanda. Their attack fizzled out fairly quickly, though they established a foothold in north-west Rwanda. But it also prompted military interventions by France and Belgium, officially to protect their nationals. The Belgians stayed only a month: news of arrests of opposition members and the militarisation of the Rwandan government sparked domestic opposition. Belgium withdrew its troops, and announced that it supported democratisation and a negotiated peace process in Rwanda.[4] It also decided to suspend the deliveries of arms and ammunition to the country – a decision that apparently fostered an 'anti-Belgian climate' among the Rwandan population, which would have tragic consequences for Belgian peacekeepers and expatriates in 1994.[5]

[3] Uvin, 'Reading the Rwandan Genocide', 78.

[4] Belgian Senate, 'Commission d'enquête parlementaire concernant les événements du Rwanda', 1–611/7 (6 December 1997), 83.

[5] Belgian Senate, 'Commission d'enquête parlementaire', 188. Ten Belgian peacekeepers and ten Belgian civilians were killed in the first days of the genocide.

The French (initially 370 men, later 670) remained until December 1993, though there were still some military advisers in the country in April 1994.[6] They trained Rwandan police and army officers, trained the Presidential Guard (which played a crucial role in the later genocide), advised the government on how to fight the RPF, checked IDs at checkpoints (since Tutsis were suspected of supporting the RPF) and supplied equipment to the Rwandan army.[7] The French government justified this as defending the 'legal government, which represented 80% of the population', against 'external aggression', which threatened the privileged position of France in Rwanda.[8] It never wavered in this support of the Rwandan government, despite news of political violence and serious human rights violations, including organised killings of Tutsis, as reported by a group of national and international human rights organisations in February 1993 and by the UN's Special Rapporteur on extrajudicial, summary or arbitrary executions in August 1993.[9] In conversations with officials in French President Mitterrand's office and the Foreign Ministry, human rights NGOs were told in March 1993 that you had to expect abuses of human rights in Africa.[10] No political conditions were attached to French

[6] According to Gérard Prunier, the French army actually kept 1100 men on the ground, though admitted only 600 to the press. Gérard Prunier, *The Rwanda Crisis: History of a Genocide* (London: Hurst & Company, 1995), p. 164. Officially the military assistance mission consisted of 25 advisers but some sources say the number was actually between 40 and 70. Daniela Kroslak, *The Role of France in the Rwandan Genocide* (London: Hurst & Company, 2007), p. 151.

[7] Kroslak, *The Role of France*, pp. 124–52. With French assistance, the Rwandan army expanded from 6000 in 1990 to 35,000 troops in 1993. International Panel of Eminent Personalities, 'Rwanda: The Preventable Genocide', Organisation of African Unity (7 July 2000), paragraph 12.24.

[8] Kroslak, *The Role of France*, p. 105, p. 130 and p. 144. Supplies of arms apparently continued well into May 1994 (p. 243).

[9] The first report was published by the Fédération Internationale des Ligues de Droits de l'Homme in February 1993; the second was an addendum to a report for the UN Commission on Human Rights, by the special rapportuer, Bacre Waly Ndiaye, recounting his visit to Rwanda in April 1993. Ndiaye famously suggested that Tutsis had been targeted and killed because they were Tutsis and therefore article 2, paragraphs a and b, of the Genocide Convention appeared to apply. Economic and Social Council document E/CN.4/1994/7/Add.1, pp. 22–3. His report was ignored, even by the Commission on Human Rights itself; furthermore, his report was not forwarded to UNAMIR as background information.

[10] International Panel of Eminent Personalities, 'Rwanda: The Preventable Genocide', Organisation of African Unity (7 July 2000), paragraph 12.21.

military or economic aid to Rwanda, and there is no evidence that the French ever pressed Habyarimana to change his policies.[11]

For Gérard Prunier, the French reaction to the 1990 RPF invasion illustrated the extent to which the 'Fashoda syndrome' is embedded in French political thinking: the RPF came from Uganda (a former British colony, and perceived as falling under American influence, therefore in the 'Anglo-Saxon orbit') to destabilise a Francophone country; France therefore had to support one of their own:

> This is how Paris found itself backing an ailing dictatorship in a tiny distant country producing only bananas and a declining coffee crop without even asking for political reform as a price for its support. This blind commitment was to have catastrophic consequences because, as the situation radicalised, the Rwandese leadership kept believing that *no matter what it did*, French support would always be forthcoming. And it had no valid reasons for believing otherwise.[12]

But in response to domestic and donor pressure,[13] the Habyarimana regime in mid 1990 did launch a process of (semi-) democratisation, allowing the creation of other political parties. So in a situation of military insecurity, a period of political instability ensued, as political parties vied for political power. Added to this came an economic slowdown and debt problem. Throughout this period, Hutu extremists not only had their own party, but were scattered in several other parties, and attempting to exercise influence on them.

Under pressure from various countries (including Belgium, France and the USA) and the OAU, the Habyarimana regime agreed to engage in peace negotiations with the RPF. These began in July 1992, in Arusha, Tanzania. France had apparently decided that the Rwandan government could not defeat the RPF militarily, and therefore a negotiated settlement was the best way to safeguard its interests.[14] The Arusha Accords, signed in August 1993, provided for a broad-based transitional government to

[11] Kroslak, *The Role of France*, pp. 155–6.

[12] Prunier, *The Rwanda Crisis*, p. 107. This view persisted even though the USA and UK were largely uninterested in Rwanda at the time.

[13] Including from the French, though their pressure was nominal, and they remained loyal to Habyarimana.

[14] International Panel of Eminent Personalities, 'Rwanda', paragraph 8.1 See also Kroslak, *The Role of France*, pp. 114–20. Belgium, France, Germany, the USA, Senegal and the OAU sent observers to the talks.

govern until democratic elections could be held. The transitional government would include Habyarimana's political party and allies, opposition parties, and the RPF; the RPF and the Rwandan army would be integrated. An international force would be deployed to patrol the agreement and related ceasefire – and French troops would withdraw.

In response to the request for an international force, the UN Security Council agreed on 5 October 1993 to launch a small (about 2500 personnel), cheap (only $10 million a month) peacekeeping mission: the UN Assistance Mission for Rwanda, or UNAMIR. It was not a propitious moment to launch a peacekeeping mission: the UN was increasingly stretched with peacekeeping missions (UNPROFOR the largest among them), the USA was less and less willing to pay a share of them all, and moreover, the mission to Somalia had just gone badly wrong, when eighteen US troops were killed in Mogadishu on 3 October. US reticence was overcome by strong French support for UNAMIR, which 'it believed was necessary to end the civil war and desperately wanted in order to extricate itself from the situation'.[15] UNAMIR was seen as a classic, easy peacekeeping mission: it would monitor a peace agreement, and moreover, its presence had been requested by the parties to the agreement. This view prevailed even after the assassination of the Burundian President, Mechior Ndadaye in October 1993, which provoked considerable violence in that country and a refugee exodus to Rwanda.

The UNAMIR force mostly included Belgian, Ghanaian, Bangladeshi and Tunisian soldiers, as well as small numbers of troops or observers from twenty other countries – but the Belgians were the best armed and equipped. There had been an unwritten rule that former colonial powers should not send troops on UN missions in their former colonies, but the Rwandan government and the RPF requested Belgian participation in UNAMIR. Belgium also wished to show its strong support for the Arusha Accords.[16] The UN requested 800 troops – the Belgian government agreed in principle to send troops on 22 September 1993, but two months later, announced that it would send only 370–450 troops, rather than 800.[17]

[15] Michael Barnett, *Eyewitness to a Genocide: The United Nations and Rwanda* (Ithaca: Cornell University Press, 2002), p. 69.

[16] Belgian Senate, 'Commission d'enquête', p. 189.

[17] See the chronology of the decision process in Belgian Senate, 'Commission d'enquête', pp. 175–82. The Belgian detachment never numbered more

It soon became apparent that neither Habyarimana nor the Hutu extremists wanted the Arusha Accords to succeed, as they sought to delay its implementation over the next few months. In the meantime, the extremist forces grew stronger, and there were sporadic killings (including the assassination of leading politicians) and violence. In January, the UNAMIR force commander, General Roméo Dallaire, sent a cable to UN headquarters indicating that an informant had come forward: the informant was a trainer of the Interahamwe militia (extreme Hutu militants), and claimed that there was a strategy to kill Belgian soldiers and thus force Belgium to withdraw its troops, that he had been ordered to register all Tutsi in Kigali (presumably for their extermination), and that he knew where there was a major weapons cache. Dallaire wanted to take action to seize the weapons, but was told by the UN's Department of Peacekeeping Operations (DPKO) that this would be beyond his mandate. In addition, Belgium, France and the USA all refused to offer protection to the informant and his family.[18]

Belgium, however, pressed for a stronger mandate for UNAMIR. On 11 February, the Belgian Foreign Minister, Willy Claes, wrote to UN Secretary-General Boutros Boutros-Ghali to call for UNAMIR to take a firmer stance. And after Claes visited Kigali in February (and witnessed how insecure the situation on the ground was), the message became stronger. A telex from the Belgian Foreign Ministry to the Belgian representation at the UN in New York on 25 February set out the Belgian position: public opinion in Belgium would not accept it if the Belgian Blue Helmets were to become passive witnesses to genocide; if conditions were to deteriorate further, neither Belgium

than 428, however (p. 295). Because Belgium sent fewer than the 800 troops requested, and because the troops from other contributing countries lacked the right capabilities and training, UNAMIR could not assemble a quick reaction force. This proved catastrophic when Belgian troops were threatened on the morning of 7 April 1994.

[18] The famous 'genocide fax' (though it does not mention the word genocide) of 11 January 1994 is available from The National Security Archive website: www.gwu.edu/~nsarchiv/NSAEBB/NSAEBB53/ [last accessed 8 May 2009]. See also Roméo Dallaire, *Shake Hands with the Devil: The Failure of Humanity in Rwanda* (London: Arrow Books, 2003), pp. 141–51. Michael Barnett has argued that the DPKO's response was 'to focus not on the threat to peacekeepers but rather on Dallaire's planned action and its threat to the operation and the UN'. The UN had to avoid jeopardising its impartiality and neutrality. Barnett, *Eyewitness to a Genocide*, p. 85.

nor the UN could withdraw from Rwanda, so UNAMIR needed to adopt a more assertive profile. But Belgium's diplomatic efforts were always going to be hamstrung because at the time it was not a non-permanent member of the Security Council, and despite being a troop contributor to UNAMIR, its access to the 'corridors of power' was limited.[19] The UN Security Council was disinclined to reinforce the mandate. Instead, on 5 April 1994, it prolonged UNAMIR for six weeks, and stated that it would only extend the mission beyond that if there was sufficient progress in implementing the Arusha Accords. It did not change the actual mandate. The European Union also publicly expressed concern at the insufficient implementation of the Arusha Accords, and intimated that its 'support for the peace process' depended on implementation of the accords.[20] There was thus some pressure on Habyarimana to comply with the accords.

Late on 6 April 1994, following a regional meeting in Tanzania to discuss the implementation of the Arusha Accords, Habyarimana flew back to Kigali. His plane was blown up by two missiles as it approached the airport; all aboard were killed.[21] Within hours, an 'interim government' led by Colonel Théoneste Bagosora had taken control, roadblocks had been set up, and killings of moderate Hutu politicians and Tutsis began. Among those killed initially were the Prime Minister, Agathe Uwilingiyimana, and ten Belgian peace-keepers who had been sent to protect her. In response to the killings, the RPF broke the ceasefire and launched an attack from their base in the north-west of the country on 8 April. The re-launching of the

[19] Belgian Senate, 'Commission d'enquête', pp. 392–7.

[20] On 3 April. Prunier, *The Rwanda Crisis*, p. 209.

[21] Habyarimana had given a lift to the Burundian President, Cyprien Ntaryamira. There were also three French crew on board and several Rwandan government officials. Who downed the plane may never be known, but as Prunier notes, the most likely explanation is that members of the 'abazu circle' (extremists connected to Habyarimana's wife) did so, because they feared that the president would actually seek to implement the Arusha agreement (Prunier, *The Rwanda Crisis*, pp. 213–25). In 2004 and again in 2006, however, a French judge, Jean-Louis Bruguière, accused the current president of Rwanda, Paul Kagame (then the leader of the RPF) of having shot down the plane; he issued arrest warrants for several of Kagame's aides (one of whom, Rose Kabuye, was arrested in Germany in November 2008, extradited to France, and released on condition that she remains in France until questioned). Bruguière's evidence has been widely discredited by experts on the Rwandan genocide. As a result of the indictments, Kagame broke off diplomatic relations between France and Rwanda in November 2006 (they

civil war distracted many outsiders from recognising the genocide, which spread from Kigali to other areas of the country the day after the presidential plane was downed. The genocide continued until the RPF captured the whole of the country in mid July.

The killing of the Belgian peacekeepers led to the outcome predicted by UNAMIR's informant a few months before. Although Belgium initially (on 8 April) called for UNAMIR's mandate to be reinforced and for additional troops (not Belgian) to be sent, once it was clear the UN Security Council would not take such a step, Belgium not only withdrew its forces from UNAMIR, but also demanded that the UN withdraw UNAMIR (on 12 April).[22] At the Belgian Senate enquiry in 1997, several witnesses – including the Prime Minister and Foreign Minister at the time of the genocide, Jean-Luc Dehaene and Willy Claes – declared that the attempt by Belgium to strengthen UNAMIR's mandate after the start of the genocide was really just to permit the safe evacuation of expatriates.[23] Once this attempt failed, Belgium demanded the withdrawal of UNAMIR. Claes admitted that the fear of losing face played a role in this decision. In public, though, the government argued that UNAMIR was useless from a political point of view and untenable from a military point of view.[24] The decision to withdraw the Belgian contingent from Rwanda was well-received in Belgium – only one newspaper argued that there was a duty to try to stop the bloodshed in Rwanda and to protect the lives of civilians. But public opinion was less clear: one poll taken in the wake of the killing of the ten peacekeepers reported that 80 per cent

were restored three years later). He also set up a commission to investigate France's role in the genocide, which concluded in August 2008 that France's support for the genocide was of a political, military, diplomatic and logistical nature. France rejected the report as unacceptable.

22 Belgian Senate, 'Commission d'enquête', pp. 525–55. The Belgian Foreign Ministry heavily lobbied the Security Council to withdraw UNAMIR, apparently phoning the ranking officials in all of the foreign ministries of the 15 UN Security Council members, which the Czech ambassador to the UN (the Czech Republic was a non-permanent member of the Security Council at the time) described as 'highly unusual'. Interview on PBS Frontline document, 'The Triumph of Evil', available at www.pbs.org/wgbh/pages/frontline/shows/evil/etc/script.html [last accessed 13 May 2009].

23 Belgian Senate, 'Commission d'enquête', pp. 536.

24 Belgian Senate, 'Commission d'enquête', pp. 548 and 551. See also the letters from Claes to the President of the Security Council, S/1994/430 (13 April 1994) and S/1994/446 (15 April 1994).

of those polled in Flanders felt the government should not send troops to intervene in the Rwandan conflict, but another poll found that 40 per cent felt that the situation in Rwanda justified the risk of military casualties, and 48 per cent supported sending more troops to try to re-establish peace there.[25] And the peacekeepers on the ground wanted to stay; the Belgian commander of the Kigali sector, Col Luc Marchal, told his superiors that they should not leave: 'Our political leaders should have known that in leaving UNAMIR, we would condemn thousands of men, women, and children to certain death.'[26]

In the meantime, on 9 and 10 April respectively, the French sent 190 paratroopers and the Belgians sent 250 soldiers to rescue foreign nationals; within a few days, almost all the foreigners and the rescue troops were gone. As Prunier notes, 'The hurried evacuation was a disgrace'.[27] Tutsis who worked for various embassies or aid agencies, or who were married to foreign nationals, were left behind (to certain death), while some members of the 'akuzu' circle of Hutu extremists were evacuated by the French. On 11 April, in preparation for the evacuation, the Belgian contingent camped out at the École Technique Officielle was ordered to regroup at the airport. Almost all of the 2000 Rwandans who had sought refuge there were murdered when the Belgians left.

The USA agreed with Belgium that UNAMIR should be withdrawn entirely. The UK was inclined to agree, but thought a compromise solution was to keep a token force. Some of the non-permanent members, namely New Zealand, the Czech Republic and Nigeria, favoured keeping UNAMIR in, but had to admit that without the Belgian contingent, UNAMIR was severely weakened. The French, according to the French ambassador the UN, Jean-Bernard Mérimée, thought that withdrawing the UN force altogether would merely have removed 'any obstacle to the Tutsi advance' and Rwanda 'would then escape French influence'.[28] So on 21 April, the Security Council agreed a compromise solution, to reduce the troop level of UNAMIR to 270 and restrict its mandate to trying to negotiate a ceasefire – as the situation was

[25] Belgian Senate, 'Commission d'enquête', pp. 563–4.

[26] Quoted in Linda Melvern, *A People Betrayed: The Role of the West in Rwanda's Genocide* (London: Zed Books, 2000), p. 163.

[27] Prunier, *The Rwanda Crisis*, p. 235.

[28] As reported in an interview with Daniela Kroslak, in *The Role of France*, p. 208.

seen to be one of civil war, not genocide.[29] This sent a clear signal to the *genocidaires* that the UN was not going to stop them.

Little accurate information on Rwanda was being reported in the press (the contemporaneous South African elections drew in the journalists instead), and the dearth of television pictures in particular has been linked to the lack of a strong international reaction to the genocide. 'During the whole conflict, but especially after the coup on 6 April, the overall failure of the media to report accurately and adequately on a crime against humanity significantly contributed to international disinterest in the genocide and the consequent inadequate response.'[30] But reports were still coming in from UNAMIR and the few NGOs on the ground (including the Red Cross), and from a few foreign journalists.

As the horror of the genocide sank in over the weeks following the 21 April reduction in UNAMIR, the Security Council reversed its decision. On 17 May, at the same time as it imposed an arms embargo on Rwanda, it authorised UNAMIR troop levels to rise to 5500. However, UN member countries were slow to promise and deploy troops, and on 19 June, UNAMIR's troop strength was still only 504.[31] In June, the French decided to intervene unilaterally. On 22 June, the Security Council approved the controversial French plan: 2500 troops would stay for two months, and contribute to the security and protection of displaced persons, refugees and civilians at risk in Rwanda.[32] These decisions are analysed more fully below.

Similar to what happened in the case of Bosnia and Herzegovina, the UN moved to investigate genocide and human rights violations in Rwanda. In early June, Spain called for a UN commission to investigate the abuses, and report back to the Security Council so that those

[29] Dallaire convinced other contingents to stay, and ultimately 454 peacekeepers remained on the ground. Dallaire, *Shake Hands with the Devil*, p. 328.

[30] Joint Evaluation of Emergency Assistance to Rwanda, 'The International Response to Conflict and Genocide: Lessons from the Rwanda Experience', Synthesis Report, March 1996, p. 20. See also Allan Thompson, ed., *The Media and the Rwanda Genocide* (London: Pluto Press, Fountain Publishers and International Development Research Centre, 2007).

[31] Dallaire, *Shake Hands with the Devil*, p. 432. In fact, UNAMIR II would not reach its full deployment until December 1994. Dallaire, *Shake Hands with the Devil*, p. 433.

[32] UN Security Council Resolution 929 (1994).

responsible for them could be brought to justice.[33] The UK, France and New Zealand then joined Spain in co-sponsoring a Security Council resolution to set up the commission (Resolution 935 of 1 July), which began work at the end of July. That commission recommended that individuals responsible for genocide and human rights abuses be tried in an international tribunal sitting outside Rwanda. On 8 November 1994, the Security Council voted to create the International Criminal Tribunal for Rwanda (ICTR), with its seat in Arusha, Tanzania.[34] As Kingsley Moghalu, a special counsel and spokesman for the ICTR, notes:

> Faced with its moral failure, the society of states did the next best thing – establishing a mechanism of juridical intervention to ensure that those responsible for the massacres were brought to justice. It was the path of least resistance, for it did not offer up the prospect of body bags that accompanied the far more risky option of sending in troops to stop the slaughter under a Chapter VII mandate. And the society of states could look itself in the face and say: 'we did do something'.[35]

In the wake of the RPF's final advance in July, several hundred thousand Hutus – including members of the genocidal regime and militias – fled across the borders, mostly to Zaire. The ensuing humanitarian crisis prompted a considerable humanitarian response from the outside world, thus understandably angering the survivors inside Rwanda, struggling to recover from the genocide. From April to December 1994, $1.4 billion (half of which came from the EU and USA) was donated for refugees; two-thirds of that assistance was provided to refugees outside Rwanda (among whom were a considerable number of *genocidaires*, who controlled the camps).[36] The

[33] 'Spain Proposes Panel to Investigate Genocide in Rwanda', *Agence France Presse* (10 June 1994).

[34] In Resolution 955. Rwanda (a non-permanent member of the Security Council) voted against the resolution because it objected to trials taking place outside Rwanda, and to the non-use of the death penalty (which would mean the 'big fish' would escape the death penalty).

[35] Kingsley Moghalu, *Rwanda's Genocide: The Politics of Global Justice* (Houndmills: Palgrave, 2005), p. 49.

[36] International Panel of Eminent Personalities, 'Rwanda', paragraph 19.17; Joint Evaluation of Emergency Assistance to Rwanda, 'The International Response to Conflict and Genocide: Lessons from the Rwanda Experience', Synthesis Report, Copenhagen (March 1996).

presence of *genocidaires* in Zaire/DRC led to yet more cross-border violence and war, as Rwanda tried to defeat the extremist forces on its borders.[37]

Naming genocide?

The US refusal to use the term genocide at all until late May and the contortions that US State Department officials went through to avoid doing so are infamous.[38] The State Department cautioned against the use of the word because it could commit the US government 'to do something', even though using it would not have any particular legal consequences under the Genocide Convention.[39] It is also the case that the OAU failed to call it a genocide for the entire time it lasted. Only in early June did fourteen African heads of state condemn the genocide.[40] And few non-western governments ever used the term in the UN Security Council – even after the Secretary-General and other governments had done so.[41] What about European governments: how willing were they to use the term?

[37] In May 2002, the DRC made a claim against Rwanda at the ICJ, in which it invoked several treaties including the Genocide Convention in addressing massacres that took place during the war. The ICJ ruled that it did not have jurisdiction with respect to the Genocide Convention because Rwanda had made a reservation to article IX of the Convention (on ICJ jurisdiction) when it ratified it in 1975. Schabas, *Genocide in International Law*, 2nd edition, pp. 511–12.

[38] On this see Samantha Power, 'Bystanders to Genocide', *The Atlantic Monthly* (September 2001).

[39] See Power, *'A Problem from Hell'*, pp. 358–64. See also the memorandum released under the US Freedom of Information Act: Has genocide occurred in Rwanda? (21 May 1994), and Discussion paper: Rwanda (1 May 1994). Available through the National Security Archive: www.gwu.edu/~nsarchiv/NSAEBB/NSAEBB53/ [last accessed 8 May 2009].

[40] But just days later, the OAU invited the Rwandan interim government to a summit. Furthermore, as did other international actors, the OAU urged a ceasefire and negotiations in response to the killings. International Panel of Eminent Personalities, 'Rwanda', paragraph 15.86.

[41] At the end of May, in a report to the Security Council, Secretary-General Boutros Boutros-Ghali stated clearly: 'The magnitude of the human calamity that has engulfed Rwanda might be unimaginable but for its having transpired. On the basis of the evidence that has emerged, there can be little doubt that it constitutes genocide, since there have been large-scale killings of communities and families belonging to a particular ethnic group.' UN Security Council, Report of the Secretary-General on the situation in Rwanda, S/1994/640 (31 May 1994), p. 11. The first time 'genocide' was

Much of the international diplomacy regarding Rwanda centred around the UN Security Council, on which several European governments served: France and the UK of course, but also the Czech Republic and Spain. This section thus looks at the positions those countries took in the debates on Rwanda, and whether and at what point they described the situation in Rwanda as genocide. It then considers the first time European Union governments used the term, and the positions of various European governments at the UN Commission on Human Rights in mid May.

On 29 April, New Zealand, in its position as outgoing president of the UN Security Council, attempted to push through a presidential statement which would have said the following:

> [T]he horrors of Rwanda's killing fields have few precedents in the recent history of the world. The Security Council reaffirms that the systematic killing of any ethnic group, with the intent to destroy it in whole or in part constitutes an act of genocide as defined by the relevant provisions of international law.[42]

The New Zealand ambassador, Colin Keating, was supported in this by the Czech Ambassador, Karel Kovanda. At the Security Council meeting, Kovanda said that brokering a ceasefire in Rwanda 'was like wanting Hitler to reach a cease-fire with the Jews'.[43] But the UK ambassador, Sir David Hannay, objected to the use of the word genocide, and said that the Security Council would become a 'laughing stock': 'To name this a genocide and not to act on it would be ridiculous.'[44] The USA and China were also opposed to using the word. After several hours of debate (lasting until 1.15 am), the statement was watered down as follows:

used in a Security Council Resolution on Rwanda was on 8 June 1994, in a preamble: 'noting with the gravest concern the reports indicating that acts of genocide have occurred in Rwanda, and recalling in this context that genocide constitutes a crime punishable under international law' (Resolution 925). But non-European governments (with the exception of New Zealand) still avoided the use of the term at the 8 June meeting of the Security Council. UN Security Council, Record of the 3388th meeting (8 June 1994), S/PV.3388.

42 Cited in Barnett, *Eyewitness to a Genocide*, p. 134.

43 Cited in Barnett, *Eyewitness to a Genocide*, p. 134.

44 Cited in Melvern, *A People Betrayed*, p. 180.

The Security Council condemns all these breaches of international humanitarian law in Rwanda ... the Security Council recalls that the killing of members of an ethnic group with the intention of destroying such a group in whole or in part constitutes a crime punishable by international law.

Thus the statement uses the language of the Genocide Convention but not the term genocide. It also, however, contains language desired by the French, to establish the 'moral equivalence' of the two sides:[45]

The Security Council demands that the interim government of Rwanda and the Rwandese Patriotic Front take effective measures to prevent any attacks on civilians in areas under their control.[46]

So as late as 30 April, the principal members of the Security Council – including France and the UK – were seeking to avoid use of the term genocide. And this was apparently because if they did use the term, they would have to act on it, which they were not prepared to do.

The pressure to use the term grew from the beginning of May. By then, it was estimated that 200,000 people had been killed, and 40,000 bodies had been fished out of Lake Victoria alone.[47] On 28 April, Oxfam called for international action against the 'genocidal slaughter'; on the same day, Médecins sans Frontières Belgium said that a 'veritable genocide' was under way in Rwanda; a European network of NGOs, Eurostep, on 1 May also called for action against the genocidal slaughter; the Pope used the term with respect to Rwanda on 27 April; Boutros-Ghali even did so in an interview with a US news show 'Nightline', on 4 May.[48] On 6 May, a group of European NGOs sent a statement to the EU's Development Council calling on the EU to try to end the genocide in Rwanda; it called for pressure

[45] Melvern, *A People Betrayed*, p. 180.

[46] UN Security Council, statement by the President of the Security Council (30 April 1994), S/PRST/1994/21. We now know that both sides were killing, it is just that only one side (the Rwandan government's) was carrying out a genocide.

[47] UN Security Council, Report of the independent inquiry into the actions of the United Nations during the 1994 genocide in Rwanda, in S/1999/1257 (16 December 1999), 22; Linda Melvern, *Conspiracy to Murder: The Rwandan Genocide* (London: Verso, 2004), p. 224.

[48] See 'Un genocide en course au Rwanda, selon MSF', *Agence France Presse* (28 April 1994); Kroslak, *The Role of France*, p. 181; des Forges, *Leave None to Tell the Story*, chapter on 'Acknowledging Genocide'.

to be put on the UN and OAU to bring the parties to the negotiating table, and to strengthen UNAMIR.[49]

The first time the word was mentioned in a public meeting of the Security Council was by the Czech ambassador, Karel Kovanda. In a debate on Mozambique on 5 May, he stated:

> Different countries of the cone of Africa south of the Equator are facing an exceptionally broad array of political circumstances at this moment. On the one end of the spectrum, there is the hell of Rwanda. My delegation is appalled by the situation in that country and has been shocked by the fact that neither the Security Council nor the Secretariat has so far managed to describe the massacres in Rwanda by the only word that fits them – namely, genocide.[50]

According to Daniela Kroslak, the French Foreign Minister (Alain Juppé) was the first western minister to use the term 'genocide' to describe the killings in Rwanda – on 15 and 16 May.[51] But the Czech ambassador was actually the first to do so in public. Furthermore, Juppé's remarks were in connection with an EU declaration on Rwanda, in which all twelve member states agreed to a formulation which included the word genocide.[52] The Declaration by the European Union on Rwanda was approved by the General Affairs Council (composed of the foreign ministers), which met on 16 and 17 May 1994.[53] The declaration begins: 'The European Union,

[49] 'EU/Rwanda: NGOS Call on EU Development Council for Action', *European Report* (7 May 1994). The Development Council decided only to send a mission of development ministers to neighbouring countries to evaluate the humanitarian situation of refugees from Rwanda.

[50] UN Security Council, Record of the 3375th meeting (5 May 1994), S/PV.3375, p. 8.

[51] Kroslak, *The Role of France*, p. 178.

[52] The connection between the two declarations is evident in des Forges, *Leave None to Tell the Story*, chapter on 'Acknowledging Genocide', and in 'L'Union soutient les initiatives pour arreter le genocide au Rwanda', *Agence France Presse* (16 May 1994). The latter article begins: 'On Monday in Brussels, the Twelve sought to increase their efforts in favour of the populations of Rwanda and agreed an arms embargo on the country. The intransigence of the warring parties paralyses all action in Rwanda, theatre of an actual genocide, affirmed the French Foreign Affairs Minister, Alain Juppé.' (My translation.)

[53] At that time, the EU member states were: Belgium, Denmark, France, Germany, Greece, Ireland, Italy, Luxembourg, the Netherlands, Portugal,

recalling its declaration of 18 April 1994 on Rwanda, again appeals urgently to all parties to the conflict to bring an end to the genocide now taking place in the country.'[54] It then expresses support for a number of measures to address the situation (analysed in the next section).

This Declaration was largely ignored by the press at the time (as many EU declarations are); it has also been ignored by scholars of EU foreign policy and of the Rwandan genocide. But insofar as it mentions 'genocide' so explicitly – and moreover, specifies that the genocide is ongoing – it merits some attention. This is the first acknowledgement by twelve European governments that the atrocities in Rwanda do constitute genocide. This is in and of itself rather curious – particularly because several of the EU member states continued to resist using the term after the declaration was agreed. It is also a mystery as to how the declaration came to include the term, as there are almost no press accounts (other than an occasional mention that a declaration had been agreed) and no academic or other investigations on the EU decision-making process that led to this declaration. According to one of the very few press accounts of the declaration, the EU used the term because it 'will have legal implications for the Rwandese government'. Those responsible for the slaughter could be held responsible under the Genocide Convention.[55] Thus the use of the term is linked to the legal norm of the Genocide Convention – and to the obligation 'to punish' under that Convention. But as far as

Spain and the UK. The press release states that all but Greece were represented by their foreign ministers at the meeting. The Greek deputy Foreign Minister, Theodoros Pangalos, chaired the meeting (the EU presidency at the time was held by Greece).

[54] Council of the European Union, press release, 'General Affairs Council, 16–17 May 1994', document no. 6883/94 (Presse 88-G), p. 5. The 18 April 1994 declaration had expressed the EU's dismay at the violence and atrocities, and urged the opposing forces to end violence and resume peace negotiations – but did not mention genocide. Council of the European Union, press release, 'General Affairs Council, 18–19 April 1994', document no. 6294/94 (Presse 70). A later declaration by the European Council (heads of state or government), on 24–25 June 1994, began: 'The European Council expresses its horror at the genocide taking place in Rwanda'. European Council, 'Presidency conclusions on Rwanda', Corfu (24–25 June 1994).

[55] Debra Percival and Bob Mantiri, 'Rwanda-Europe: Africa Should Handle Rwanda – Belgium', *Inter Press Service* (17 May 1994).

I have been able to discern, there was no such deliberate intention by all the Twelve to use the word in this way.

Documents released to me by the UK Foreign Office, following a Freedom of Information request, do not shed much light on the matter. I asked for documents on the UK position on the Declaration. None of the documents released even mention the word 'genocide' – including those documents that summarise the EU Declaration after it was agreed. Instead, references are made to the 'humanitarian tragedy' and 'appalling situation' and 'crisis'.[56] The UK wanted to ensure that the EU would only support the UN Security Council and the Secretary-General: it should not 'cut across the efforts of the United Nations', and any support for regional peace efforts should be pursued in cooperation with the UN.[57] And any peace efforts should aim to end the fighting by *all* parties and to bring them all to the negotiating table.[58] However, the fact that the Declaration used the term 'genocide' had implications for the UK's position in the Commission on Human Rights, discussed below.

The absence of any reference to the word 'genocide' in the released Foreign Office documents is puzzling – it would almost appear that the word was slipped in, either without the UK government noticing, or at least objecting. Indeed, drafts of the Declaration which were circulated among the member states until 13 May did not include the term genocide.[59] I have tried to contact participants present at the EU Council meeting in May to ask how the inclusion of genocide in the

[56] 'Humanitarian tragedy', in document entitled 'Foreign Affairs Council, Brussels, 16/17 May 1994: Rwanda'; 'appalling situation', in document entitled 'Cabinet: Thursday 19 May: Rwanda: points to make'; 'crisis', in document entitled 'Baroness Chalker's evidence to House of Lords Select Committee 14 June 1994: Rwanda; bull points'.

[57] As stated in the document entitled 'Foreign Affairs Council, Brussels, 16/17 May 1994: Rwanda', and a copy of a COREU (COREUs are telexes circulated by and between the EU member states' foreign ministries) 'Subject: COAFR: Rwanda: stability and security in Central Africa; Ref: PESC/COM/204' (6 May 1994).

[58] As indicated in the documents cited in the two previous notes, as well as in a memorandum to the Secretary of State, on 16 May 1994 on 'Rwanda', and a memorandum from the African Department (Equatorial) to Baroness Chalker on 23 May 1994, regarding a draft of a speech for use by Mr Lennox-Boyd in an adjournment debate in parliament.

[59] Interview with UK Foreign Office official, 19 July 2009.

Declaration came about, but have so far not received a response from any of them. Given that Juppé went public with the term in conjunction with the EU Council meeting, it is likely that the term genocide was included because of a French initiative. Given French interests in Rwanda, and deference to those interests by other EU member states, if France did suggest including the word, it would probably not have been opposed. But why it did so is a question which may have to wait until the relevant documents are released to archives.

Meanwhile, the Security Council was also in session. At the 16 May meeting of the Security Council (which after midnight approved the increase in UNAMIR troops levels), the Spanish ambassador, Yañez Barnuevo, associated Spain 'with all the other members of the Council in recalling that the killing of members of an ethnic group with the intention of destroying that grouping whole or in part constitutes a crime which is punishable under international law'. He did not use the term genocide – even though he referred to the EU declaration on Rwanda. Likewise at the same meeting, neither the French nor British ambassadors used the term – or referred to the EU declaration. Instead the French ambassador described a 'humanitarian catastrophe' and 'massacres', and the British ambassador referred to a 'tragedy' and 'bloodshed'. In contrast, at the same meeting of the Security Council, the Czech ambassador did call it a genocide: 'This situation is being described as a humanitarian crisis as though it were a famine, or perhaps a natural disaster. In the view of my delegation, the proper description is genocide.'[60] The Security Council resolution (918) decided at that meeting did not use the term genocide, but in the preamble used the formulation agreed a few weeks earlier, which repeated the definition of genocide in the Genocide Convention (the USA in particular was at this stage still allergic to using the word).

So even though the twelve EU foreign ministers had declared there was a genocide ongoing in Rwanda on 16–17 May, some European governments in the UN Security Council remained hesitant to use the term, while one European country not in the EU – the Czech Republic – was not.

Avoidance of the term 'genocide' was also apparent in the UN Commission on Human Rights special session on the human rights

[60] United Nations Security Council, record of the 3377th meeting (16 May 1994), S/PV.3377.

situation in Rwanda, which was held the week after the EU and Security Council meetings, on 24 and 25 May 1994. Even at this late stage of the genocide, the resolution adopted (by consensus) did not unambiguously condemn the killings in Rwanda as genocide. One of the preambular paragraphs noted merely 'believing that genocidal acts may have occurred in Rwanda', while the body of the resolution itself condemned the killings, called for a ceasefire, affirmed that individuals should be held accountable for violations of human rights and international humanitarian law, and requested the appointment of a Special Rapporteur, whose brief would include gathering information on possible violations of human rights, including acts of genocide.[61] Most countries in the Western Europe and Other Group (WEOG) apparently did not want the CHR to issue a 'finding' that genocide had taken place, but there was support for mentioning the term genocide – and the text of the resolution reflects this position.[62]

European representatives did not all use the term at the CHR – not even those from EU member states – and did not all use it in the same way. Several non-EU European states said that it was imperative to investigate whether 'the crime of genocide' (Austria) or 'acts of genocide' (Finland on behalf of the five Nordic group countries) had been committed in Rwanda. In both cases, the use of the past tense is striking – as all the delegates recognised the killings were ongoing. The Czech Republic made no statement. The observer for Switzerland, however, stated that the CHR 'resolution should also point out that the massacres in Rwanda and the destruction of an ethnic group amounted to genocide'.[63]

[61] Resolution S-3/1, in UN Economic and Social Council, Report of the Commission on Human Rights on its third special session (Geneva, 24 and 25 May 1994), E/CN.4/S-3/4 (30 May 1994). Canada had called for the special session. At this meeting, several non-European governments did call the situation in Rwanda a genocide or possible genocide, including Australia, New Zealand, Pakistan, Tunisia, Egypt, Ghana, Colombia, Ecuador – and the USA. The resolution was co-sponsored by all EU member states.

[62] Document released to me by the Foreign Office following a Freedom of Information request (I requested minutes and correspondence regarding the UK position at the CHR special session). Fax from the UK mission to the UN in Geneva, dated 18 May 1994, Rwanda: CHR special session, apparently sent at 17.53. This document reports on the WEOG meeting.

[63] UN Economic and Social Council, Summary record of the second meeting, third special session, Commission on Human Rights, E/CN.4/S-3/SR.2 (1 June 1994), p. 27.

The Greek representative, speaking on behalf of the EU, repeated the wording from the EU declaration on Rwanda, and 'appealed for an end to the acts of genocide taking place in that country' (note the present tense). The UK mission to the UN in Geneva accepted such terminology, because it recognised that in the wake of the EU declaration it could not oppose such a reference, but it wished to 'go no further' than the exact language used by the EU.[64] In EU coordination meetings regarding the EU statement to the CHR, the UK

> expressed doubts about the tactical wisdom of the reference to genocide in the EU statement, and pointed also to the legal implications of the finding of genocide. Thus while acknowledging that the term had been used in the FAC [Foreign Affairs Council] statement, the EU should think very carefully about whether to use it in the context of the CHR special session. Greece agreed with our concerns and the Irish 'took the UK point'.[65]

The UK agreed to the language even though 'Legal Advisers are unhappy'; the UK sought to avoid any firm determination that a genocide was taking or had taken place, so preferred the use of 'acts of genocide' to '**the** genocide'.[66]

Apparently Germany and Belgium wanted the EU statement to be clearer about who was responsible for the killing, but the UK sought a more balanced statement, because there were allegations of atrocities in RPF-controlled areas.[67] The German and Belgian view was supported by Finland and the Netherlands in the WEOG discussions about the CHR resolution.[68] The Netherlands – together with the

[64] Document released to me after a Freedom of Information request. Fax from the FCO in London to the UK mission in Geneva, dated 18 May 2004, Special session on rwanda: revised EU statement.

[65] Fax from the UK mission in Geneva to the Foreign Office in London, dated 18 May 1994, Rwanda: CHR special session, apparently sent at 18.25. This fax discussed an EU heads of mission meeting, and is thus a different document to the one cited in note 62.

[66] Fax from the FCO to UK mission in Geneva, dated 19 May 1994, Special session on Rwanda.

[67] Fax from the FCO in London to the UK mission in Geneva, dated 18 May 2004, Special session on Rwanda: revised EU statement and fax from the UK mission in Geneva to the Foreign Office in London, dated 18 May 1994, Rwanda: CHR special session, sent at 18.25.

[68] Fax from the UK mission to the UN in Geneva, dated 18 May 1994, Rwanda: CHR special session, sent at 17.53.

USA and Australia – also pushed for language calling on the Special Rapporteur to gather information on possible acts of genocide.[69]

At the CHR, the UK was keen to avoid language in the resolution that would open the way towards the creation of an international criminal tribunal on Rwanda. Thus, for instance, the UK did not want the CHR to declare 'categorically that genocide has taken place in Rwanda, with the resultant implication that an international tribunal should be considered.'[70] In this, they were backed by Sweden and France.[71] Thus the UK delegation was pleased that the resolution stopped short of doing so, and furthermore, affirmed that 'the primary responsibility for bringing perpetrators to justice rests with national judicial systems.'[72] The UK objected to an international tribunal because it was 'hard to see how it will work practically, its failure would undermine the credibility of international law and of the UN, huge costs, more viable to re-establish order and encourage national tribunals to bring individuals to justice'.[73]

Other EU states, including Germany, did not mention genocide in their interventions at the CHR. The German representative only referred to 'horrendous massacres', though he endorsed the Greek declaration. Neither the Netherlands nor the UK made a public statement at the CHR.

France and Belgium, though, went further in their statements with respect to the 'genocide' question. The French representative was quite emphatic, declaring, 'The reports received were damning for the militia, their systematic nature deserved a name whose legal consequences she

[69] Telex to FCO; sender blacked out, dated 25 May 1994: Subject: MIPT: third special session of UN Commission on Human Rights (CHR) on Rwanda, 24/25 May. Document released to me under the Freedom of Information Act.

[70] Note from the Human Rights Department, 26 May 1994, 'UN Commission on Human Rights: special session on Rwanda'. Document released to me under the Freedom of Information Act.

[71] Telex sent on 26 May 1994 – both the sender and recipient have been blacked out – with the subject line: 'MIPT: Our TELNO 334 (Not to all): special session of UN Commission on Human Rights (CHR) on Rwanda, 24/25 May 1994'. Document released to me under the Freedom of Information Act.

[72] Paragraph 17 of Resolution S-3/1, in Economic and Social Council, 'Report of the Commission on Human Rights on its third special session (Geneva, 24 and 25 May 1994)', E/CN.4/S-3/4, 30 May 1994.

[73] Fax from Foreign Office, Human Rights Policy Department; recipient blacked out, dated 24 May 1994, 'CHR resolution: Rwanda'. Document released to me under the Freedom of Information Act.

fully weighed: genocide.' She also stated that France had supported the strengthening of UNAMIR (see below on this), which should protect civilians, and also reiterated the general support for an investigation into the human rights violations and holding individuals accountable for them.[74] The observer for Belgium declared, 'The genocide and other human rights violations being committed in Rwanda since 6 April were the result of ethnic tensions that had already caused other bloody conflicts in the past and that had recently been exploited for political purposes.' He then called for an enquiry into the human rights situation, and the identification and trial of those responsible for violations, and particularly for all acts having the characteristic of genocide.[75]

Even after all these meetings, some governments remained reluctant to use the term. Germany largely kept quiet about Rwanda for most of the duration of the genocide – and in contrast to its occasional outspokenness on the matter of genocide in Bosnia, did not make public denunciations of genocide in Rwanda.[76] German ministers did not use the term in several Bundestag debates, even though other MPs did.[77]

The UK government remained squeamish about using the term. In parliament, it was pressed to do so by opposition MPs but on 17 May (*after* the EU Declaration), for example, Prime Minister John Major referred only to the 'civil war' in Rwanda, for which a ceasefire was needed.[78] In fact, as Linda Melvern and Paul Williams note, 'from the start of the genocide until the Conservative Party was voted out of office [in May 1997], neither Major, [Foreign Secretary] Hurd nor [Defence

[74] UN Economic and Social Council, 'Summary record of the first meeting, third special session, Commission on Human Rights', E/CN.4/S-3/SR.1 (21 June 1994), pp. 9–11.

[75] UN Economic and Social Council, 'Summary record of the third meeting, third special session, Commission on Human Rights', E/CN.4/S-3/SR.3 (16 June 1994), pp. 5–6.

[76] For example, on 18 May, German Foreign Minister Klaus Kinkel claimed that the 'civil war' in Rwanda had already caused 500,000 deaths – but did not describe these killings as genocide (despite the fact that the EU Council in which he had participated the previous day had done so). Marie Sanz, 'Klaus Kinkel fait etat d'un bilan de 500.000 morts au Rwanda', *Agence France Presse* (18 May 1994).

[77] The situation in Rwanda was discussed in Bundestag debates on 13 April, 28 April, 19 May and 29 June 1994 (translations by DM). On 29 June, Gerd Poppe from the Greens criticised the EU for being silent for too long about genocide in Rwanda (translation by DM).

[78] Hansard, House of Commons debates (17 May), vol. 243, col. 672.

Secretary] Rifkind ever mentioned the word "genocide" in Parliament in connection with Rwanda'.[79] On 23 May, the Parliamentary Under-Secretary of State for Foreign and Commonwealth Affairs, Mark Lennox-Boyd, was asked by a Labour MP, Tony Worthington, if the Foreign Secretary had made an assessment as to whether the Rwandan government was contravening the Genocide Convention. Lennox-Boyd responded that the EU 'Foreign Affairs Council' on 16 May had appealed for an end to the genocide.[80]

The UK government made no statements in parliament on Rwanda and the House of Commons held no proper debates on it, though an exchange between Worthington and Lennox-Boyd (only) took place on the floor of the House of Commons at around midnight on 24 May.[81] In the draft speech prepared for Lennox-Boyd by the Foreign Office's African Department (Equatorial) on 23 May, there is a paragraph on genocide, which was not ultimately used in the House of Commons because the question was not raised, but which reveals more of the UK government's thinking on the issue:

> Is it genocide? Genocide is a crime under international law. The Genocide Convention defines it as including the killing of members of an ethnical or racial group with intent to destroy that group as such, either in whole or in part. However, at this stage it is difficult to identify specifically which of these atrocities amount to individual acts of genocide, as defined by the Convention.[82]

The UK's position is obviously very cautious (even after the term had been used by the EU twice, in the declaration on Rwanda and in the statement to the CHR) – and very much influenced by the legal norm.

In the House of Lords almost two months later, the Minister for Overseas Development, Lynda Chalker, was asked specifically whether the government considered that 'any persons in Rwanda

[79] Linda Melvern and Paul Williams, 'Britannia Waived the Rules: The Major Government and the 1994 Rwandan Genocide', *African Affairs*, vol. 103, no. 410 (2004), footnote on p. 13.

[80] Hansard, House of Commons, written answers (23 May 1994), vol. 244, col. 44W.

[81] Hansard, House of Commons (24 May 1994), vol. 244, cols. 308–16.

[82] Note from African Department (Equatorial), of 23 May 1994: 'Adjournment debate, 24 May 1994: HMGS policy towards Rwanda'. Document released to me after a Freedom of Information request (I requested information on the UK's position in the special session of the CHR).

have engaged in genocide'. Her response states merely that the UN's Special Rapporteur on human rights in Rwanda, Degni Segui, 'makes a convincing case that events in Rwanda constitute genocide'. The UK supported the investigations of a Commission of Experts into grave violations of international humanitarian law, including genocide.[83] The government thus retreated into the position that 'genocide' was a determination made by experts, and judged after the fact. According to a former UK ambassador to Rwanda (who arrived there on 4 October 1994), the British government was 'being a little difficult' about recognising that genocide had taken place, and 'didn't in fact recognise the precise definition of genocide until the end of September 1994.'[84] (But it should be reiterated that the UK did agree to the EU declaration on Rwanda on 16–17 May, which used the term.)

The French position on the use of the word is an odd one, to say the least: it was prominent among those first describing the atrocities as genocide, yet this quite apparently contradicts its ongoing support for the 'interim government', and its contemporaneous description of the situation as a 'humanitarian catastrophe' and a 'civil war'.[85] Daniela Kroslak surmises that the reason Juppé used the term in mid May was because 'For the French government it became clear that the situation in Rwanda was becoming untenable.'[86] In the beginning of May, the press and NGOs were increasingly speaking of genocide and Bernard Kouchner, the former Minister for Humanitarian Action, visited Rwanda from 10 to 17 May, and called for humanitarian intervention.[87] Most of these calls were for a ceasefire (thus illustrating continued confusion between the civil war and genocide),

[83] Hansard, House of Lords, written answers (21 July 1994), vol. 557, col. 43WA.

[84] Presentation by Lillian Wong at The Rwanda Forum, 27 March 2004, held at the Imperial War Museum, London.

[85] On 27 April, two high-ranking members of the 'interim government' visited Paris and met with Mitterrand, Prime Minister Edouard Balladur and Foreign Minister Alain Juppé – with little consternation in the press. (In contrast, the Belgian government refused visas to the two men.) Prunier, *The Rwanda Crisis*, pp. 277–8. In late May, the Minister of Health, Philippe Douste-Blazy, after a visit to refugee camps outside Rwanda, was asked about whether it was a genocide committed by Tutsis or Hutus, and responded that 'it is not up to me to take sides'. Cited in Kroslak, *The Role of France*, p. 195.

[86] Kroslak, *The Role of France*, pp. 185–6.

[87] Kroslak, *The Role of France*, p. 198. The French newspaper *Libération* was the first to use the term genocide, on 11 April, to describe the killings, though there was no widespread usage of the term in the press until several weeks later.

though MSF called for intervention to stop the genocide on 16 May.[88] As seen below, the French reaction to the events in Rwanda illustrates the contradictions in its rhetoric.

After the genocide, several members of the French government – including President Mitterrand – repeated the 'theory of the double genocide'. This was the argument that the RPF also engaged in a genocide against Hutus. In fact, the RPF did kill numerous civilians – estimates range from 30,000 to 100,000 – behind its lines. But the UN Commission of Experts (among others), which investigated the atrocities, stated that while the RPF did commit atrocities and crimes against humanity, they did not commit genocide: 'The Commission did not uncover any evidence to indicate that Tutsi elements had perpetrated acts committed with the intent of destroying the Hutu ethnic group as such.'[89]

In November 1994, the French refused to invite the new government of Rwanda to a Franco-African summit in Biarritz. At a press conference there, President Mitterrand was asked about the genocide, but answered, 'The genocide or the genocides? I don't know what I should say!'[90] Almost a decade later, in September 2003, the French Foreign Minister, Dominique de Villepin, spoke in a radio interview of the Rwandan 'genocides'. This so incensed the journalist Patrick de Saint-Exupéry that he wrote a book, *L'Inavouable: La France au Rwanda* (Shameful: France in Rwanda), in the form of a letter to Villepin recounting what had really gone on in Rwanda.[91]

So while European governments were the first governments publicly to use the term genocide to describe the atrocities in Rwanda (well ahead of the USA), the endorsement of the legal term was by no means emphatic across the board. And as has already been hinted at above, what the European states appear to suggest should follow such an endorsement is quite limited: investigation and possible legal action, but nothing more.

[88] Melvern, *A People Betrayed*, p. 194. On the confusion of foreign observers between the war and genocide, see also Prunier, *The Rwanda Crisis*, p. 269.

[89] UN Security Council document S/1994/1125 (4 October 1994), p. 2. This was repeated in the final report of the Commission, UN Security Council document S/1994/1405 (9 December 1994).

[90] Cited in Prunier, *The Rwanda Crisis*, p. 339.

[91] Patrick de Saint-Exupéry, *L'Inavouable: La France au Rwanda* (Paris: les Arènes, 2004).

Governments' response

The initial reticence to use the term genocide to describe what was happening in Rwanda appears to be related to the consequences that were believed to follow from such use. At least, we know this was the case in the USA because memoranda indicating this have been released to the public. But similar memoranda (if they exist) have never been released by European governments – and the two parliamentary investigations (France, Belgium) do not dwell on the point at which the government used the term and why. But it seems reasonable to assume that in some cases (such as that of Belgium and the UK), the reticence to use it is connected to concern about pressure that might arise in consequence.[92] This pressure stems from the social norm – that something drastic must be done to stop genocide – rather than the legal norm. When they did use the term, European governments linked the legal definition of genocide under the Convention to the punishment of individuals responsible for genocide, and little more.

So, once the term *was* used, in mid May, what then happened? Arguably, not much. Governments that had been reluctant to intervene remained so. Certainly there was no rush to attempt to stop the genocide in course. The French intervention, Operation Turquoise, in June is a case apart, and will be discussed further below.

The 16 May EU Council declaration on Rwanda gives us the best indication of what EU member states felt should be done in response to an *ongoing* genocide. It is thus worth citing in full (see Box 5.1). First of all, the continuing confusion between civil war and genocide is apparent. There is an emphasis on measures which would be perfectly reasonable to suggest in the case of a civil war, but seem quite

[92] According to Roméo Dallaire, at the 30 April Security Council meeting on the New Zealand presidential statement, the UK thought that the Security Council should avoid terms such as 'forceful action' and 'intervention' (Dallaire, *Shake Hands with the Devil*, p. 351); this was the same meeting where the UK objected to the use of the word genocide. Belgium, having just pressed for the withdrawal of UNAMIR, could hardly turn around quickly and argue that a genocide was ongoing, without getting itself into an awful public moral quandary. On 10 April 1994, Claes would not use the term genocide even though he was aware of the organised mass killings of Tutsi; he told the Belgian Senate inquiry that he could not specify the date on which he was convinced it was genocide. Belgian Senate, 'Commission d'enquête', pp. 560–1.

Box 5.1: Rwanda – Declaration by the European Union

The European Union, recalling its declaration of 18 April 1994 on Rwanda, again appeals urgently to all parties to the conflict to bring an end to the genocide now taking place in the country.

The European Union expresses its full support for the United Nations' humanitarian efforts and in this context welcomes the resolution that is currently before the Security Council. The European Union looks forward to an urgent decision on measures which can be implemented soon.

The European Union welcomes the initiative of the United Nations High Commissioner on Human Rights to conduct a mission to both Rwanda and Burundi and supports the call for a special meeting of the UN Commission on Human Rights.

The European Union expresses its appreciation and support for the efforts of the OAU and to President Mwinyi of Tanzania for their initiatives in convening a regional conference, in which both the authorities of Rwanda and the RPF will be invited.

The European Union urges the two sides to agree on the need to respect the Arusha agreement, which, through the way of negotiation, offers the best available basis for national reconciliation. In this context the European Union supports the call for an early imposition of an arms embargo in Rwanda, and calls on all concerned to refrain from any action that is liable to exacerbate the situation.

The European Union is eager to increase its humanitarian aid whenever and where such aid can be brought to the populations that have suffered so cruelly from the violence. In this respect it will continue its immediate assistance to refugees in the neighbouring countries and will endeavour to equally assist the stricken populations within Rwanda, whenever conditions allow this.

The European Union decided on 6 May 1994 to dispatch a Troika mission, on a Development Ministers level, to visit as soon as possible the countries neighbouring Rwanda, with a view to evaluating the humanitarian situation vis-à-vis the influx of the refugees.

Source: Council of the European Union, press release, 'General Affairs Council', document 6883/94 (Presse 88-G), 16/17 May 1994.

perverse when the case is that of genocide: there should be negotiations between the parties (even though one of those parties is genocidal) and an arms embargo.[93] Secondly, the UN should conduct missions to investigate human rights abuses. Thirdly, humanitarian aid should be delivered, but only where it is safe to do so. Fourthly, refugees outside Rwanda should be helped (granted this was before the extent to which Hutu extremists and *genocidaires* were in those refugee camps was known). Finally, there was support for the UN Security Council's forthcoming decision to increase UNAMIR's strength.

There was no appetite for any stronger measures – and the declaration does not demand that the party actually carrying out the genocide, the Rwandan interim government, cease its actions, though there was ample evidence at this stage that it bore considerable responsibility for the killings (at the very least, for tolerating the atrocious incitements to kill being broadcast on the RTLM radio station). In the EU declaration (as well as in the CHR and Security Council resolutions that also mention genocide), this appears to be a crime with only victims but no perpetrators (unless one really believes that 'all parties' were carrying out the genocide). This rhetorical move means that it is difficult to argue for specific measures to be taken to stop the genocide, because it is not clear *who* has to be stopped. It also justifies an approach of investigation and later punishment (perfectly in line with the Genocide Convention), because it implies that firstly individuals have to be identified and only then can action be taken to bring them to justice.

As for military measures, they were off the agenda. The Greek Deputy Foreign Minister, Theodoros Pangalos, declared before the meeting that member states did not want to risk sending European troops to be killed in Rwanda; instead they would help 'if possible' the OAU's capabilities.[94] After the Council meeting a Belgian Foreign Ministry spokesman declared that OAU troops 'would be better suited for peacekeeping operations in Rwanda than European troops.'

[93] Yet the European Council declaration on Rwanda agreed on 24–25 June 1994 (almost three months into the genocide) still appealed 'urgently to all parties to the conflict to stop the wanton killing of civilians and to come back to the negotiating table to work for peace and security for all'. European Council at Corfu, 24–25 June 1994, Presidency Conclusions on Rwanda.

[94] 'UE/Rwanda: L'UE ne veut pas s'engager dans un violent conflit', *Europolitique* (12 May 1994).

And 'under no circumstances' would Belgium send troops to Rwanda; instead it would give financial and logistical support to UN peacekeeping operations.[95] The German government declared that it would not send troops but would help a UN mission in Rwanda with a military transport plane – *if* the security situation at the airport improved, and if the German constitutional court allowed them to do this. The UN had asked Germany for logistical help in the form of a medical unit – but while the Foreign Ministry was in favour of sending doctors and nurses, the Ministry of Defence was opposed.[96]

After the UN Security Council approved the increase of UNAMIR's strength, to 5500 troops, not one single European country offered troops. The UK government argued that the UN had not asked it to do so, but had only asked it to supply logistical support. Yet Boutros Boutros-Ghali *had* asked UN Security Council members to send troops, and a total of fifty-five states were contacted by Kofi Annan, then the head of the DPKO. Only African countries offered troops; and only the Netherlands, Italy and the UK offered some means of transport (the UK offered unarmoured trucks, which never arrived).[97]

At this point it is difficult not to conclude that European governments were mere bystanders to an acknowledged ongoing genocide. The fact that acknowledgement that a genocide was ongoing did not create momentum for an intervention to stop it can only be seen as reflecting a strict view of what the Genocide Convention actually obliges states to do – a narrow view of the legal norm, and a dismissal of the social norm. This does raise the question as to why there was reticence to use the term in the first place (in this or in any other case): governments seem quite capable of justifying their actions on

[95] Debra Percival and Bob Mantiri, 'Rwanda-Europe: Africa Should Handle Rwanda – Belgium', *Inter Press Service* (17 May 1994).

[96] 'Bonn prêt a soutenir une operation d'aide de l'ONU mais ne veut pas envoyer de troupes', *Agence France Presse* (19 May 1994). There was little support for sending soldiers to Rwanda: one opposition MP (Gernot Erler, SPD) did ask on 19 May why Germany had sent soldiers to Somalia, but not to Rwanda, and was told by the Minister of State Helmut Schäfer that the UN had not requested soldiers from Germany (translation of Bundestag debate by DM). But an SPD motion in the Bundestag on 31 May only called on the government to work for a ceasefire and peace negotiations, and to support the UN peacekeeping mission financially.

[97] Melvern and Williams, 'Britannia Waived the Rules', 16–17; Melvern, *A People Betrayed*, p. 232; Bassir Pour Asfane, 'Rwanda: Comme si nous étions devenues insensibles', *Le Monde* (25 May 1994).

the basis of the legal norm, brushing aside any pressure to 'do something' arising from the social norm.

But in mid June, one government appeared to react more forcefully. On 14 June, France announced that it would send troops unilaterally to Rwanda, because UNAMIR was still not up to strength. The fact that France did not decide to boost UNAMIR remains a controversial issue to this day. Instead it asked the UN Security Council to endorse its intervention, and requested support from its European and African allies. Support for the French action in the Security Council was weak: ten countries voted for the resolution endorsing it, while five abstained (Brazil, China, New Zealand, Nigeria and Pakistan). Only Senegal agreed to send a few troops. In two meetings held at France's request, the Western European Union discussed supporting the French mission. Italy initially responded enthusiastically, and said it would consider sending troops, but rowed back from that commitment fairly quickly, setting strict (and unreachable) conditions for its involvement (including the RPF's agreement). Belgium, Germany, the Netherlands, Portugal, Spain and the UK said they would provide logistical assistance – but France later stated that none of them had actually done so.[98]

The French intervention was viewed extremely suspiciously (if not with outright hostility), given its overt support for the interim government. Indeed, when they heard the news that France would intervene, the interim government's forces in Kigali 'went mad with joy at the prospect of imminent rescue by the French'.[99]

Gérard Prunier attributes France's decision to intervene to continuing media pressure and NGO lobbying, and the need to avert a possible intervention by South Africa (a member of the 'Anglo-Saxon world').[100] Daniela Kroslak analyses the French government's motivation to launch Operation Turquoise as threefold:

[98] The Western European Union was a defence alliance which at the time was supposed to serve as the European Union's 'military arm'. Its full members in 1994 were Belgium, France, Germany, Greece, Italy, Luxembourg, the Netherlands, Portugal, Spain and the UK. Paul Ames, 'European Allies Reject French Troops Request, May Give Logistics Support', *Associated Press* (21 June 1994); 'Heavy Fighting in Kigali', *Agence France Presse* (24 June 1994); 'Paris says WEU Members Offered no Help so Far over Rwanda', *Agence France Presse* (19 July 1994).

[99] Dallaire, *Shake Hands with the Devil*, p. 426.

[100] Prunier, *The Rwanda Crisis*, p. 281.

to be seen to be doing something, that is save their own face; diplomatically, to maintain the credibility of the interim government, at least to the extent that it would be involved in subsequent negotiations; militarily, to fight the RPF.

Once it was clear that they could not confront the RPF, 'they therefore established the Safe Humanitarian Zone (SHZ)' in the southwest of the country.[101] Certainly the French sought to justify publicly their intervention as a purely humanitarian one. The French Prime Minister Edouard Balladur told the UN that 'France has sent its soldiers out of a moral duty to act without delay in order to stop the genocide and provide immediate assistance to the threatened populations.'[102] But as Alan Kuperman notes, 'ironically, Turquoise was triggered by concern for the Tutsi but implemented by a French military establishment hoping to help the Hutu.'[103]

French troops did save Tutsi lives, but a lack of trucks (and a surplus of armoured cars more appropriate for a war situation) meant that often they did not have the capacity to carry many people to safety. Estimates of the numbers of Tutsi who were saved by the French range from 10,000 to 13,000 (though the French government claims 15,000–17,000).[104] But French forces also allowed several prominent members of the interim government to escape out of the SHZ, and helped Rwandan government troops escape into Zaire.[105] Kroslak criticises the French intervention: 'Paris disregarded the victims and the consequences of the genocide when the killings were at their height, and only intervened politically and militarily after several hundred thousand people had been slaughtered, and with very marginal effect.'[106]

[101] Kroslak, *The Role of France*, p. 228. One of the objectives assigned to French soldiers was to 'be ready to control progressively the extension of Hutu territory'. This was apparently not an attempt to counter the RPF victory, but to stabilise a front line between the two parties, to enable negotiations between them. Assemblée Nationale de France, Mission d'information commune, Enquête sur la tragédie rwandaise (1990–1994), rapport no. 1271, vol. 1 (15 December 1998), 362–3.

[102] Cited in Prunier, *The Rwanda Crisis*, p. 296.

[103] Kuperman, *The Limits of Humanitarian Intervention*, p. 44.

[104] Kuperman, *The Limits of Humanitarian Intervention*, pp. 50–1.

[105] Prunier, *The Rwanda Crisis*, p. 308; Kroslak, *The Role of France*, p. 233.

[106] Kroslak, *The Role of France*, p. 246.

The attitude of European countries after the genocide merits brief consideration. Kroslak argues that 'there is abundant evidence to hold the French government collectively accountable for its failure to act to prevent or stop the Rwandan genocide.'[107] The French parliamentary information mission in 1998 did raise numerous questions about French involvement with the Habyarimana regime and the interim government, and Operation Turquoise. But the conclusions exonerate France: 'France is neither responsible nor guilty', claimed the parliament's rapporteur.[108] In response to this, a French federation of NGOs and private individuals organised a 'citizens' inquiry commission' into France's role in the genocide; its conclusions were published in February 2005 and argued that the French state and some of its representatives might have been accomplices to genocide. It called for further enquiries, and possibly judiciary complaints.[109] But there has been no official government acknowledgement of France's responsibility – and certainly no apology. For much of 1994, the French government even blocked EU aid to Rwanda, and as noted above, did not invite Rwanda to the France-Africa summit in 1994 (but did do so in 1996).[110] Relations since then have been tense, although in February 2010, French President Nicolas Sarkozy visited Kigali, briefly, and acknowledged that France and the international community had made mistakes during the genocide. But he did not offer a full apology.

In contrast to France, the Belgian Senate report did find that Belgium, the UN and the international community as a whole bore responsibility for some of what happened after 6 April 1994 in Rwanda. And the Belgian government has apologised to Rwanda. On 7 April 2000, at a ceremony in Gisozi, Rwanda on the anniversary of the start of the genocide, the Belgian Prime Minister, Guy Verhofstadt, said, 'I don't know if I will ever know if the terrible events of 1994 could have been avoided, but I am convinced that we could have done

[107] Kroslak, *The Role of France*, p. 273.

[108] Kroslak, *The Role of France*, p. 272. Instead, an obstructive USA, traumatised Belgium, and powerless UN were all more culpable than France. See the trenchant analysis of the French report in International Panel of Eminent Personalities, 'Rwanda', paragraph 12.7 The French parliamentary report is in four volumes: Assemblée Nationale de France, Mission d'information commune, Enquête sur la tragédie randaise (1990–1994), rapport no. 1271 (15 December 1998).

[109] Beigbeder, *Judging War Crimes and Torture*, pp. 294–5.

[110] International Panel of Eminent Personalities, 'Rwanda', paragraph 17.24.

more, and we could have done better ... A dramatic combination of negligence, incompetence and hesitation created the conditions for the tragedy.'[111] Verhofstadt also attended the tenth anniversary ceremony in 2004, and repeated Belgium's apology.

In the UK, there has been no parliamentary investigation, and no admission of any responsibility for international inaction. Linda Melvern notes that Rwanda was not even mentioned in Prime Minister John Major's memoirs of his time in office, nor discussed in memoirs by Foreign Secretary Douglas Hurd and Defence Secretary Malcolm Rifkind. Hurd did later state in parliament that 'I do not think any of us, looking back, can be satisfied with the way in which the international community responded.'[112]

On the tenth anniversary of the Rwandan genocide, the EU presidency released a declaration entitled, 'NEVER AGAIN', which admitted that mistakes were made by 'the international community' before and during the genocide. It further declared that: 'The challenge to never again fail to prevent such horrors lies at the heart of the European Union's policy. The European Union is ambitious in its objective to avoid the recurrence of genocide anywhere in the world, yet humble in knowing that whatever it does, it may not be enough.'[113]

As for the ICTR, some European governments were not keen on setting up an international tribunal, as noted above. Even as late as early June, the UK's official position was that it would not be 'in the forefront of those opposing it', but that 'it is too early to determine the best way' to ensure that those responsible for the atrocities

[111] 'Belgium Apologizes for Inaction During Genocide', *The Gazelle* (Montreal), 9 April 2000. President Bill Clinton and UN Secretary-General Kofi Annan also issued apologies (of sorts).

[112] Cited in Melvern and Williams, 'Britannia Waived the Rules', 11–12. See also Linda Melvern, 'The UK Government and the 1994 Genocide in Rwanda', *Genocide Studies and Prevention*, vol. 2, no. 3 (2007), and Paul D. Williams, 'The Peacekeeping System, Britain and the 1994 Rwandan Genocide', in Phil Clark and Zachary D. Kaufman, eds., *After Genocide: Transitional Justice, Post-Conflict Reconstruction and Reconciliation in Rwanda and Beyond* (London: Hurst & Company, 2008).

[113] The last phrase gives the EU an obvious justification for any perceived failings in future. European Union, 'Declaration by the Presidency on behalf of the European Union on the occasion of the 10th anniversary of the genocide in Rwanda: NEVER AGAIN', press release 8219/1/04 REV 1 (Presse 102), Brussels, 8 April 2004.

are brought to justice.[114] But since its creation, European governments have generally been quite supportive of the ICTR, though the Rwandan government still accuses France of 'harbouring' *genocidaires.*[115] Kingsley Moghalu states that 'European countries have been firmly supportive of the ICTR... European countries have also been favourite hiding places for Rwandan *genocidaires*. These countries, such as Belgium, Switzerland, and the Netherlands, have been quick to apprehend genocide suspects and indictees at the tribunal's request.'[116] This is somewhat in contrast with the initial attitude towards ICTY of some European states, as noted in the previous chapter.

The ICTR was initially plagued with numerous problems (some stemming from the fact that for many years it shared a prosecutor with ICTY), and was quite slow at issuing indictments and judgements. In September 1998, the first ever judgement for the crime of genocide was delivered by the ICTR (a conviction of the former mayor of a Rwandan town, Jean-Paul Akayesu); since then there have been numerous convictions for genocide.[117]

The ICTR – like ICTY – is to wrap up all its cases by 2010. As a result, Rwanda will try all remaining suspects, though its judicial system has been criticised by human rights groups. In April 2009, the UK High Court blocked the extradition of four Rwandans to Rwanda, where they were to face charges of genocide. It did so on the grounds that defence witnesses in Rwanda were afraid to give evidence in the men's favour, and therefore they would be denied a fair trial. It ordered the release of the four men.[118] At the time, the UK could not exercise jurisdiction over the crime of genocide if the crime was committed before 2001, though this law was later revised in April 2010 (as noted in chapter 2). Belgium, however, has prosecuted some Rwandans for their role in the genocide.[119]

[114] Note from the Foreign Office Human Rights Policy Department on 3 June 1994, recipient blacked out, subject 'Rwanda Secretary-General's report'. Document released to me under the Freedom of Information Act.

[115] Schabas, *Genocide in International Law*, 2nd edition, p. 442.

[116] Moghalu, *Rwanda's Genocide*, pp. 162–3.

[117] The Akayesu ruling is also significant because it stated that rape was a genocidal crime.

[118] 'Rwanda Accused Win Court Case', BBC News online (8 April 2009).

[119] Beigbeder, *Judging Criminal Leaders*, p. 116.

Conclusion

In contrast to the Bosnia case, in the Rwanda case virtually all European governments used the term 'genocide' to describe the killings while they were still ongoing. There were still variations, however, in how willing governments were to use the term – and how often they did so – but in mid May the bodies piling up in Rwanda and the pressures from NGOs in particular led them to acknowledge the patent fact of an ongoing genocide. But the way in which they defined the crime – without an apparent perpetrator – and the confusion with the ongoing civil war, had the effect of justifying a cautious approach to the practical implications of using the term. The legal norm here provided a cover: by continuously expressing the need to bring the individuals responsible for the genocide to justice, governments could claim full compliance with the Genocide Convention (they were abiding by the directive to 'punish' under the Convention), but because such individuals were not identified, action could not be taken to stop them at the time. There was no appetite to intervene militarily to try to stop the killings. Of course, it may be that the French position on Rwanda helped to block a stronger approach by the EU as a whole (as it resisted identifying the 'interim government' as the party responsible for the genocide), but the other EU member states did not express stronger views outside the EU context. Reluctance to use the term and to blame the *genocidaires* goes deeper than any consideration of intra-European diplomatic negotiations.

Operation Turquoise was sold to the international community as an intervention to stop the genocide, but this justification was viewed with considerable suspicion by France's European partners and more widely in the UN, given the French government's continuing support for the interim government. In the end, the French did save some Tutsi – but as many have argued, this was 'too little too late'. No other European government even attempted to do more. No European government volunteered to send forces to the strengthened UNAMIR, and even the logistical help that was promised was paltry if it arrived at all.

The Rwanda case tells us quite a bit about the power of the legal and social norms against genocide. In the most clear-cut case of genocide in the post-Cold War era, European governments could (grudgingly) acknowledge that a genocide was ongoing but nonetheless limit their response to declaratory measures, humanitarian aid and support for a process of justice (which by definition is post hoc). This may illustrate compliance with the letter of the Genocide Convention but certainly not the spirit. The social norm had almost no impact at all, except, belatedly, on France in launching Operation Turquoise (but there its motives were also quite mixed). The next two cases consider whether the shaming experience of Rwanda had an influence on how European governments would respond later to two possible cases of genocide, in Kosovo and Darfur.

6 *Kosovo*

By the mid 1990s, the importance of the non-interference norm seemed to be much reduced among European governments. Unlike in the cases of Bangladesh, Cambodia and elsewhere during the Cold War, European governments were no longer holding to the line that 'we should not interfere in the internal affairs of another country' if there were massive human rights violations being committed there. Furthermore the cases of Bosnia and Rwanda illustrated the impact of the legal norm against genocide on European governments: to punish individuals responsible for genocide, they helped to set up the ICTY and ICTR. But the social norm apparently had little impact on governments – as seen not only in the strict definitions of genocide employed (with the exception of Germany in the Bosnia case) but also in their reluctance to do more than what is clearly required by the Convention. In both Bosnia and Rwanda, European governments had shown little or no willingness to intervene with coercive military measures to stop the violence.

But in the years following the Rwanda and Srebrenica genocides, there was some soul-searching about what could or should have been done in response. As noted in the previous chapters, the Dutch government requested a study into Srebrenica, the Belgian Senate conducted an inquiry into Belgium's role in Rwanda, and the French National Assembly undertook two 'information missions' regarding the French role in both Srebrenica and Rwanda. The Belgian Prime Minister apologised to Rwanda for not doing more. The UN also looked into its own role in both cases, and the OAU commissioned a report on the international reaction to Rwanda.

Although the UN and OAU reports were issued after the Kosovo War, their conclusions reflected a substantial strain of international opinion of the late 1990s. The OAU report called for a re-examination of the 1948 Genocide Convention, including 'the process for determining when a genocide is occurring' and 'the legal obligation of states when genocide is declared'.[1] The UN's report on Rwanda argued that the 'United Nations – and in particular the Security Council and troop contributing countries – must be prepared to act to prevent acts of genocide or gross violations of human rights wherever they may take place. The political will to act should not be subject to different standards.'[2] Its report on Srebrenica concluded: 'The cardinal lesson of Srebrenica is that a deliberate and systematic attempt to terrorize, expel or murder an entire people must be met decisively with all necessary means, and with the political will to carry the policy through to its logical conclusion.'[3] In June 1998, the UN Secretary-General, Kofi Annan (who had been the Under-Secretary General for Peacekeeping during the Rwanda and Srebrenica genocides), gave a talk at the Ditchley Foundation, which called into question the norm of non-intervention in the case of mass atrocities. He noted that preventing genocide is impossible without intervening in a state's internal affairs. But he also argued that only the Security Council 'has the authority to decide that the *internal* situation in any state is so grave as to justify forceful intervention.'[4]

In 1997 and 1998, two new left-wing governments took office in the UK and Germany. The new UK Foreign Secretary, Robin Cook, announced that the UK would henceforth pursue a 'foreign policy with an ethical dimension', and that human rights would be at the heart of British foreign policy; the new Germany Foreign Minister, Joschka Fischer, had argued forcefully in the wake of Srebrenica that only military means can stop genocide. Therefore, by the late 1990s, it seemed that the time was ripe for European governments to act in accordance with the social norm against genocide: they would have to 'do something' in response to genocide, beyond the legal requirements of the Convention.

Is the Kosovo War an example of the force of the social norm against genocide? The Kosovo War has generated enormous debate,

[1] International Panel of Eminent Personalities, 'Rwanda', paragraph 30, chapter 24.

[2] UN Security Council, Report of the independent inquiry into the actions of the United Nations during the 1994 genocide in Rwanda, in S/1999/1257 (16 December 1999), p. 53.

[3] 'The fall of Srebrenica', p. 108.

[4] Emphasis in original. Kofi Annan, 'Intervention', Ditchley Foundation Lecture XXXV (26 June 1998), available at www.ditchley.co.uk [last accessed 28 May 2009].

and NATO's aims in conducting air strikes against Serbia have been dissected repeatedly in the academic literature. Whether Serbia was waging genocide against Kosovar Albanians has also generated debate in the academic literature, with quite a lot of doubt expressed as to whether it was genocide.[5] Did European governments consider Kosovo to be a case of genocide? This chapter considers this question in more detail, after first reviewing the background to the war.

NATO goes to war

The Dayton agreement, which ended the Bosnian war, had two consequences, neither of which were properly foreseen: firstly, it solidified Milošević's position as a linchpin of Balkan stability; secondly, it proposed no solution for the situation in Kosovo, thus leaving the province unhappily – and ultimately tragically – within Serbia's 'domestic jurisdiction'. Slobodan Milošević had forced the Bosnian Serbs to accept the Dayton agreement, and his continued cooperation was seen as necessary to hold Bosnia together in the years after Dayton. Furthermore, Serbia had the largest economy in the former Yugoslavia and so was seen as the guarantor of stability and possible engine of future prosperity in the region.[6] Justice was sacrificed

[5] Those who doubt it is a genocide generally do not consider ethnic cleansing to be genocide. William Schabas argues that it was not, because ethnic cleansing may be 'cultural genocide', but is not genocide under the Genocide Convention because it does not entail the intent to destroy the group. Martin Mennecke argues that genocide was not committed in Kosovo and furthermore that the political utilisation of the term in the case of Kosovo reinforces concerns about its abuse. Jason Abrams argues that many of the killings of Kosovar Albanians qualify as acts of genocide, but the difficulty is proving the intent to destroy the group. See William A. Schabas, 'Problems of International Codification – Were the Atrocities in Cambodia and Kosovo Genocide?' and Jason Abrams, 'The Atrocities in Cambodia and Kosovo: Observations on the Codification of Genocide', both in *New England Law Review*, vol. 35, no. 2 (2001); Martin Mennecke, 'Genocide in Kosovo?', in Totten, Parsons and Charny, eds., *Century of Genocide*, 2nd edition (London: Routledge), 2004.

[6] Between 1992 and 2003 Serbia was the largest of the two republics that made up the Federal Republic of Yugoslavia (FRY), the other being Montenegro. Kosovo was a province of Serbia, and Serb forces (police, or as part of the FRY army) were responsible for the violence in the province. The Montenegrin president criticised Serbia for atrocities committed in Kosovo, but also condemned the NATO air strikes. Officially NATO's actions were against the FRY, but Montenegro was not targeted, and in fact

to try to ensure peace. And 'stability' entailed several years of tolerance of Serb repression in Kosovo. Milošević was not indicted by the International Criminal Tribunal for the former Yugoslavia until May 1999, when the Kosovo War was well under way, and that was only for crimes committed in Kosovo; he was first indicted for crimes committed in Croatia in October 2001 and in Bosnia and Herzegovina in November 2001 (by which time he was in custody in The Hague).

Kosovo did not feature in the Dayton agreement despite the fact that it had long been considered a potential 'flashpoint' for widespread violence in the region: because its population is largely ethnic Albanian, the fear was that violence there would trigger a confrontation between a 'greater Serbia' and a 'greater Albania', dragging in other neighbours as well. Furthermore, Milošević's moves against Kosovo's autonomy in the late 1980s were the trigger for the breakup of Yugoslavia. Kosovo had been an autonomous province within Serbia since 1974; in March 1989, that status was revoked. Ethnic Albanians made up the vast majority of Kosovo's 1.9 million inhabitants; throughout the 1980s, ethnic Serbs living there accused the Albanians of trying to eliminate them in a 'genocide'. Milošević stoked Serb nationalism, and after 1989, imposed repressive measures against Kosovar Albanians (including restricting the use of the Albanian language in schools).[7]

In response, the Kosovar Albanian government established a 'parallel', underground political and educational system. In September 1991, the parallel parliament adopted a resolution declaring Kosovo an independent republic; in a covert referendum, this was approved by almost 100 per cent of the 87 per cent of registered voters participating. The government then requested diplomatic recognition from the European Community in December 1991 – along with most of the

NATO even gave Montenegro a temporary security guarantee to stave off a possible Serb coup against its government (Ivo H. Daalder and Michael E. O'Hanlon, *Winning Ugly: NATO's War to Save Kosovo* (Washington, DC: Brookings Institution Press, 2000), p. 128). Between 2003 and 2006 Serbia and Montenegro formed a 'State Union'; in May 2006 a referendum in Montenegro supported independence and in June the country declared its independence and joined the UN. Serbia then became an independent state, with the official name of the Republic of Serbia. Milošević was the President of Serbia between 1989 and 1997, and the President of the Federal Republic of Yugoslavia from 1997 to 2000.

[7] See Silber and Little, *The Death of Yugoslavia*, chapters 1–5.

other Yugoslav republics. But the EC refused to consider the request, as Kosovo was not a 'constituent republic' of Yugoslavia, but only a province of Serbia – a rather arbitrary distinction considering that until 1991 the idea that the violent break up of a federation could be accepted along any lines at all would have been considered a violation of the non-interference norm.[8]

Throughout the 1990s, Kosovo was led by a pacifist president, Ibrahim Rugova, who hoped that by leading non-violent resistance to Serbian rule, the international community would recognise Kosovo's independence.[9] While Rugova's strategy was much admired, 'the international community has always made it very clear that it would not support an independent Kosovo because it would not support secession and a redrawing of international borders which might awaken latent or historical claims elsewhere in the region'.[10] Dayton, therefore, was a defeat for Kosovar Albanian hopes: not only did Kosovo not feature on the agenda of the negotiations, but the agreement also gave considerable autonomy to the Republika Srpska, a territory that had not existed before Dayton and that had arguably been created on the battlefield. Furthermore, when the European Union recognised the Federal Republic of Yugoslavia (consisting of Serbia and Montenegro) in April 1996, it merely noted that improved relations with the FRY would depend on a 'constructive approach' to the granting of autonomy for Kosovo.[11] For Kosovar Albanians, the non-violent route appeared to have led nowhere, and support instead grew for the separatist Kosovo Liberation Army (KLA).

In 1998, the KLA launched several attacks on Serbian police, prompting over-reactions by the police and Yugoslav army forces, resulting in civilian deaths. Between February and September 1998 an estimated 1000 civilians were killed, with an unknown but probably smaller number killed between September 1998 and March 1999. Over 400,000 Kosovar Albanians were driven from their

[8] See Tim Youngs and Tom Dodd, 'Kosovo', House of Commons research paper, 98/73 (7 July 1998). The sole exception during the Cold War was the acceptance of Bangladeshi independence.

[9] The Serbian government tolerated this, largely because it kept the province quiet.

[10] Richard Caplan, 'International Diplomacy and the Crisis in Kosovo', *International Affairs*, vol. 74, no. 4 (1998), 751. Not least of which Bosnia, but Macedonia was also considered vulnerable to secessionist forces.

[11] Caplan, 'International Diplomacy', 750.

homes during this entire period, half of whom fled into neighbouring countries.[12] Refugees fleeing into neighbouring countries appeared to be escaping not just the civil war, but also ethnic cleansing by Serb forces. While the death toll is relatively low, the number of refugees is not. However, it is also estimated that by mid July 1998, the KLA controlled 40 per cent of Kosovo's territory.[13]

The violence prompted a response from the Contact Group (France, Germany, Italy, Russia, the UK and the USA), condemning violence on both sides, but also growing pressure – particularly from the USA – on Yugoslavia to halt the violence and enter into dialogue with the Kosovar Albanians. On 31 March 1998, the UN Security Council imposed an arms embargo on the FRY (Resolution 1160). Beginning in April 1998, the European Union imposed a series of sanctions on the FRY, including an asset freeze, visa ban (for individuals considered responsible for the violence), and flight ban, eventually culminating in an oil embargo imposed a year later. On 23 September, UN Security Council Resolution 1199 demanded that all parties cease hostilities and enter into dialogue, and that the Federal Republic of Yugoslavia withdraw all security forces engaged in civilian repression. In October 1998, NATO threatened air strikes unless Milošević withdrew some of his forces from Kosovo and allowed in 2000 unarmed ceasefire monitors from the Organization for Security and Cooperation in Europe (OSCE). He complied initially, and most of the refugees returned home. But violence nonetheless increased over the next few months, as the KLA moved in to take over from departing Serb forces which in turn were sent back into Kosovo.[14]

[12] The numbers of dead and displaced are notoriously contested in the Kosovo case. These figures are generally considered among the most reputable, and are from the Independent International Commission on Kosovo, *The Kosovo Report* (Oxford: Oxford University Press, 2000), Executive Summary. For a variety of other reputable estimates, see Youngs and Dodd, 'Kosovo', 17–18; Michael MccGwire, 'Why did we Bomb Belgrade?', *International Affairs*, vol. 76, no. 1 (2000), 4; Daalder and O'Hanlon, *Winning Ugly*, p. 12.

[13] Daalder and O'Hanlon, *Winning Ugly*, p. 35.

[14] At this point, some observers concluded that the international community's response to violence in Kosovo was similar to its initial response to violence in Bosnia: ineffective. The OSCE verification mission was chosen over a more robust approach, because of US refusal to contemplate the latter. See Nicholas Morris, 'Humanitarian Intervention in the Balkans', in Jennifer M. Welsh, ed., *Humanitarian Intervention and International Relations* (Oxford: Oxford University Press, 2004), pp. 110–14.

In January 1999, it was alleged that Serb forces had killed forty-five civilians in the village of Racak. The Contact Group reacted forcefully, and convened a conference at Rambouillet, France in which they presented a non-negotiable solution: Serbia would withdraw most troops from Kosovo, grant autonomy, and allow NATO troops to be deployed to ensure peace. If Serbia did not accept, NATO would bomb. After meetings in February and March, Serbia still did not accept the deal.[15] On 20 March, the OSCE observers were ordered to withdraw; on 22 March, Serb forces launched a pre-emptive offensive, aimed at driving out Kosovar Albanians – and the KLA – from the southern and western parts of Kosovo.[16]

On 24 March 1999, NATO launched air strikes against the Federal Republic of Yugoslavia, though its targets were Serb forces and military infrastructure in Kosovo and Serbia (not Montenegro). The NATO action was widely dubbed a 'humanitarian war'.[17] On 12 April, the North Atlantic Council stated that NATO air strikes would continue until President Milošević did the following:

- ensured a verifiable stop to all military action and the immediate ending of violence and repression;
- ensured the withdrawal from Kosovo of the military, police and paramilitary forces;
- agreed to the stationing in Kosovo of an international military presence;
- agreed to the unconditional and safe return of all refugees and displaced persons and unhindered access to them by humanitarian aid organisations;

[15] The KLA almost refused to go along with the deal (which is why the talks were convened again in mid March) – unhappy with the provisions only for 'autonomy' and not for full independence. Apparently the US Secretary of State Madeline Albright convinced them to sign by promising informally that a referendum on self-determination would be held after three years. MccGwire, 'Why did we Bomb Belgrade?', 7–8.

[16] MccGwire, 'Why did we Bomb Belgrade?', 10; Tim Youngs, Mark Oakes and Paul Bowers, 'Kosovo: Operation "Allied Force"', House of Commons Library research paper 99/48 (29 April 1999), 8; Lawrence Freedman, 'Victims and Victors: Reflections on the Kosovo War', *Review of International Studies*, vol. 26, no. 3 (2000), 352.

[17] Adam Roberts, 'NATO's "Humanitarian War" over Kosovo', *Survival*, vol. 41, no. 3 (Autumn 1999).

– provided credible assurance of his willingness to work on the basis of the Rambouillet Accords in the establishment of a political framework agreement for Kosovo in conformity with international law and the Charter of the United Nations.[18]

Despite the references to the 'international community' and the UN Charter in that statement, NATO acted without specific authorisation from the UN Security Council to use force as China and Russia had signalled they would veto such authorisation. Furthermore, it took 78 days of bombing – far more than anticipated – to convince Milošević to withdraw Yugoslav forces from Kosovo. In the meantime, Serb forces continued to 'drain the swamp', that is, to empty villages of Kosovar Albanians and thus deprive the KLA of support. By the war's end 863,000 Kosovar Albanians had fled into neighbouring countries and an estimated 590,000 were internally displaced (the combined total is over 90 per cent of the Kosovar Albanian population), though almost all refugees and displaced persons returned to their homes after the end of the war.[19] In addition, an estimated 10,000 Kosovar Albanians had been killed mostly by Serb forces; while 500 Serb civilians had been killed by NATO airstrikes.[20] No NATO personnel were killed during the air campaign. The aftermath was messy: in the nine months after the war ended, at least 100,000 Kosovar Serbs were expelled by Kosovar Albanians and perhaps 300 Kosovar Serbs killed.[21] Peacekeepers had to be deployed specifically to protect remaining Serbs from violence.

The war generated controversy within NATO: at times the NATO member countries strained to maintain their unity, and several governments publicly voiced their concerns about the bombing

[18] North Atlantic Council, 'The situation in and around Kosovo', statement issued at the extraordinary ministerial meeting of the North Atlantic Council held at NATO headquarters, Brussels, on 12 April 1999, press release M-NAC-1(99)51.

[19] Organization for Security and Cooperation in Europe, 'Kosovo/Kosova: As Seen, As Told. An Analysis of the Human Rights Findings of the OSCE Kosovo Verification Mission, October 1998 to June 1999' (1999), chapter 14.

[20] Independent International Commission on Kosovo, *The Kosovo Report*, Executive Summary. NATO air strikes were not always accurate – notoriously hitting the Chinese embassy in Belgrade, but also killing civilians in a train crossing a bridge in Serbia, and killing Kosovar Albanians in a refugee convoy fleeing Serb forces.

[21] Daalder and O'Hanlon, *Winning Ugly*, pp. 193–6.

campaign. Bombing targets had to be approved by all the NATO member countries. But as one observer pointed out, '[a]t least in the Balkans, a regional organization took a unanimous decision to deploy military force for human protection.'[22] However, the war was also heavily criticised in the press, by academics, MPs in many NATO countries, and by non-NATO governments, for numerous reasons:

- the war was illegal, given that NATO had launched air strikes without a specific Security Council resolution authorising it to do so;[23]
- it was an illegitimate intervention in a civil war, in support of secessionist forces, namely the KLA;
- the war was conducted unjustly because NATO would not risk the lives of its own soldiers, but only engage in hostilities from the air, and at high altitudes which entailed a greater risk of 'collateral damage' to civilians and civilian infrastructure;[24]
- the war was conducted unjustly because NATO air strikes killed civilians, specifically because it targeted 'dual-purpose' (military and civilian) targets;[25]
- NATO bombing caused Serb forces to accelerate their 'ethnic cleansing' of Kosovar Albanians, thus a war that had been launched to avert a humanitarian catastrophe ended up creating one;

[22] Weiss, *Humanitarian Intervention*, p. 153.

[23] This was the conclusion of the Independent International Commission on Kosovo (*Kosovo Report*, Executive Summary); it also argued, however, that 'the intervention was justified because all diplomatic avenues had been exhausted and because the intervention had the effect of liberating the majority population of Kosovo from a long period of oppression under Serbian rule.'

[24] Human Rights Watch and Amnesty International both argued that NATO had violated international humanitarian law: for Human Rights Watch this was because NATO targeted civilian assets, for Amnesty International, because it unlawfully killed civilians. But the ICTY prosecutor, Louise Arbour, decided that there had been no deliberate targeting of civilians or unlawful military targets. See the discussion about these contrasting interpretations of international law in Nicholas J. Wheeler, 'The Kosovo Bombing Campaign', in Reus-Smit, ed., *The Politics of International Law*, pp. 207–13.

[25] This is Henry Shue's argument in 'Bombing to Rescue? NATO's 1999 Bombing of Serbia', in Deen K. Chatterjee and Don E. Scheid, eds., *Ethics and Foreign Intervention* (Cambridge: Cambridge University Press, 2003).

– after the war ended, Kosovar Albanians ethnically cleansed Serbs from several parts of Kosovo, thus NATO's war could be seen as having been fought for the illegitimate principle of ethnic homogeneity.

It is not the intention here to dwell on such arguments, though it is necessary to keep in mind how controversial the war was and continues to be. The rest of this chapter focuses only on the extent to which the UK, France and Germany felt that there was a risk of genocide or an actual genocide ongoing in Kosovo (and at what point in time), and that the military action against Serbia was therefore justified. Did they 'name' genocide in this case? If so, did they refer to the legal norm, to the Genocide Convention, to justify coercion? Is the influence of the social norm apparent?

Naming genocide?

For Ivo Daalder and Michael O'Hanlon, the situation before the war 'was not an attempted genocide' – '2000 people' had been killed, a relatively low level of violence. But 'there was good reason to believe that, without intervention, things would have gotten much worse.'[26] They point out that 'no NATO country formally made the charge of genocide, or invoked the 1948 UN convention against genocide, at any time during the war', and argue:

> Nonetheless, NATO probably handled this issue correctly during the conflict over Kosovo, raising its concerns about the possibility of genocide without in the end invoking that weighty term to describe killings that, although ruthless, were not on a scale to compare with the century's – or even the decade's – worst massacres.[27]

However, while no NATO country 'formally' made the charge of genocide – if that is supposed to mean action charging Serbia with genocide before the ICJ or Security Council – several officials from NATO countries and the organisation itself did use the term frequently, and not just to raise concerns about the possibility of a genocide in Kosovo but to describe the killings. But in all of these cases, the

[26] Daalder and O'Hanlon, *Winning Ugly*, p. 12.
[27] Daalder and O'Hanlon, *Winning Ugly*, pp. 111–12.

term was used by governments or NATO officials *after* the airstrikes began on 24 March.[28] NATO governments did not use the term in relation to any of the massacres or ethnic cleansing that occurred in 1998 or early 1999. It is thus inaccurate to argue, as one scholar does, that 'Labeling the conduct of the Serb forces in Kosovo genocidal undoubtedly smoothed the way for armed intervention without the requisite UN Security Council mandate.'[29] Armed intervention was already under way when the 'label' was applied.

The first uses of the term coincided with an escalation in the NATO bombing campaign: NATO had not anticipated that it would take more than three days of bombing to force Milošević back into negotiations, and thus on 27 March it entered into 'phase 2' involving a wider set of military targets.[30] The first use of the term genocide also, however, coincided with the escalation in Serb violence against Kosovar Albanians, and a marked increase in the number of killings and of refugees fleeing across the borders into neighbouring territories. Was the term used to legitimise continued bombing or was it an appropriate descriptor?

US and NATO officials used the term from 30 March. On that day, US State Department spokesman James Rubin stated, 'We have very clear indications that genocide is unfolding in Kosovo. Clearly there are crimes against humanity.'[31] Also on the same day, a White House spokesman repeated that 'we are beginning to see evidence of a potential genocide' and that there was no reason to believe that those

[28] There was some usage by parliamentarians beforehand. Some US Senators (Dole, Biden), a backbench Labour MP (Ben Bradshaw) and a member of the House of Lords (Baroness Ludford) used the term before the war began. In the Bundestag on 19 November 1998, Christian Schwarz-Schilling of the CDU/CSU indicated that the agreement on the OSCE mission had prevented a new genocide (Amtliche Protokolle, 19 November 1998, 008.Sitzung; translation by DM). UK Foreign Secretary Robin Cook told the press in May 1998 that 'no one is going to tolerate genocide' in Kosovo, but at no point before the war did he indicate that a genocide had already begun. David Buchan, 'Europe: NATO Prepares for Crisis in Kosovo', *Financial Times* (29 May 1998). The term *was* used by journalists and various commentators in the months before the war began – but *not* by governments.

[29] Mennecke, 'Genocide in Kosovo?', 453.

[30] Daalder and O'Hanlon, *Winning Ugly*, p. 117.

[31] Joseph Fitchett, 'Denouncing Serbs, NATO Intensifies Attacks on Troops; U.S. Cites "Clear Indications" of Genocide Unfolding in Kosovo', *International Herald Tribune* (31 March 1999).

carrying out ethnic cleansing were 'not acting on orders'.[32] This formulation of words 'indications', 'potential genocide', and so on, was repeated by US officials during the war. And on 25 June, President Clinton stated there were fears of 'deliberate, systematic efforts at genocide'. According to Samantha Power, there had been a debate within the State Department about what language to use, and 'indicators of genocide' was judged a more appropriate finding than a direct accusation that genocide was ongoing.[33]

Others went further. On 30 March, NATO spokesman Jamie Shea said the situation in Kosovo resembled a 'modern version of the Great Terror' in the USSR in the 1930s, and that Serb forces were forcibly emptying cities and towns just as the Khmer Rouge had forcibly evacuated Phnom Penh in 1975.[34] A few weeks later, in a question and answer session organised by BBC World Service, Shea stated that bombing was the 'only way the international community can stop the genocide in Kosovo'.[35] NATO press statements and declarations, however, did not use the term, though they condemned 'appalling violations of human rights' and the 'massive humanitarian crisis' in Kosovo.[36]

Even UN Secretary-General Kofi Annan raised the possibility that genocide was ongoing in Kosovo. In an address to the UN Commission on Human Rights on 7 April, he stated that the delegates were meeting 'under the dark cloud of genocide'. And 'although there were no independent observers on the ground', there were signs that genocide was happening in Kosovo. 'The odious campaign of ethnic cleansing conducted by the Serbian authorities in Kosovo appeared to have just one aim: to expel from Kosovo or kill as many ethnic Albanians as possible, thereby denying a people their most basic rights to life, liberty and security.'[37]

32 'NATO Rejects Serb Offer, Vows to Continue Strikes', *Agence France Presse* (31 March 1999).

33 Power, *'A Problem from Hell'*, pp. 467–8; Clinton quote on p. 468.

34 Joseph Fitchett, 'Denouncing Serbs, NATO Intensifies Attacks on Troops; U.S. Cites "Clear Indications" of Genocide Unfolding in Kosovo', *International Herald Tribune* (31 March 1999).

35 'NATO Answers your Questions', BBC World Service, 'Talking Point on Air' (20 April 1999), available at news.bbc.co.uk/1/hi/talking_point/talking_point_on_air/319293.stm [last accessed 2 July 2009].

36 See, for example, North Atlantic Council, 'The situation in and around Kosovo'.

37 Paragraph 7 of UN Economic and Social Council, 'Commission on Human Rights, fifty-fifth session, summary record of the 19th meeting held at the

Did European governments use the term? Did they come under pressure to do so? Of the three European governments considered here, Germany and the UK did use the term – early in the war and thereafter. But references to the Genocide Convention, and its definition of the term, were rare if completely absent. In fact, as we will see, exactly what Germany and the UK were defining as genocide is not terribly clear in the public pronouncements of ministers. In contrast, the French government did not use the term genocide.

The new left-wing German government, in office in October 1998, agreed that Germany had to be involved in NATO military action against Milošević. Chancellor Gerhard Schröder wanted to ensure continuity and dependability in foreign policy, while Foreign Minister Joschka Fischer initially felt torn: he was under contrasting pressures from his Green Party members and coalition partners, the SPD. But Fischer was also strongly convinced that 'never again Auschwitz' had to be a guiding principle of German foreign policy and that force might have to be used as a result – a conviction that arose after the Srebrenica genocide.[38] Schröder too argued that because Germany had been guilty of genocide in the past, 'we must not tolerate violations of human rights and stand aside with the cheap excuse that our abstinence is justified by our history'.[39] For Brendan Simms, 'by the late 1990s, the lessons of history had been reinterpreted in favour of a special German mission to prevent genocide in Europe.'[40]

Germany (along with the UK) was the first western government to use the term genocide with respect to Kosovo. The German understanding of the term seems to be that of an expansive definition of genocide (as per the social norm) in which ethnic cleansing comes very close to, or indeed is, genocide. This is consistent with the use

Palais de Nations, Geneva, on Wednesday, 7 April 1999 at 10 a.m.' E/CN.4/1999/S.R.19 (9 July 1999).

[38] Alister Miskimmon, 'Falling into Line? Kosovo and the Course of German Foreign Policy', *International Affairs*, vol. 85, no. 3 (2009), 563–4. Miskimmon cites Schröder's and Fischer's memoirs.

[39] Quoted in Brendan Simms, 'From the Kohl to the Fischer Doctrine: Germany and the Wars of the Yugoslav Succession, 1991–1999', *German History*, vol. 21, no. 3 (2003), 413. Schröder's statements on Kosovo in the Bundestag often take this line: see, for example, his comments in the debate on 24 February 1999 (Amtliche Protokolle, 24 February 1999, 021.Sitzung; translation by DM) and on 15 April 1999 (Amtliche Protokolle, 15 April 1999, 032.Sitzung; translation by DM)

[40] Simms, 'From the Kohl to the Fischer Doctrine', 413.

of the term by German government ministers to describe events in northern and eastern Bosnia in 1992.

On 28 March, German Defence Minister Rudolf Scharping stated that 'genocide has begun' in Kosovo and that a humanitarian catastrophe was unfolding.[41] This was before the US State Department used the term, and was considerably more emphatic in describing the events as genocide. On 30 March Schröder and Scharping described Serb actions in Kosovo as genocide, and Scharping declared that NATO bombing would continue until Serbia's 'capability to continue its genocide in Kosovo' had been destroyed.[42] On 15 April, Scharping told the Bundestag that indifference in the face of genocide destroys the foundations of society and that Europe would damage its soul if it accepted genocide and ethnic cleansing.[43]

In early April 1999, Schröder, Fischer and Scharping jointly condemned Yugoslav President Slobodan Milošević for 'planned deportations' and 'genocide' in Kosovo.[44] Schröder accused Serb paramilitary groups of 'waging genocide' against ethnic Albanians.[45] Fischer told journalists, 'When you are confronted by genocide and mass human suffering, you cannot sit passively with your hands folded and ignore the killing of innocent civilians. I believe there are certain human values that are more important than pacifism, and those are rooted deeply in my conscience.'[46]

In several interviews, Fischer used 'never again Auschwitz' to justify his support for military action against Serbia. Germany had to act to prevent the beginning of a possible genocide: in Kosovo, people were being expelled and there was an attempt to exterminate their cultural identity, and 'from there it is only a small step towards genocide.'[47] In

[41] BBC Worldwide Monitoring, 'German Minister Sees "Genocide" in Kosovo but Rules out Ground Forces' (30 March 1999).

[42] Roger Cohen, 'Crisis in the Balkans: The Diplomacy', *New York Times* (31 March 1999).

[43] Amtliche Protokolle, 15 April 1999, 032.Sitzung (translation by DM).

[44] Jerome Daquin, 'Kosovo Crisis Restores Germany to Military Power Status', *Agence France Presse* (3 April 1999).

[45] 'Schroeder demands end to "genocide campaign" in Kosovo', *Agence France Presse* (3 April 1999).

[46] William Drozdiak and Anne Swardson, 'Support for Bombing Spreading in Europe; Refugees' Suffering Stifles Pacifist Qualms', *The Washington Post* (4 April 1999).

[47] Matthias Geis and Gunter Hoffman, 'Serbian gehört zu Europa', *Die Zeit* (15 April 1999) (translation by DM).

response to criticisms (particularly from within his own Green Party), he declared in an interview with *Newsweek*:

> There are many pacifists who cannot accept it, but, on the other hand, my generation was brought up with two experiences. The first is 'Never Again War.' And the second is 'Never Again Auschwitz.' It means standing up against genocide. It's a contradiction, but we have to live with it. If we accept Milosevic as a winner, it would be the end of the Europe I believe in.[48]

At a tumultuous Green party conference on 13 May, Fischer restated this position – and came in for considerable criticism for it, though in the end the conference vote approved the position of the Greens in the government.[49]

The term genocide was also used by other MPs and leading members of the opposition. The chairman of the SPD parliamentary group, Peter Struck, declared that preventing genocide was more important than respecting the veto of two members of the UN Security Council (so NATO was right to act without Security Council authorisation), and that Europe could not allow a second Srebrenica.[50] Just as NATO launched the air strikes, the CDU party chairman, Wolfgang Schäuble, stated that there was no disagreement between the government and his party over the Kosovo question, and that NATO's intervention aimed at preventing murder in Kosovo. Expulsions, ethnic cleansing and genocide must not be tolerated, which meant using force, he reiterated in a debate in the Bundestag on 15 April.[51]

But there was some domestic unease with the language used. Fischer's reference to Auschwitz was criticised in Germany, and further afield (including by Holocaust survivor Elie Wiesel), for trivialising

[48] Lally Weymouth, 'We Have to Win This', *Newsweek* (19 April 1999). Some German Foreign Ministry officials told me that Fischer was expressing public sentiment – though this raised the obligations on Germany to respond appropriately to ensure genocide was not repeated. Interviews with officials from the German Foreign Ministry, Berlin, 10 October 2008.

[49] Fischer was hit with red paint at the conference. Miskimmon, 'Falling into Line?', 564–5.

[50] In Bundestag debate on 26 March 1999 (Amtliche Protokolle, 26 March 1999, 031.Sitzung; translation by DM).

[51] See the debates in the Bundestag on 25 and 26 March 1999 (Amtliche Protokolle, 25 March 1999, 030.Sitzung, 26 March 1999, 031.Sitzung), and 15 April 1999 (032.Sitzung) (translation by DM).

the Holocaust. He did tone down his rhetoric, and was careful in the interviews and speeches cited above to state that Auschwitz was incomparable, and that the catastrophe in Kosovo was not on the same level as Auschwitz. Schröder too clarified that ethnic cleansing in Kosovo could not be compared to the Nazis' genocide of Jews.[52]

The UK was also early in its denunciation of an ongoing genocide in Kosovo. The use of the term in British discourse seems closer to the legal norm: it is the killing that is genocide, not necessarily the ethnic cleansing. On 28 March, Defence Secretary George Robertson declared that 'we are confronting a regime intent on genocide'.[53] In the House of Commons, Foreign Secretary Robin Cook indicated that the UK fully supported bringing to justice 'those who have stained Kosovo with ethnic cleansing and genocide'.[54] George Robertson used the term several times in the House of Commons, and argued that NATO's military action was the only way to stop the genocidal *killing* in Kosovo.[55] The Shadow Foreign Secretary, Conservative MP John Maples, seemed to agree with the government on the question of genocide, declaring at one point: 'There has been an organised campaign of atrocities – genocide, dare one say – against the Albanians in Kosovo.'[56] But in general there was no debate in the House of Commons on whether the use of the term 'genocide' was appropriate or not. And a parliamentary report on Kosovo, published almost a year after the war, does not mention the word 'genocide' at all, much less comment on its use in the debates inside the House of Commons.[57]

[52] 'Kosovo Crimes not Comparable to Holocaust: Schroeder', *Agence France Presse* (18 April 1999). The PDS accused Scharping of diminishing the uniqueness of Auschwitz, and waging a war to compensate for what happened in Auschwitz. Intervention by Wolfgang Gercke in the Bundestag debate on 22 April 1999 (Amtliche Protokolle, 22 April 1999, 035.Sitzung; translation by DM).

[53] Carol Lin and Christiane Amanpour, 'Strike against Yugoslavia', CNN Sunday morning (transcript), 28 March 1999.

[54] Hansard, House of Commons debate on Kosovo (19 April 1999), vol. 329, col. 573.

[55] Hansard, House of Commons: 10 May 1999, vol. 331, cols. 5–6; 18 May 1999, vol. 331, cols. 966 and 968; 26 May 1999, vol. 332, cols. 363 and 364; and 19 July 1999, vol. 335, cols. 781 and 784.

[56] Hansard, House of Commons (17 June 1999), vol. 333, col. 596.

[57] UK House of Commons, Select Committee on Foreign Affairs, fourth report: Kosovo (23 May 2000).

Prime Minister Tony Blair also used the term in the House of Commons. On 26 April, he declared that 'we cannot allow a policy of racial genocide to go unchecked in Europe.'[58] A few weeks later he accused Milošević of pursuing a policy of 'racial genocide'.[59] On 21 June, Blair declared that 'racial genocide' had been committed in Kosovo.[60] His persistent use of the adjective 'racial' is baffling: not only is it inappropriate (are the Albanians and Serbs different 'races'?), but it is superfluous, given that the official definition of genocide encompasses racial, ethnical, religious and national groups.

Blair did not, however, describe events in Kosovo as genocide in his important speech on the 'Doctrine of the International Community', given in Chicago on 22 April 1999. Instead, he used the terms, 'ethnic cleansing, systematic rape, mass murder'.[61] In fact the only mention of genocide in that speech was his insistence that 'acts of genocide can never be a purely internal matter' – and therefore this would justify intervention by the international community (an articulation of the social norm against genocide).

In contrast, the French government did not use the term genocide to describe the situation in Kosovo, though it did use strong language condemning Serbian actions in the province. For example, President Jacques Chirac declared that NATO was right to act: '(Europe) cannot accept on its soil a man and a regime that, for nearly 10 years, has conducted … operations of ethnic cleansing, murders and massacres, of destabilization in the entire region, resulting in more than 200,000 deaths and millions left homeless. It is enough.'[62] Prime Minister Lionel Jospin told the National Assembly that the recourse to force was necessary to respond to Belgrade's persistent violations of UN Security Council obligations and to counter grave violations of fundamental human rights.[63] But the French government did not use

[58] Hansard, House of Commons (26 April 1999), vol. 330, col. 32. He repeated the same sentiment on 12 May (Hansard, vol. 331, col. 311).

[59] Hansard, House of Commons (26 May 1999), vol. 332, col. 348.

[60] Hansard, House of Commons (21 June 1999), vol. 333, col. 767.

[61] Speech available at www.pbs.org/newshour/bb/international/jan-june99/blair_doctrine4–23.html [last accessed 4 July 2009].

[62] George Jahn, 'NATO Bombing Escalates while Russians Seek Negotiations', *Associated Press* (29 March 1999).

[63] 'Intervention du Premier ministre, M. Lionel Jospin, à l'Assemblée nationale', Paris, 26 March 1999, in Ministère des Affaires Étrangères, *La Politique Étrangère de la France: Textes et Documents*, March –April 1999, p. 209.

the term genocide, and nor did MPs from both opposition and government benches; the government was not under any parliamentary pressure to use the term.[64]

Indeed, the Foreign Minister Hubert Vedrine clearly ruled out the use of the term in an interview on 7 April. He was asked by a journalist whether he agreed with Kofi Annan's use of the term genocide. He responded, in a way which indicates a very strict reading of the definition of genocide:

I think that we should keep to an extremely rigorous definition of the word genocide. For now what has happened in Kosovo is utterly atrocious. There are various abominations, aimed at terrorising the population, not to suppress it on a grand scale but to make it leave. This is already horrible enough as it is without having to use words that define other historical events that come to mind. The problem is not one of words ... What we have been trying to do for some months, and what we will succeed in doing, is enabling people to return to their homes one day, in a secure Kosovo.[65]

Pierre Rousselin, the foreign editor of *Le Figaro*, noted in an interview on American television on 8 April that the rhetoric in France was less strong – there was no talk of genocide: 'people are very careful with words, and are not – we are trying not to be critical, to be not saying there is a genocide, for instance. Maybe this sounds a little too nitty, but words have a very particular sense, and people would be shocked if we went overboard, I guess, in France.' He surmised this could also be because while there had been a shift in French foreign policy under

[64] Despite the apparent reluctance of French government officials to use the term genocide, in an infamous letter to Chirac, the leftist writer Regis Debray reported that on a recent visit to Kosovo he had seen no evidence of genocide or ethnic cleansing against Kosovar Albanians, and that this did not correspond to the words Chirac was using. Debray was immediately criticised by other French intellectuals, notably Bernard-Henri Levy and Alain Joxe, for backing the aggressors and ignoring the crimes committed in Kosovo. Regis Debray, 'Lettre d'un voyageur au President de la Republique', *Le Monde* (13 May 1999); 'Guevara's French Friend under Heavy Fire for pro-Serb stand', *Agence France Presse* (13 May 1999).

[65] 'Entretien du ministre des Affaires étrangères, M. Hubert Védrine, avec "France Info"', 7 April 1999, in Ministère des Affaires Étrangères, *La Politique Étrangère de la France: Textes et Documents*, March –April 1999, p. 287 (my translation). As far as I can tell, no journalist asked why French officials were not using the term while British and German ones were.

Chirac away from the traditional friendship with Serbia, the ties were still strong.[66] But the term wasn't entirely absent from the French public debates. For example, early in the war, *Le Monde* used it: 'It is to be welcomed that NATO is substituting the UN in order to assure regional stability and stop a genocide.'[67]

A brief word is in order on whether any other European governments used the term. The Italian government used it to describe developments in Kosovo – again after the start of NATO's air strikes. In a television interview on 30 March, the Italian Prime Minister Massimo D'Alema described Milošević's policy in Kosovo as genocide, and the following day, the Italian Defence Minister Carlo Scognamiglio declared that NATO's action was the lesser evil compared with the genocide under way in Kosovo.[68] But there was hardly any use of the term later. And as far as I can tell from a search of the Nexis database, the Dutch and Belgian governments did not use the term. In contrast, politicians from some Central and East European countries used the term from early in the war onwards. On 2 April, Czech President Vaclav Havel said that 'the most important task we have to deal with is to ensure that the genocide of the Kosovo Albanians is stopped.'[69] The Slovak Prime Minister, Mikulas Dzurinda, also used the term frequently to describe the events in Kosovo.[70]

This absence of consistent use of the term genocide by European (and western) governments helps to explain why it was not used in

66 *The News House with Jim Lehrer* (transcript) (8 April 1999).

67 Nathalie Duclos, 'Oui, il fallait intervenir au Kosovo', *Le Monde* (30 March 1999) (my translation).

68 Augusto Minzolini, 'Primakov, la grande illusione', *La Stampa* (31 March 1999); Maurizio Molinari, 'Dini: Trovare un accordo è ora più difficile', *La Stampa* (1 April 1999).

69 BBC Summary of World Broadcasts (Czech Radio), 'Milosevic's Regime a Threat to Europe, says President' (2 April 1999); BBC Monitoring – Europe (CTK News Agency). See also 'Czech President Says G8 Peace Initiative for Kosovo Best Plan So Far' (14 May 1999). The Czech Prime Minister, Milos Zeman, also echoed that language. BBC Monitoring – Europe (CTK News Agency), 'Premier Says Czechs May Participate in Economic Blockade of Yugoslavia' (27 April 1999).

70 BBC Summary of World Broadcasts (CTK News Agency), 'Slovakia, Bulgaria Express Solidarity with NATO Action in Yugoslavia' (8 April 1999); CTK National News Wire, 'NATO Defending Kosovo Albanians – Dzurinda' (21 April 1999); Czech News Agency, 'Slovakia Supported by France on Road to Europe – Dzurinda' (5 May 1999). At the time, the Czech Republic had just joined NATO; Slovakia was still waiting to join.

NATO statements – nor, for that matter, by the EU. The language used by both organisations was nonetheless strong. As already indicated above, NATO denounced the 'humanitarian catastrophe' in Kosovo. The EU condemned the 'extreme and criminally irresponsible policies and repeated violations of United Nations Security Council Resolutions by the Federal Republic of Yugoslavia.'[71]

In all three countries, France, Germany and the UK, there was little domestic pressure on the governments to use the specific term 'genocide', and where there were MPs or commentators or NGOs using the term they were largely in synch with (rather than anticipating) governments.[72] In fact, there was actually considerable scepticism about the use of the term (outside of the UK). This is the first case considered in this book in which the social norm against genocide was contested: the wide definition of genocide used in public discourse and whether military force should be used were questioned in the press. In some of the public debates, doubt was expressed as to whether 'ethnic cleansing' was genocide. But the real controversy was over whether the rhetoric was instrumental, just a form of propaganda. Several observers and critics argued that the term was being used cynically, to justify the war.

On 31 March, US National Public Radio host Ray Suarez dedicated a show to the topic 'persuasion, language, politics and Kosovo', and asked:

> Try to think of the number of times you've heard the word 'genocide' over the past several weeks. There are two million people in Kosovo, some 3000 have been killed in recent years. Some 125,000 have fled their homeland. Is it genocide? Have you heard a gradual change in the rationale for the Kosovo mission since the bombs started to fall last week?[73]

[71] Council of the European Union, 'Common position of 10 May 1999 concerning additional restrictive measures against the Federal Republic of Yugoslavia (99/318/CFSP)', in Official Journal of the European Union L123 (13 May 1999).

[72] Thus two key NGOs used the term to describe what was happening in Kosovo from late March (not before): International Helsinki Federation for Human Rights and Physicians for Human Rights. See the International Helsinki Federation for Human Rights press release, 'Genocide and ethnic cleansing in Kosovo' (30 March 1999), and Physicians for Human Rights, *War Crimes in Kosovo* (August 1999), p. 13. But others – Amnesty International, Human Rights Watch – did not describe the situation in Kosovo as genocide.

[73] National Public Radio, Talk of the Nation, 'Persuasion, language, politics and Kosovo' (31 March 1999). Note that the numbers Suarez uses are contestable,

On that show, the NPR diplomatic correspondent, Tom Gjelten, argued that 'the testimony from refugees is so compelling that it is very difficult, really, to question whether these terms are legitimate or not. They seem wholly legitimate to describe what's going on.' One of Suarez's guests, Professor Paul Williams agreed, stating that 'Kosovo actually provides a fairly clear case for crimes of genocide.' But another guest, Philip Gourevitch (who wrote extensively about the Rwandan genocide) pointed out that the administration was using the term because it was acting militarily, 'so they want it to be a genocide, rhetorically. I'm not saying they want to see a genocide in Kosovo, but they would rather call what's happening by its strongest possible name, and in times when they don't act, they'll want to call it by its least-powerful name because they will want to justify inaction.'[74]

Other observers at the time argued that the strong accusations of genocide were for domestic consumption. For *Le Monde*, the German press engaged in a 'demonization' of Serbia and Milošević to ensure support for German participation in the war even though it lacked a UN Security Council mandate.[75] *Le Temps* (Geneva) argued that the denunciations served to bolster support for NATO's action in general:

> The need to convince public opinion seems to justify these linguistic emphases. It seems that this terminology, fed by the witnesses to the horror of the refugees and those images of the packed trains evoking memories of evil, has had an effect, as much on opinion as on the political class. It has succeeded in painting an image of Milosevic as barbarous and bloody with whom the west cannot decently negotiate.[76]

Fischer's references to Auschwitz came in for criticism in parts of the press (and his party) – and were seen as 'just part of an attempt to calm a guilty conscience and justify NATO's bombs'.[77]

as his contention that for 'several weeks' the term had been used (by journalists and commentators, yes, but not by governments before 28 March).

74 National Public Radio, Talk of the Nation, 'Persuasion, language, politics and Kosovo' (31 March 1999).

75 Reiner Grundmann, Dennis Smith, and Sue Wright, 'National Elites and Transnational Discourses in the Balkan War: A Comparison Between the French, German and British Press', *European Journal of Communication*, vol. 15, no. 3 (2000), 309.

76 'Washington met Slobodan Milosevic à l'index', *Le Temps* (8 April 1999) (my translation).

77 'Joschka Fischer, a Sterner Shade of Green', *The Economist* (15 May 1999).

After the war, academics also criticised the use of the term. Michael MccGwire stated that 'the continued bombing was justified by describing what was happening in Kosovo (which was terrible enough) using exaggerated and emotive language, including talk of genocide which, in common parlance, clearly did not apply'.[78] (Actually in common parlance – if this is understood to be the use of the term by journalists, opposition MPs, NGOs, etc – the term would apply.) David Chandler excoriated the over-emphasis on 'genocide' in his trenchant critique of human rights and western foreign policy, *From Kosovo to Kabul.*[79]

The claims that Serbia had engaged in a genocide against Kosovar Albanians were met with counter-claims: first of all, Serbia had long (and dubiously) claimed that Albanians in Kosovo were trying to wipe out Serbs in Kosovo; this had been the core argument in the moves against Kosovo's autonomy in the late 1980s. In addition, Serbia claimed that NATO was engaging in genocide against Serbs (a claim that was sometimes repeated by Russian government officials[80]). On 25 April 1999, Serbia and Montenegro filed ten applications in the International Court of Justice against ten NATO members, for using force illegally against it, and for violating the obligations in the Genocide Convention. The ICJ argued that there was no case for violation of the Genocide Convention sufficient to justify provisional measures. Eventually the cases were dropped or dismissed on legal technicalities.[81] Such counter-claims muddied the debates on genocide, and seemed to indicate only that such language was always used instrumentally (and cynically).

The absence of international legal proceedings specifying genocide added to the controversy over the language used. On 24 May 1999, the International Criminal Tribunal for the former Yugoslavia indicted Milošević – for crimes against humanity and violations of the rules or customs of law in Kosovo, but not for genocide. In total,

[78] MccGwire, 'Why did we Bomb Belgrade?', 1.

[79] David Chandler, *From Kosovo to Kabul: Human Rights and International Intervention* (London: Pluto Press, 2002).

[80] For example, the Russian Foreign Minister Igor Ivanov accused NATO of genocide against the Serb people, shortly after the air strikes began. 'NATO Launches Third Day of Air Strikes on Yugoslavia, Russians Furious', *Agence France Press* (26 March 1999).

[81] Schabas, *Genocide in International Law*, 2nd edition, pp. 507–10.

ICTY has indicted nine Serbs for crimes committed in Kosovo – but none for genocide. In September 2001, the UN-supervised Supreme Court in Pristina, Kosovo, ruled that Serbian troops did not carry out genocide against Kosovar Albanians, but did engage in crimes against humanity and war crimes, and overturned the conviction for genocide of a Serb.[82]

However, the charges that 'emotive language' was used purely for cynical, instrumental motives are far too simplistic. Fischer's conversion to the 'intervention camp' cannot be dismissed as just an instrumental move. This criticism unfairly overlooks Fischer's long-standing position on the lessons of Srebrenica: only force can stop genocide.[83] Furthermore, Blair's views too were fundamentally shaped by his perceptions of the suffering on the ground. John Kampfner reports how shaken Blair was after visiting refugee camps in Macedonia and Albania, in April and May. Afterwards he 'likened the packing of Kosovans into trains and trucks to the fate of Jews in the Holocaust' and spoke of a battle between good and evil. Kampfner notes, 'As the scale of the human suffering became ever more apparent, so his language became more biblical.'[84] But to argue that this is purely a cynical use of language is simply too cynical itself.

So in the Kosovo case, some European governments used the term, while others did not. The term, however, was employed only after air strikes had been initiated, and it was an important part of the public debate on the war only in Germany (and to a much lesser extent, in the UK). In Germany, the definition of genocide seemed to fit the wider definition of the social norm; in the UK, the definition seemed closer to the legal norm. But the use of the term in debates about Kosovo also generated controversy (fuelled by the counter-claims from Serbia) – with doubts expressed about whether it was an appropriate descriptor, and suspicions that it was used only instrumentally

[82] 'Kosovo Assault "Was Not Genocide"', *BBC News online* (7 September 2001).

[83] See Paul Berman, *Power and the Idealists or, the Passion of Joschka Fischer and its Aftermath* (Brooklyn, NY: Soft Skull Press, 2005). It should be reiterated that Srebrenica is the main reference point (and interestingly, not Rwanda), which was what prompted Fischer to change his mind regarding military intervention.

[84] John Kampfner, *Blair's Wars* (London: Free Pres, 2003), p. 56. It should be noted that the chapter on Kosovo contains no references at all to 'genocide' – another indication of the relatively uncontroversial role that the term played in the British debates on Kosovo.

by governments. The next section examines more closely whether the use of the term altered the response to the events on the ground.

Governments' response

First of all, the influence of the legal norm is clear here: European governments pushed for investigations by the ICTY prosecutor into allegations of genocide, crimes against humanity, war crimes and so on. Those suspected of such crimes should be brought to justice. But the legal norm in the Kosovo case plays a much less important role in policy-making; punishing genocide was a side-show compared to the action that was being taken to stop it (according to the British and German governments, at least).

Plainly, however, European governments did not use 'preventing or stopping genocide' as a justification for launching NATO action against Serbia in the first place, because no one in government used the term before the war began. Human rights issues were at the forefront of their justifications, but not genocide as such. There were also other justifications for the NATO bombing, including stopping the civil war, preventing instability in the Balkans, confronting Milošević once and for all, and maintaining NATO's credibility and resolve by carrying out its threats to take action.[85]

Inserting the accusations of genocide into this mix arguably did not shift NATO's strategy in any perceptible way – not least because NATO as a whole never agreed to use such a term. And those officials and politicians who did use the term genocide did not argue for a different military strategy – instead they argued that they were already doing what was necessary to ensure that genocide did not go 'unchecked' (as Tony Blair stated in the House of Commons on several occasions), or to weaken the military machine carrying out genocidal killings (as George Robertson and Rudolf Scharping often

[85] Severe critics of the war have cited other rather more outlandish reasons, including: Clinton launched the war to distract from his troubles regarding the Monica Lewinsky sex scandal; Germany participated because it is traditionally anti-Serb; Blair was desperate to boost his domestic legitimacy on foreign policy issues; the USA was asserting its dominance over European affairs, and so forth. The problem with such arguments is that they are made without consideration paid to the international dimension, to the position of other NATO countries: why, for example, would other countries have taken so many risks just to get Clinton out of hot water?

repeated). Schröder told his Social Democratic party that 'the genocide in Yugoslavia cannot be met with pacifism'.[86] This is an example of the social norm against genocide: confronting genocide requires states to 'do something'. But the social norm in this case doesn't justify intervention to prevent genocide, but to stop it – once military action has already been initiated.

The use of the term genocide did not lead either Germany or the UK to suggest a different military strategy – even as the air strikes did not cause Serbia to capitulate quickly, and as the Serb offensive against Kosovar Albanians continued. The specific charge of genocide was not, in the public rhetoric, linked to the specific proposal that ground troops needed to enter Kosovo – a position that the UK pushed for from quite an early stage in NATO's discussions, in early to mid April.[87] In Germany, where ministers also used the term, there was outright opposition from the government – and little support from public opinion – for deploying ground troops.[88] Some of this was undoubtedly due to the widespread preference for 'zéro mort' (as was the case in Bosnia), but the opposition to German troops going into war on the ground came not only from the attachment to 'never again war' but also the historical sensitivities regarding the actions of German troops in Yugoslavia in the Second World War. Furthermore, there was concern that such a military intervention would make it more difficult to reconstruct the region afterwards.[89]

Both the German and British governments had considerable support for their positions on Kosovo from their own backbenches and the conservative opposition in parliament, and thus it is unlikely that they felt it necessary to use stronger terms to describe events in order to shore up their own positions in parliament. In general in Germany there was much cross-party support for the government's position on the NATO action over Kosovo. Opposition came from the Party

[86] 'Crisis in the Balkans: In Germany, An Echo of Kosovo in Bonn', *New York Times* (13 April 1999).

[87] Daalder and O'Hanlon, *Winning Ugly*, p. 132; Gerard Baker and George Parker, 'Reluctant Crusaders', *Financial Times* (24–25 April 1999).

[88] Likewise in the USA, where – despite the rhetoric about 'indicators of genocide' – the 'bodybag effect' influenced the American, and therefore the NATO, position: extreme reluctance to send in ground troops; avoidance of low altitude air strikes; and resistance to using Apache helicopters. Freedman, 'Victims and Victors', 339.

[89] Miskimmon, 'Falling into Line?', 565.

of Democratic Socialism (the legal successor to the old East German ruling communist party), and some members of Alliance '90/The Greens.[90]

In the UK, the government was criticised for its handling of the war – but not for agreeing to the NATO action in the first place. The Conservative Party leader, William Hague, accused the government of insufficient planning for handling the refugee crisis, while other Tories argued that NATO should have bombed more extensively from the start and that ground forces should have been deployed. The Liberal Democrat Party was on the whole supportive of the NATO action, even judging it legal under international law, though it too thought ground forces needed to be sent in.[91] For Daniel Keohane, there was support for the war because 'most Labour [MPs] and Liberal Democrats were strongly attracted by its humanitarian purpose'.[92] That humanitarian purpose could have included the view that the war was necessary to stop genocide (given the absence of contestation of the term 'genocide' in the parliamentary debates) but more likely involved the view that the war was necessary to stop the human rights violations in general (given that the term was not used frequently in debates).

A further question is whether preventing or stopping genocide became part of the public justification for some states and officials after NATO action began. Did they feel that it was necessary to use such a term to ensure public support for the war, to legitimise the war? Certainly some of the commentators cited above thought so. Answering this question in any definitive way is impossible: when government archives are opened we may have a better idea of the reasoning behind the use of the term. But we also do not know what the impact of the rhetoric was on public opinion: as far as I can tell, there were no polls involving questions specifically on 'genocide' in Kosovo and whether this increased support for the war. There are, however,

[90] Representative views of the parties are apparent in the debates in the Bundestag on 25 and 26 March 1999 (Amtliche Protokolle, 25 March 1999, 030.Sitzung, 26 March 1999, 031.Sitzung, and 15 April 1999, 032.Sitzung; translation by DM). On the parliamentary debates, see also Miskimmon, 'Falling into Line?', 565–6.

[91] See Dan Keohane, 'The Debate on British Policy in the Kosovo Conflict: An Assessment', *Contemporary Security Policy*, vol. 21, no. 3 (2000), 83–8.

[92] Keohane, 'The Debate on British Policy in Kosovo', 91.

numerous polls on public support for NATO's campaign, and these show substantial support in several countries – right from the beginning of the campaign.

The German Ministry of Defence conducted a weekly poll during the air campaign, asking the same questions. The percentage agreeing with NATO's intervention in the Kosovo conflict with air strikes never dipped below 52.1 per cent (in mid May). On 26–27 March, 62.6 per cent agreed with NATO's intervention; a few days later, on 10–12 April, 59.1 per cent still did. These polls would suggest that the use of the term genocide from 28 March actually caused support to dip (a bit) – but again, we simply don't know why it dipped.[93]

The Economist reported the polls a few weeks into the campaign, showing general and rising support for air strikes in some countries, with the exception of Italy (see Table 6.1). Is the rise in support between the final days of March and beginning of April due to the use of the term genocide? The answer to that question is unknowable, and it is worth pointing out that support rose also in France, where the government conspicuously avoided the term. Support remained strikingly low in Italy, where the government used the term briefly at the end of March.

Philip Everts has analysed public opinion on the war in several NATO countries, and argued that there were initial hesitations but that support for the war grew in the early phases of the war, and was then largely maintained until the war ended. He concludes that:

> Apart from the obvious reason that public opinion was willing to follow its leaders in supporting or even joining in NATO's air strikes because of a basic feeling of solidarity with other countries in the Atlantic alliance, the most important parameters of the evolution of support for the military actions in their various forms seem to be: (1) the perceived legitimacy of the actions and the interests involved; (2) the perceived effects of the actions, i.e. perceptions of success or failure; and (3) the sustainability of the idea

[93] Detlef Puhl, 'Addendum: Kosovo and German Public Opinion', in Wolfgang-Uwe Friedrich, ed., *The Legacy of Kosovo: German Politics and Policies in the Balkans*, German Issues no. 22 (American Institute for Contemporary German Studies, The Johns Hopkins University, 2000), pp. 51–56. The percentage opposed to an operation involving ground troops never dipped below 62.3 per cent.

Table 6.1. *Public support for air strikes (%)*

UK	26 March	2 April
	69	75
France	27 March	7 April
	40	50
Germany	24 March	1 April
	57	63
Italy	24 March	31 March
	25	37

Source: 'Troops or no troops? Not by Bombs Alone', *The Economist*, 10 April 1999.

of a 'clean war', a war without bloodshed, first of all on one's own side, but perhaps also with respect to civilian casualties on the other side.[94]

What is not clear is whether the 'perceived legitimacy' of NATO's actions is linked to the increased rhetoric on genocide (or in general on crimes against humanity, ethnic cleansing, and so forth) from the end of March, or the news and images of the developments on the ground in Kosovo (Serb assaults on civilians, ethnic cleansing, the flight of refugees, and so forth). We simply don't have the polling evidence with specific reference to the issue of genocide.

Conclusion

This is the one case considered in this book where the term genocide was used by some governments at the same time that strong military action was taken – but the connection between the two is hard to discern. This was not a war launched to prevent or stop genocide per se. Once air strikes began, and the term was used by some policy-makers, the military strategy did not shift – even though air strikes were not having the desired effect and may even have accelerated human rights abuses on the ground. There was too much opposition to ground troops – and the argument that deploying them might have

[94] Philip Everts, 'War Without Bloodshed? Public Opinion and the Conflict over Kosovo', in Philip Everts and Pierangelo Isernia, eds., *Public Opinion and the International Use of Force* (London: Routledge, 2001), p. 253.

been necessary to stop a genocide (or ethnic cleansing) was never made forcefully. In a sense, then, the accusations that Serbia was conducting a genocide in Kosovo are peripheral in the war.

At the same time, Gourevitch's point about the language used merits further consideration: when governments don't want to act, they avoid using strong language such as 'genocide'; when they are acting, it's in their interests to use the strongest language possible. In the case of Kosovo, where NATO acted without UN Security Council authorisation, then legitimising the war on the basis of a 'higher law' may have been seen as necessary. Certainly a strong normative case could be made for intervening forcefully to prevent a genocide – if there are reasonable grounds indicating that such an outcome is likely but not yet reality. But neither the UK nor Germany invoked the legal or social norm in such a direct manner. And it should be left as an open question whether they really maintained that the term described subsequent events appropriately (perhaps the archives will reveal the answer to that question). In any event, not all European governments used the term so that not all governments felt it necessary to justify NATO action in such a manner.

The Kosovo case may, however, signal the high point for the social norm against genocide on policy-makers. The war was so controversial that it generated a backlash against humanitarian intervention, or more specifically, against the use of military force for 'humanitarian purposes'.[95] US policy after the 9/11 terrorist attacks only strengthened that backlash, with the wars in Afghanistan and Iraq further discrediting military intervention in general. The impact this may have had on the Darfur case is discussed in the next chapter.

[95] Interviews with officials from the German Foreign Ministry, Berlin, 10 October 2008.

7 *Darfur*

Darfur has been the first purported genocide to come along during all the international discussions on the 'responsibility to protect' – itself the end result of discussions about the legitimacy and legality of humanitarian intervention after the Kosovo War. It has often been seen as a test case for the principle, but a failed one, given that violence continues to wrack the region. It also is the first purported genocide to come along after wars were launched in Afghanistan and Iraq (the latter spectacularly controversially). The occasional use of humanitarian arguments justifying intervention in those two countries coloured the debates on the responsibility to protect – stoking suspicions that such justifications really served only to mask the interests of powerful western states, and therefore fostering resistance to the general principle of the responsibility to protect. The fact that Saddam Hussein was also accused of perpetrating genocide against the Kurds fuelled suspicions that allegations of genocide could be used to justify intervention.

The legal norm against genocide remained the same. As already noted, the principle of the responsibility to protect, as articulated by the UN in September 2005, does not provide for any 'automatic' intervention to protect a people from genocide, war crimes or crimes against humanity. Thus the only clear legal obligation on governments remains that of punishing perpetrators of genocide. But what developments since 2001 have done is to make the social norm against genocide even more controversial: the principle of the responsibility to protect seems to bolster the case for 'doing something' in the event of a genocide, which heartens some activists but terrifies opponents of intervention in general and in the specific case of Darfur.

The Darfur case has sparked an extraordinary debate – amongst academics, policy-makers, activists, bloggers – about whether it is one of genocide, and what the policy response should be. This debate marks out the Darfur case from the other post-Cold War cases considered in this book, though the extent of activism on Biafra is similar. Most of the debate really centres not on the genocide question, but on what should follow: those who oppose intervention tend to argue that it is not a genocide; those who argue that it is a genocide tend to support some form of military intervention, though not always.[1] A rather disturbing proportion of the debate in the 'blogosphere' is vitriolic and vituperative.

The divisions on the question of genocide are apparent amongst academics, commentators and NGOs. Four experts on African politics told the UK House of Commons International Development Committee that they were all 'uncomfortable with the portrayal of the Darfur conflict as genocide and *with the consequence* that Sudan should be subject to punitive sanctions and military intervention.'[2] The British columnist Jonathan Steele argued that the conflict in Darfur was just a brutal civil war, in which the Sudanese government had overreacted, but his overall argument was that 'sending foreign troops into Sudan without Khartoum's consent would be nothing short of disaster.'[3] One critic of such views says that this is an example of 'the latest tactic to defuse pressure over Darfur: presenting one extreme option – Western military intervention – as the only alternative and then explaining that it would not be feasible because it would bring down the wrath of the Arab world, especially after Iraq.'[4] What it certainly shows is the force of the social norm against genocide: if there is a genocide ongoing, then intervention should follow. Those

[1] For example, in August 2009, Save Darfur called for US and international community support for peace talks, impunity for perpetrators of human rights violations, and support for the full deployment of the AU-UN hybrid operation in Darfur (UNAMID) – not for forcible intervention by western troops. See the pages on 'Responding to Genocide' on the website www.savedarfur.org (accessed 5 August 2009).

[2] Emphasis added. Suliman Baldo, James Morton, Roland Marchal and Alex de Waal, 'Darfur in 2004: the many faces of a conflict', in United Kingdom House of Commons, International Development Committee, 'Darfur, Sudan: the responsibility to protect', fifth report of session 2004–05, vol. II, HC-67-II, p. EV109.

[3] Jonathan Steele, 'Sorry George Clooney, but the Last Thing Darfur Needs is Western Troops', *The Guardian* (19 September 2006). Steele, however, seems to ignore that UN missions have repeatedly found the Sudanese government mainly responsible for heinous crimes. He also interprets – incorrectly – the Genocide Convention as requiring forcible intervention to stop genocide.

[4] Lebor, '*Complicity with Evil*', p. 245.

opposed to intervention turn it around to argue there is no genocide and therefore there should be no intervention.

Another well-known African expert, Gérard Prunier, concludes that it is not a counter-insurgency gone wrong, nor is it just an ethnic conflict. He further argues it is not genocide but his definition of genocide is far stricter than that of the Genocide Convention, in that he thinks genocide is an attempt at total obliteration. 'If we use the December 1948 definition it is obvious that Darfur is a genocide, but if we use the definition I proposed in my book on Rwanda it is not.'[5] Some human rights NGOs, such as Justice Africa and the Aegis Trust, argue that it is genocide or at least 'genocidal';[6] others, such as Amnesty International and Human Rights Watch have not used the term.

All of the debate about whether or not it is genocide prompted one observer to suggest that 'It is as though one man is clubbing another on a street corner while bystanders respond with a prolonged reflection on whether the incident is premeditated murder or simple assault or even self-defense. Meanwhile, the crime continues.'[7] To what extent have European governments been reflecting while the crime continues? This chapter first summarises the background of the conflict in Darfur, and then considers the position of European governments on the 'naming' debate. It then analyses their responses to the conflict.

The conflict in Darfur

Sudan, the largest country in Africa, became independent from British-Egyptian rule in January 1956. Political instability followed, and the current President, Omar al-Bashir, came to power in a military coup in 1989. The country has been wracked by serious violence for almost three decades. From 1983, rebels from the south of

[5] Gérard Prunier, *Darfur: The Ambiguous Genocide* (London: Hurst & Company, 2007), p. 156.

[6] 'Justice Africa background briefing note: Darfur conflict, June 2004', and 'Memorandum submitted by the Aegis Trust: Darfur: management of a genocidal crisis', in UK House of Commons, 'Darfur, Sudan: the responsibility to protect'.

[7] Jerry Fowler, 'A New Chapter in Irony: The Legal Implications of the Darfur Genocide Determination', *Genocide Studies and Prevention*, vol. 1, no. 1 (2006), 36.

the country (the Sudan People's Liberation Army) battled government forces in a conflict estimated to have killed over two million people. The conflict had religious, economic and political roots; the SPLA were mainly Christian and animist, and revolted after the government tried to impose sharia law on the whole country, but the south's political and economic marginalisation and a fight to control oil resources also fuelled the conflict. In January 2005, a peace agreement was signed at Naivasha, Kenya, which provides for substantial autonomy for the south and a referendum on independence for the south in 2011. Thus far, the peace agreement has largely been respected, despite the August 2005 death of John Garang, a rebel leader and co-vice president in the new unity government.[8]

Economic and political marginalisation has also fuelled the more recent conflict in Darfur. Darfur was an independent sultanate until it fell under British rule in 1917 and was incorporated into Sudan. Tribal violence had been common in the region before 2003, particularly as drought and desertification caused conflicts over fertile land and water; Darfur has also been negatively affected by spillover from conflicts in Chad and Libya. But large-scale violence erupted in Darfur in early 2003, when two rebel groups, the Sudanese Liberation Movement/Army (SLM/A) and the Justice and Equality Movement (JEM), began a campaign against the Sudanese government. The conflict is sometimes characterised in the press as an Arab vs. black African conflict, but the population of Darfur is 'a complex ethnic mosaic',[9] though uniformly Muslim. Predominant ethnic groups include the Fur, the Masalit and Zaghawa, who are non-Arab, but there are Arab groups too, including the Baggara. With intermarriage, 'the "Arabs" are all quite black', and the groups are mainly distinguished by native tongues.[10]

In response to the rebel attacks, the government of Sudan reacted brutally: villages were bombed from the air, while the 'janjaweed'

[8] Heavy fighting did break out in Abyei, on the border between north and south Sudan, in May 2008, and there are concerns that violence may escalate in the run-up to the referendum for southern independence in 2011. 'A Gleam Among the Ruins', *The Economist* (22 November 2008).

[9] Prunier, *Darfur*, p. 4.

[10] Gérard Prunier, 'The Politics of Death in Darfur', *Current History* (May 2006), 195.

militia (and sometimes the Sudanese army) carried out ground attacks, mostly against the Fur, Masalit and Zaghawa tribes. The janjaweed (often translated as 'devils on horseback') were recruited from Arab tribes by the government to help it fight the rebel forces.[11] Civilians were deliberately targeted, with mass killings and rapes common. By May 2004, perhaps 80,000 people had been killed, 100,000 refugees had fled to Chad and one million people were internally displaced.[12] Since then, violence has continued – despite various ceasefires and peace processes – though it has become more unpredictable and widespread, as both the janjaweed and rebel forces have fragmented. At the end of 2008, it was reported that there were 2.7 million internally-displaced refugees and 300,000 refugees in Chad, and that 300,000 people had died as a result of the conflict (though from all causes, including disease and hunger, as well as violence). The Sudanese government is still considered responsible for continuing to violate human rights in Darfur, and for failing to protect civilians in Darfur from conflict, starvation and disease.[13]

In 2003 and the first half of 2004, there was little international response to the violence in Darfur. Ending the north-south war – the longest-running conflict in Africa – was the focus of diplomatic efforts and western policies towards Sudan for many years. Maintaining the momentum towards peace is often said to be a reason why the conflict in the western region of Darfur was widely ignored for many months and why there was reluctance to take any

[11] For background on the conflict, see, among others, International Commission of Inquiry on Darfur, Report of the International commission of Inquiry on Darfur to the United Nations Secretary-General, pursuant to Security Council Resolution 1564 of 18 September 2004 (Geneva, 25 January 2005), pp. 17–25.

[12] Prunier, *Darfur*, p. 91. As is usually the case, the numbers of dead are hotly contested; the numbers of refugees are more easily calculated. On the background to the conflict, see René Lemarchand, 'Unsimplifying Darfur', *Genocide Studies and Prevention*, vol. 1, no. 1 (2006).

[13] 'A Gleam Among the Ruins', *The Economist* (22 November 2008). For recent assessments of the situation in Darfur, see UN Human Rights Council, Report of the Special Rapporteur on the situation of human rights in the Sudan, Sima Samar, A/HRC/1114 (June 2009), and UN Human Rights Council, Report of the high-level mission on the situation of human rights in Darfur pursuant to Human Rights Council Decision S-4/101, A/HRC/4/80 (9 March 2007).

action which might jeopardise the north-south peace agreement.[14] As Gérard Prunier argues:

> The whole of 2003 and of early 2004, when the usual violence of the GoS [Government of Sudan] progressively metamorphosed into a quasi-genocide, were lost months during which all eyes remained fixed on Naivasha. As casualties piled up and hundreds of thousands fled their incinerated villages in Darfur, the international media and the Western chanceries kept congratulating themselves on the 'successful' development of the North-South talks, chronicling each new paper advance on the diplomatic front as if it were a great victory for peace.[15]

In addition, of course, the war in Iraq, and the tensions that created within the UN and between states, not only distracted diplomats and policy-makers but inhibited collective international action, and certainly removed the option of coercive military intervention from feasible policy responses (both for logistical reasons and because intervention was so controversial).

In 2003, the UN humanitarian coordinator in Sudan, Mukesh Kapila, became convinced that the government of Sudan was sponsoring a deliberate campaign of atrocities against civilians in Darfur; the government denied his claims. Kapila sent numerous memoranda and reports to UN headquarters that year, reporting on the atrocities, but received little by way of interest. On 5 December 2003, however, the UN head of humanitarian affairs, Jan Egeland, called Darfur 'one of the worst humanitarian crises in the world'. A few months later, in March 2004, a frustrated Kapila told BBC radio that 'This is ethnic cleansing, this is the world's greatest humanitarian crisis, and I don't know why the world isn't doing more about it.'[16] Kapila also

[14] Cooperation between Sudanese intelligence services and the CIA after the 9/11 terrorist attacks is another such reason. 'It'll Do What it Can Get Away With', *The Economist* (3 December 2005).

[15] Prunier, *Darfur*, p. 90.

[16] All quotes from the chronology on the website for the PBS Frontline programme, 'On Our Watch' www.pbs.org/wgbh/pages/frontline/darfur/etc/cron.html [last accessed 20 July 2009]. Kapila left Khartoum and the UN that same year. Some in the UN thought he had been irresponsible in speaking of genocide without consulting UN headquarters. Julie Flint and Alex de Waal, *Darfur: A New History of a Long War*, revised edition (London: Zed Books, 2008), p. 180.

compared Darfur to Rwanda (the tenth anniversary of the genocide fell in the following month).[17]

In April, UN Secretary-General Kofi Annan sent three fact-finding missions to the region, two by the Acting High Commissioner of Human Rights (to Chad, Khartoum and Darfur); and a high-level mission, to assess the humanitarian situation. The report of the Acting High Commissioner gave details of atrocities and attributed responsibility for human rights violations – 'many of which may constitute war crimes and/or crimes against humanity'[18] – primarily to the government and the militia forces, rather than to the rebel forces. It called for the dismantling of the janjaweed, access for humanitarian aid organisations, national reconciliation and an international commission of inquiry to look into the allegations of human rights violations in Darfur and identify precisely which crimes have been committed and by whom.[19] The high-level mission also described human rights violations and set out priorities for humanitarian operations.[20]

At this point, the three main European countries were not agreed on whether the matter should be put before the Security Council: Germany (a non-permanent member of the Security Council in 2003–4) was pushing for this, but France (initially) and the UK were not, because they prioritised trying to resolve the north-south conflict in Sudan.[21] France, however, then successfully lobbied for a reference to Darfur to be made in UN Security Council Resolution 1547 of 11 June 2004, which mainly addressed the Naivasha peace process, in spite of British and American opposition to mentioning Darfur. According to one account, France's position went from 'we don't want to do this' to 'we can't let this go on', because it feared the conflict would spread to Chad.[22]

[17] Hugo Slim, 'Dithering over Darfur? A Preliminary Review of the International Response', *International Affairs*, vol. 80, no. 5 (2004), 815.

[18] UN Economic and Social Council, Report of the United Nations High Commission for Human Rights and follow-up to the world conference on human rights: situation of human rights in the Darfur region of the Sudan, E/CN.4/2005/3 (7 May 2004), 22.

[19] UN Economic and Social Council Report E/CN.4/2005/3, 24–5.

[20] Slim, 'Dithering over Darfur?', 818.

[21] Lebor, '*Complicity with Evil*', pp. 160–1.

[22] Lebor, '*Complicity with Evil*', pp. 185–7; quotes on p. 187.

On 30 July 2004, the UN Security Council issued its first major resolution (no. 1556) on Darfur, which, among other things, demanded that the government of Sudan disarm the janjaweed militias and requested that the Secretary-General report monthly on progress on that matter. It also imposed an arms embargo on non-governmental entities and individuals in Darfur. This was the first of many Security Council resolutions on Darfur, most of which have been ignored by the parties on the ground, to little reaction by the Security Council. The possibility of using sanctions to press the Sudanese government into complying with Security Council resolutions was opposed by China (with a veto on the Security Council) and the African countries. In March 2005, the UN Security Council imposed a travel ban and assets freeze on individuals who constitute a threat to stability, or commit violations of humanitarian or human rights law. But over a year later, in April 2006, the first individuals targeted by the 'smart sanctions' were finally named – and there were only four of them, from both sides of the conflict (thus scrupulously adhering to the usual discourse of 'moral equivalency' of all sides in a conflict).[23] These are the only sanctions that the Security Council has approved with respect to the Darfur conflict. From September 2004, the African Union sent a mission to Darfur, to try to monitor and discourage violence, but the AU mission has always been overstretched, with too few personnel spread out across a large territory, and highly dependent on western financial and logistical aid. From early 2008, the UN joined the AU in the UN African Mission in Darfur (UNAMID), but it too has been 'impotent' and overstretched.[24]

In the meantime, in mid 2004 a 'genocide debate' took off in the USA. In March 2004, the *New York Times* columnist Nicholas Kristof began publishing a series of articles accusing the Sudanese government of committing genocide in Darfur. In July, the Committee of

[23] UN Security Council Resolution 1591 (2005); on the list of individuals affected by the sanctions, see the information page of the Sudan Sanctions Committee: www.un.org/sc/committees/1591/index.shtml [last accessed 28 July 2009]. See Samuel Totten, 'Saving Lives in Darfur, 2003–06?: Lots of Talk, Little to No Action', in Amanda Grzyb, ed., *The World and Darfur: International Response to Crimes against Humanity in Western Sudan* (Montreal and Kingston: McGill-Queen's University Press, 2009), p. 193.

[24] 'A Gleam Among the Ruins', *The Economist* (22 November 2008).

Conscience of the US Holocaust Memorial Museum in Washington, DC issued a 'genocide emergency' (the highest level of warning, indicating that genocide is imminent or ongoing) regarding Darfur. Numerous human rights and civil rights groups called for use of the genocide label, as did newspaper editorials, with the expectation that doing so would prompt intervention. Several activist groups created the Save Darfur Coalition, which included the Genocide Intervention Network and a student group called 'Students Taking Action Now! – Darfur (STAND)'. A million Americans sent postcards to US President Bush asking for intervention to end the 'first genocide of the 21st century'.[25] On 22 July, the House of Representatives and the Senate passed concurrent resolutions calling the situation in Darfur a genocide and requesting the USA to take either multilateral or unilateral action to end it.[26] The domestic debate in the USA is a classic example of the social norm against genocide: the situation in Darfur was widely considered to be a genocide, and intervention to stop it was demanded.

Yet it was also clear at this stage that other international actors were less sure about the question of genocide. On 10 June 2004, UN Secretary-General Kofi Annan gave the commencement address at Harvard University; protesters against the genocide in Darfur demonstrated in Harvard Square and told him he should have gone to Darfur, not Harvard. He declared: 'Based on reports that I have received, I can't at this stage call it genocide ... There are massive violations of international humanitarian law, but I am not ready to describe it as genocide or ethnic cleansing yet.'[27] Gérard Prunier argues that Annan wanted to avoid using the term because doing so would force the

[25] Flint and de Waal, *Darfur*, p. 180; see pp. 179–87 for more on the debate in the USA. They cite one policymaker who called the campaign 'the largest American activist movement on Africa since the anti-Apartheid campaign' (p. 184). The involvement of actors such as Mia Farrow, Don Cheadle and George Clooney has attracted considerable media attention. There was a concerted effort to characterise the 2008 Beijing Olympics as the 'Genocide Olympics', to put pressure on the Chinese government to put pressure on Sudan to halt the violence. China may indeed then have convinced Sudan to accept UN involvement in the AU peacekeeping efforts.

[26] On the US debate, see Scott Straus, 'Darfur and the Genocide Debate', *Foreign Affairs*, vol. 84, no. 1 (January/February 2005).

[27] Doug Saunders, 'Is the Brutality in Sudan Genocide?', *The Globe and Mail* (19 June 2004); Prunier, *Darfur*, p. 142.

UN to act, with no guarantee that states would provide him with the means to do so.[28]

In July 2004, the US Department of State and US Agency for International Development hired an NGO, the Coalition for International Justice, to investigate the question of whether genocide was taking place in Darfur. It should be noted that this is the first time since Biafra that a state sent a team specifically to investigate whether a genocide was taking place (although the team that was sent to Biafra was sent to prove a genocide was not taking place). The 'Atrocities Documentation Team' interviewed 1,136 refugees from Darfur who were in camps in Chad. Their report, published in September 2004, stated that the government and janjaweed forces were coordinating attacks on villages, and that there was a clear pattern of atrocities in the region.[29] Following this, on 9 September, US Secretary of State Colin Powell told the Senate Foreign Relations Committee that the Sudanese government and janjaweed were committing genocide in Darfur:

> we concluded – I concluded – that genocide has been committed in Darfur, and that the government of Sudan and the Janjawid [sic] bear responsibility, and that genocide may still be occurring ... we believe the evidence corroborates the specific intent of the perpetrators to destroy a group 'in whole or in part' – the words of the [genocide] convention. This intent may be inferred from their deliberate conduct.[30]

However, at the same time, Powell declared that 'no new action is dictated by this determination'. It would not alter US policy, and certainly not lead to unilateral intervention. In 2007, the USA tightened its existing economic, trade and financial sanctions against Sudan (imposed in 1997), barring more companies and individuals from access to the US banking system and business with the USA. But that is the extent of the coercive action it has taken. It has certainly never been keen to be militarily involved, even just as part of a peacekeeping force (especially, but not only, because of the wars

[28] Prunier, 'The Politics of Death', 198.

[29] For a summary of the report, see Eric Markusen (a member of the team), 'Three Empirical Investigations of Alleged Genocide in Darfur', in Grzyb, ed., *The World and Darfur*.

[30] Cited in Markusen, 'Three Empirical Investigations', p. 99.

in Iraq and Afghanistan) – to the great disappointment of activists in the USA.

The US government has since repeated the claim that genocide is being perpetrated in Darfur; Bush, for example, said this to the UN General Assembly in September 2006.[31] The US State Department's annual human rights reports also repeated the accusation, with the 2008 report stating that 'Civilians in Darfur continued to suffer from the effects of genocide.'[32] But in June 2009, the USA softened the language: US President Obama's special envoy to Sudan, Scott Gration, said that the Sudanese government was no longer engaging in a coordinated campaign of mass murder, and that instead 'what we see is the remnants of genocide'.[33]

On the genocide question, the US government has by and large stood alone, as will be seen in the following section. This may have served its interests. Eric Heinze argues, 'when Bush administration officials began using the rhetoric of genocide to describe Darfur, accompanied by no intention whatsoever of intervening, they arguably had a better understanding of the precise nature of the legal obligation under the Genocide Convention than had Clinton administration officials during Rwanda.'[34] By referring the matter to the UN Security Council in September 2004, the USA fulfilled its obligation to prevent and punish genocide – and bumped the problem up to the UN. And once the UN commission of inquiry had decided that it was not a case of genocide, the pressure to intervene subsided. The USA could continue to talk tough, which was good for its domestic audiences, but 'the United States was employing the rhetoric of genocide *as a substitute* for more-decisive action.'[35] Similarly, two of the investigators on the US State Department's Darfur Atrocities Documentation Project argued that such investigations can 'serve as a way to display a show

[31] 'Darfur: Will they be Rescued?', *The Economist* (23 September 2006).

[32] United States Department of State, Bureau of Democracy, Human Rights and Labor, 2008 country reports on human rights practices, Sudan (25 February 2009).

[33] Colum Lynch, 'Sudan's "Coordinated" Genocide in Darfur is Over, U.S. Envoy Says', *The Washington Post* (18 June 2009).

[34] Eric A. Heinze, 'The Rhetoric of Genocide in U.S. Foreign Policy: Rwanda and Darfur Compared', *Political Science Quarterly*, vol. 122, no. 3 (2007), 374.

[35] Heinze, 'The Rhetoric of Genocide', 376.

of action while still skirting the responsibility to take decisive action to stop the killing.'[36]

In September 2004, the USA requested the UN Security Council – under article 8 of the Genocide Convention – to take action as it considers 'appropriate for the prevention and suppression of genocide'. This is the only time article 8 has ever been activated. As a result of the US request, the UN Security Council agreed on 18 September 2004 that the Secretary-General should establish an international commission of inquiry on Darfur, which would investigate the allegations of human rights violations and determine if acts of genocide had occurred. Over the next few months, the commission visited Sudan and Chad, and interviewed refugees as well as members of the Sudanese government. The commission's report was released on 25 January 2005. It established that the Sudanese government and the janjaweed 'are responsible for serious violations of international human rights and humanitarian law amounting to crimes under international law.' The crimes 'may amount to crimes against humanity'.[37] As for violations by rebel forces, the Commission 'did not find a systematic or a widespread pattern to these violations', but that some of them may amount to war crimes.[38] More controversially, the Commission argued that the Sudanese government had not pursued a policy of genocide. While it found evidence that acts prohibited by the Genocide Convention were committed against members of a group protected under the Convention, the essential element for determining genocide – intent – was lacking. Why? Because the attackers did not kill everyone but instead forced them into displaced persons' camps, villagers with mixed Arab-African populations were not attacked, and some civilians were just beaten and not killed.[39]

Some commentators have praised the UN commission of inquiry for presenting a 'clearly reasoned and accurate' analysis; others have criticised it for not recognising that 'the facts clearly suggest that the

[36] Samuel Totten and Eric Markusen, 'The US Government Darfur Genocide Investigation', *Journal of Genocide Research*, vol. 7, no. 2 (2005), 289. They also argued – perfectly in line with the social norm against genocide – that: 'nations that have ratified the UNGC [UN Genocide Convention] are morally obligated to do all they can to halt a genocide once the latter is detected' (p. 289).

[37] Report of the International Commission of Inquiry on Darfur, p. 3.

[38] Report of the International Commission of Inquiry on Darfur, p. 4.

[39] Report of the International Commission of Inquiry on Darfur, pp. 124–32.

crimes committed in Darfur are genocide'.[40] Samuel Totten noted, 'Speculation abounds as to whether the United Nations purposely avoided describing the crisis in Darfur as a case of genocide, knowing that if it did it could obligate the UN, under the UN Convention on Genocide, to take action (including, if merited, force).'[41] Eric Reeves, a well-known critic of the Sudanese government, lambasted the report as 'a document fatally compromised in its moral and intellectual integrity. It addresses the essential question of genocide in Darfur with neither logical rigor nor adequate commitment to the evidence available.'[42] Jerry Fowler argued that the UN commission erroneously applied a 'beyond reasonable doubt' standard, where it only needed to make a threshold finding on the basis of which the UN Security Council could take further action. Furthermore, the application of the standard 'is all the more erroneous in light of the constraints placed upon it by the amount of time available, as well as the continued perpetration of the very crimes it was supposed to investigate.'[43] Eric Markusen cited evidence that the head of the UN commission, Antonio Cassese, had told members of the commission before the inquiry that in his opinion genocide was not occurring, thus possibly swaying others' opinions as well. Furthermore, the Sudanese government actively tried to obstruct the commission's gathering of evidence.[44] A report published by Physicians for Human Rights at almost the same time, in February 2005, based on investigations in Chad refugee camps, concluded that genocide was ongoing, and there was ample evidence of genocidal intent.[45]

Another scholar has noted that the UN commission report had immediate consequences, as talk of genocide in Darfur died down, and attention shifted elsewhere. 'Avoidance of the signifying label

[40] For praise, William Schabas, *Genocide in International Law*, 2nd edition, p. 653; for criticism, see Jennifer Trahan, 'Why the Killing in Darfur is Genocide', *Fordham International Law Journal*, vol. 31, no. 4 (2008), 1056.

[41] Totten, 'Saving Lives in Darfur, 2003–06?', p. 192.

[42] Eric Reeves, Report of the International Commission of Inquiry on Darfur: a critical analysis (Part II), February 6, 2005, conclusion. Available at www.sudanreeves.org [last accessed 13 April 2010].

[43] Jerry Fowler, 'A New Chapter in Irony: The Legal Implications of the Darfur Genocide Determination', *Genocide Studies and Prevention*, vol. 1, no. 1 (2006), 35.

[44] Markusen, 'Three Empirical Investigations', pp. 104–5.

[45] Markusen, 'Three Empirical Investigations', pp. 106–8.

"genocide" in the media leads to a downgrading of attention to, and salience of, Darfur among the public at large, their elected representatives, and policy makers.'[46]

The UN commission recommended 'strongly' that the Security Council refer the situation in Darfur to the International Criminal Court, so that the ICC could prosecute persons responsible for the most serious crimes; it identified a number of such individuals (but kept the list out of the public domain) and recommended that the file be handed over to the ICC prosecutor.[47] These recommendations, of course, raised a particular problem for the USA: the Bush Administration's deep and vociferous hostility to the ICC was infamous, and it initially suggested that yet another ad hoc tribunal be set up.[48] European governments, particularly France and the UK, supported referral to the ICC, and in the end on 31 March 2005 the UN Security Council did refer the situation in Darfur to the ICC prosecutor (UN Security Council Resolution 1593 (2005)). The USA (along with Algeria, Brazil and China) abstained rather than block the move.

The ICC Office of the Prosecutor then opened an investigation into the situation in Darfur. In April 2007, the ICC indicted two individuals (Ahmad Harun, Sudanese Minister of State for the Interior, 2003–4, and Ali Kushayb, a janjaweed leader) for crimes against humanity and war crimes. The Sudanese government refused to arrest or surrender them. In May 2009, a rebel leader from north Darfur handed himself over to the ICC, in response to a summons to appear in court to face charges of murder and attacking peacekeepers.

More explosively, in July 2008, the ICC prosecutor applied for a warrant for the Sudanese President, Omar al-Bashir for the crime of genocide, crimes against humanity and war crimes. His case argued that from March 2003, al-Bashir tried to destroy in part the Fur, Masalit and Zaghawa groups: 'the goal was not simply to defeat a rebellion, but to destroy those ethnic groups whose members

[46] William F. S. Miles, 'Labeling "Genocide" in Sudan: A Constructionist Analysis of Darfur', *Genocide Studies and Prevention*, vol. 1, no. 3 (2006), 260.

[47] Report of the International Commission of Inquiry on Darfur, pp. 4–5, 145–49.

[48] Prunier, *Darfur*, p. 143.

challenged his power.'[49] This was the first occasion on which the ICC prosecutor has sought an indictment for genocide.

The prosecutor's request sparked concerns that pursuing an indictment against al-Bashir would endanger the chances of resolving the conflict in Darfur and the peace process between north and south Sudan, as well as the safety of UN peacekeepers and aid workers. But until the pre-trial chamber had ruled, neither UN members or the UN itself took any action. In early March 2009, the pre-trial chamber issued a warrant for the arrest of al-Bashir for crimes against humanity and war crimes, but not for genocide, as a majority of the chamber ruled that there was not yet enough evidence for genocide. The prosecutor appealed that verdict in July 2009, and in February 2010, the Appeals Chamber directed the pre-trial chamber to reconsider its decision, as the pre-trial chamber had used a standard of evidence that was higher and more demanding than what was required. On the day of the original indictment in March 2009, Sudan expelled thirteen western aid agencies and asked the UN Security Council to suspend the indictment (which under the ICC statute it can do, one year at a time). While three of the five permanent members of the Security Council are not parties to the ICC statute and might be willing to consider suspending the indictment, France and the UK are staunch supporters of the ICC and would be extremely unlikely to take such a step.

Naming genocide?

In stark contrast to the US government's use of the term genocide in relation to Darfur, no European government has used the term consistently, and almost never since the UN commission's report was published. Government ministers and officials often justified their non-use of the term by referring to the UN's classification of the conflict as not (yet, at least) a genocide; this even though the exact same governments in the case of Germany and the UK used the term genocide to describe Kosovo when few others had. As in previous cases, backbench and opposition MPs have used the term, as have activists,

[49] International Criminal Court, 'Situation in Darfur, The Sudan: public summary of prosecutor's application under Article 58', document no. ICC-02/05 (14 July 2008), paragraph 7.

journalists and editors. There is, however, also more outright opposition to the use of the term from respected human rights organisations and experts, as noted above, which means that in Europe there is less of a groundswell of public opinion pushing for governments 'to do something about genocide in Darfur'.

When the genocide debate was in full swing in the USA, in the summer of 2004, European governments were under some pressure to take a stance. In September 2004, the European Parliament passed a resolution on the Darfur region which – rather gingerly – urged the 'Sudanese authorities to end impunity and to bring to justice immediately the planners and perpetrators of crimes against humanity, war crimes and human rights violations, which can be construed as tantamount to genocide'.[50] National MPs began asking questions in parliaments about their governments' response to the conflict.

In August, the EU High Representative for the Common Foreign and Security Policy, Javier Solana, sent his special representative on Sudan, Peter Feith, and a small team to Darfur for five days. They were there to investigate the possibilities for EU assistance to the African Union mission, but on his return to Brussels, Feith told the media: 'We are not in the situation of genocide there ... But it is clear there is widespread, silent and slow killing going on and village burning of a fairly large scale.'[51] However, an EU official also stated that the team was not there to see if it was genocide, for 'it's up to the United Nations ... to make this decision.'[52] In September the Council of the EU declared that it 'would welcome steps by the UNSG to establish as soon as possible an international commission of inquiry in order to immediately investigate all violations of human rights and humanitarian law in Darfur, and to determine whether acts of genocide have occurred'.[53]

[50] European Parliament, Resolution on the Darfur region in the Sudan, 16 September 2004, in Official Journal of the European Union C 140E (9 June 2005), paragraph 16.

[51] 'No Genocide in Darfur but Large-Scale Killings: EU', *Agence France Presse* (9 August 2004). It is not clear why he felt he could make such a determination on the basis of a visit of five days.

[52] 'EU Says up to United Nations to Decide Whether Atrocities in Darfur Amount to Genocide', *Associated Press* (10 August 2004).

[53] Council of the European Union, 'External relations, 13 September 2004', press release 12068/04 (Presse 251), p. 6.

The position that it was up to the UN to decide whether it was genocide or not remained the position of most EU member states. In early August, the Swedish Prime Minister Goran Persson, declared that labelling the situation in Darfur a genocide was irrelevant, and would make no difference to those being murdered.[54] The Belgian Cooperation Minister dismissed the use of the term genocide as inappropriate and simplistic.[55] The Dutch Foreign Minister, Bernard Bot, said that the EU had to wait for the UN report: 'once we have received the report it will be clear if we are dealing with genocide or not.'[56] However, the Czech Foreign Minister, Cyril Svoboda, did suggest it was genocide, on 6 September.[57]

But once the UN commission of inquiry had decided it was not a case of genocide, then this became the official stance of European governments. When the UN commission issued its report, the EU welcomed it and condemned the crimes being committed in Darfur.[58] A string of EU declarations – and of European Parliament resolutions – since then do not use the term genocide at all. Indeed, EU declarations tend not even to single out the government side for having being primarily responsible for atrocities (in contrast to the various UN reports cited above). For example, the EU was quite even-handed in its declaration on the UN commission's report, with one sentence each on the findings regarding violations by the government and janjaweed on the one hand, and rebel forces on the other.[59] Later declarations condemned the deteriorating security situation and attacks on civilians, without singling out one side as being more responsible for such attacks, though the EU did remind the Sudanese government of its responsibility to protect its

[54] BBC Monitoring Europe (from Dagens Nyheter), 'Swedish Prime Minister Speaks out on Darfur' (6 August 2004).

[55] BBC Monitoring Europe (from De Standaard), 'Belgian Cooperation Minister Deems Military Intervention in Sudan "Unfeasible"' (6 August 2004).

[56] 'EU Renews Sanctions Threat Against Sudan', *Agence France Presse* (13 September 2004).

[57] BBC Monitoring Europe (from Czech Radio), 'Czechs to Continue to Defend Human Rights in Cuba, Burma, North Korea, Belarus' (6 September 2004).

[58] Council of the European Union, 'Declaration by the Presidency on behalf of the European Union on the report by the International Commission of Inquiry on Darfur', document no. 6072/2/05 REV 2 (Presse 19) (7 February 2005).

[59] Council of the European Union, 'Declaration by the Presidency ... on the report by the International Commission of Inquiry on Darfur'.

citizens.[60] Attribution of responsibility for violence all around, as seen particularly in the case of Rwanda, helps to justify an even-handed policy response.

As for the three countries on which this book focuses, the debate followed similar lines. In the period before the UN commission issued its report, there was some hesitation as to whether the term should be used, with the occasional use by ministers (in Germany). Afterwards, there was little hesitation that it did not apply.

In general the German government did not use the term before the UN commission's report was published – though there were members of the coalition parties (SPD, Alliance 90/The Greens) who did, and even the odd slip by members of the government. Foreign Minister Joschka Fischer, who had been so outspoken regarding genocide in Kosovo, was much less keen on using the term in the case of Darfur. In September 2004, he called it 'a humanitarian catastrophe with genocidal potential'.[61] One German journalist, Gerhard Irmler of Deutschlandfunk Radio, accused Fischer of verbal contortions, creating the term genocidal potential 'so that afterwards nobody could say that the EU was looking on while genocide was committed in Sudan'.[62] (Fischer replied only that the international community had reacted strongly and prevented an even worse situation.)

Kerstin Müller, a minister of state in the Foreign Office, preferred the terms 'humanitarian crisis' and 'ethnic expulsions'.[63] She declared that 'it is not important whether one speaks of ethnic cleansing as the German government does or of genocide as some humanitarian organizations do, in any case the international community is responsible.'[64] Following the publication of the UN commission of inquiry, she told the Bundestag that she 'would not call the situation a genocide from the point of international law; the report of the international investigating committee says explicitly that it does

[60] This before the warring parties began to fragment and violence became more widespread. See, for example, Council of the European Union, 'Council conclusions on Sudan' (30 March 2006), document no. 7035/06 (Presse 69).

[61] Constant Brand, 'European Union Urges U.N. Inquiry into Allegations of Genocide in Sudan', *Associated Press* (14 September 2004).

[62] BBC Monitoring Europe, 'German Minister Hopes for Common International Position on Iran, Darfur' (13 September 2004).

[63] As in the debate in the Bundestag on 26 May 2004 (translation by DM).

[64] A. Perger von Werner, 'Das Morden in Darfur geht weiter', *Die Zeit* (19 November 2004) (translation by DM).

not consider it to be one.' She further rejected the notion that the UN commission had not used the term because otherwise the UN would have been forced to act.[65]

But the German Overseas Development Minister, Hediemarie Wieczorek-Zeul did call it a 'genocide in slow motion', in July 2004, though in the Bundestag in December 2004 she specified that the International Crisis Group had so characterised it.[66] The German Defence Minister Peter Struck went further in September 2004, labelling the atrocities genocide, and even going so far as to imply that Germany should therefore intervene: 'For me there is no doubt that we Germans also carry a responsibility for this continent. We cannot simply look on when a part of the continent is experiencing genocide.'[67] And the chairwoman of the Bundestag human rights committee, Christa Nickels (Alliance 90/The Greens), who in May 2004 led a delegation of five German MPs to Sudan that was prohibited from going to Darfur, declared that 'what is happening in Sudan equals genocide.'[68]

Opposition MPs also used the term frequently in this period. The Free Democrat Party called it a genocide; one of its parliamentarians was Gerhart Baum, a former UN Special Rapporteur for human rights in Sudan, who stated as early as April 2004 that the massacres in Darfur were a genocide.[69] This was a position he repeated in the Bundestag, as did several of his FDP colleagues.[70] MPs from the CDU/

[65] Plenary Protocol, 16 March 2005 (translation by DM).

[66] Christine Poehlmann, 'German Foreign Minister Urges Sudan to Avert "Disaster"', *Agence France Presse* (12 July 2004); German Bundestag, Plenary Protocol (3 December 2004) (translation by DM).

[67] 'German Defence Minister Calls Atrocities in Darfur "Genocide"', *Associated Press Worldstream* (18 September 2004).

[68] A. Perger von Werner, 'Im Ergenbenis Völkermord', *Die Zeit* (24 May 2004) (translation by DM).

[69] Grill von Bartholomäus, 'Wen kümmert's', *Die Zeit* (22 April 2004) (translation by DM). Baum also called for humanitarian intervention, otherwise 'we make ourselves guilty'. Interview of Deutschlandfunk with Baum: 'Druck auf die sudaneische Regierun erhöhen', *Die Zeit* (20 August 2004) (translation by DM).

[70] On 5 May 2004, Ulrich Heinrich of the FDP asked the government whether it agreed with Kapila that a genocide was taking place in Darfur. The answer was that the government was worried about developments in Darfur (but did not use the term genocide). Plenary Protocol, 5 May 2004 (translation by DM). The FDP also put forward a motion on 4 May 2004 demanding the prevention of genocide in Sudan; the motion was not voted on.

CSU party also used the term.[71] But use of the term by politicians from all sides declined after the UN commission of inquiry published its report. Discussion about the issue – as in the government's 2005 Human Rights Report – simply refers to the commission's findings that it was not.[72] The 'impulse' to use the term genocide disappeared, in accordance with advice from within the Foreign Ministry that there were both legal and policy reasons for not using the term vis-à-vis Darfur.[73] More recently, the German Commissioner for Human Rights Policy and Humanitarian Aid, Günter Nooke, stated that 'whether or not the crimes committed in Darfur amount to genocide remains for the [International Criminal] Court to decide', thus maintaining the shift to the international level of a determination of genocide.[74]

The British debate was quite similar to the German one: the government generally avoided the use of the term, while backbench and opposition MPs did not. In April 2004, after Kapila's statements to the press, MPs asked the government whether it considered that genocide had taken place in Darfur and what action would be taken as a result. The government's standard response was: 'We and the UN agree that what is happening in Darfur cannot be described as genocide.'[75] This is a rather curious stance, given that the UN had not 'agreed' that it was not genocide; the reports of the UN missions to the region that April do not make such a definitive finding (and were in any event not published until May).

[71] In particular Andreas Schockenhooff of the CDU/CSU used the term in the Bundestag. Plenary Protocol, 26 May 2004, Plenary Protocol, 3 December 2004 (translation by DM).

[72] Auswärtiges Amt, 'Siebter Bericht der Bundesregierung über ihre Menschenrechtspolitik in den auswärtigen Beziehungen und in anderen Politikbereiche' (Seventh Human Rights Report (15/5800) 17 June 2005 (translation by DM).

[73] Interview with German Foreign Ministry officials, Berlin, 10 October 2008.

[74] Speech at conference in Marburg/Frankfurt commemorating the 60th anniversary of the Genocide Convention, 3–6 December 2008 (www.auswaertiges-amt.de/diplo/en/Infoservice/Presse/Reden/2008/081206-Nooke-GenocideConvention.html [last accessed 13 April 2010].

[75] Hansard, House of Lords (19 April 2004), vol. 660, col. 3WA (response by Baroness Symons, minister of state for foreign affairs); House of Commons debate (26 April 2004), vol. 420, col. 776 (response by Chris Mullin, minister of state for foreign affairs).

After the extensive debates in the USA that summer, a few more MPs asked whether the UK government considered the situation to be one of genocide. While one minister, Chris Mullin, openly ventured that it 'may' amount to genocide, the standard answer soon became that the UN was looking into it.[76] Furthermore, Baroness Amos, leader of the House of Lords, asserted that 'The declaration that what is happening in Sudan is genocide would make a difference to the action being taken by other countries. It would not make a difference to the action being taken by this Government.'[77] In September 2004, Foreign Secretary Jack Straw said: 'Some people call it genocide, some people call it ethnic cleansing, some people call it civil war, some people call it none of the above. Whatever it is, it's a desperate situation which requires the attention of the world.'[78]

In response to a question put down in the House of Lords on what criteria the government used to establish that a genocide had not taken place in Darfur, Lord Triesman answered that 'the UK did not have sufficient evidence to judge whether the crimes perpetrated in Sudan were undertaken with the intent necessary to constitute genocide. For this reason, we pressed for the Secretary-General of the United Nations to establish an expert international commission of inquiry (ICI) to investigate reports, of violations of international humanitarian and human rights law in Darfur in 2004, and to determine whether genocide had occurred.'[79] As the UN commission reported it was not, that was the end of the matter.

The extent to which the UN commission on inquiry 'finding' regarding genocide brought the debate to a halt is evident in a report on Darfur by the House of Commons International Development Committee. The first witness to appear before the committee appeared in November 2004 and was quizzed on whether it was genocide or

[76] Hansard, House of Commons (7 September 2004), vol. 424, cols. 620–1; Mullin written answer to question by Ann Clywd MP, Hansard, House of Commons (14 September 2004), vol. 424, col. 1549W.

[77] Hansard, House of Lords (15 September 2004), vol. 664, col. 1173.

[78] Constant Brand, 'European Union Urges U.N. Inquiry into Allegations of Genocide in Sudan', *Associated Press* (14 September 2004).

[79] Hansard, House of Lords (27 June 2005), vol. 673, col. WA9. However, the Northern Ireland Secretary Peter Hain (and a well-known former anti-apartheid activist) said in April 2007 that 'the world is looking away as genocide is committed in Darfur'. 'Genocide in Darfur Ignored – Hain', *BBC News online* (29 April 2007).

not.[80] Witnesses who appeared later – and particularly after the UN report was published – were not. The committee concluded, 'In our view, the crimes committed are no less serious and heinous than genocide' (similar to the wording of the UN commission) and criticised the UN Security Council for failing to protect the people of Darfur.[81]

Likewise France also held off calling the situation in Darfur a genocide, preferring that the UN decide. Instead, terms such as 'civil war' and 'humanitarian disaster' were used. In mid 2004, the Secretary of State for Foreign Affairs, Renaud Muselier, said he 'firmly believed' that it was a civil war, and that he agreed with Kofi Annan's comment that the situation was only 'bordering on ethnic cleansing'.[82] Michele Alliot-Marie, the Defence Minister, declared it a 'humanitarian disaster' and argued that it could only be solved by political settlement.[83] In September 2004, the French Foreign Minister, Michel Barnier, told the Foreign Affairs Committee of the National Assembly that:

> Finally, on the question of knowing whether this crisis constitutes a genocide, as has been asserted by the US, it is actually indispensable to be able to describe correctly the atrocities that are currently being committed in Darfur. France has therefore asked the UN Secretary-General to give his opinion on the reality of the situation.[84]

And once the UN commission had characterised 'correctly' the atrocities committed in Darfur, then the French government could legitimately avoid the term. And as in Germany and the UK, there were MPs who did use the term genocide,[85] but government ministers usually did not.

[80] The witness was Dr Suliman Baldo, of the International Crisis Group. He did not want to get into the debate about whether it was genocide, leaving that issue to the UN commission of inquiry to decide. UK House of Commons, 'Darfur, Sudan: the responsibility to protect', p. EV3.

[81] UK House of Commons, International Development Committee, 'Darfur, Sudan: the responsibility to protect', fifth report of session 2004–5, vol. I, HC-67 (30 March 2005), summary.

[82] Cited in Samantha Power, 'Dying in Darfur: Can the Ethnic Cleansing in Sudan be Stopped?', *The New Yorker* (30 August 2004).

[83] Michele Alliot-Marie, 'When Darfur is Safer, Seek a Political Solution: France's Role in Sudan', *International Herald Tribune* (2 September 2004).

[84] Assemblée Nationale, Commission des Affaires Étrangères, Compte Rendu no. 61, 14 September 2004 (my translation).

[85] See, for example, questions put to the government by the following MPs, all of whom used the term genocide: Thien Ah Koon André (UMP) on 4 July 2006; Paul Quiles (Socialist Party), on 29 April 2004, 22 June 2004 and 19

European governments have generally been under less domestic pressure on Darfur than their American counterpart. There are pressure groups active on the issue (in addition to human rights and development NGOs there are single-issue groups, such as the German student group SOS Darfur), and there have been rallies, concerts, protest marches and petitions aimed at pressing governments to take action to stop what is often (though not always) termed a 'genocide' in Darfur. This activism undoubtedly has made it impossible for European governments to downplay Darfur.[86] In the USA religious groups have been very mobilised on the issue and they have a particularly strong impact on political debate; in Europe, few religious groups have been active on the Darfur issue, with the exception of some Jewish organisations.[87] But domestic pressure is of less salience in Europe than in the USA, and the issue was never going to appear at the top of policy-makers agendas anyway, in an era of war in Afghanistan and Iraq, proliferation concerns in Iran and North Korea, and other similar serious crises.[88] Furthermore, the unpopularity of the Iraq War arguably reduced the appeal of intervention, even for humanitarian reasons.

There was some consideration in American circles as to whether the French refusal to use the term genocide in 2004 and to support US calls for sanctions on Sudan was aimed at frustrating the USA.[89] Certainly in that year transatlantic tensions were difficult to ignore, but European countries in the 'pro-American' camp on the Iraq War were also hesitant to follow the US lead on naming genocide in Darfur. More likely is the fact that European governments did not

October 2006; Taubira Christiane (Socialist) on 12 December 2006; and Rauolt Éric (UMP) on 30 June 2006. Available on the National Assembly website: www.assemblee-nationale.fr/ [last accessed 30 July 2009].

[86] Paul D. Williams, 'The United Kingdom', in David R. Black and Paul D. Williams, eds., *The International Politics of Mass Atrocities: The Case of Darfur* (London: Routledge, 2009), pp. 202–3.

[87] As pointed out to me by James Smith, Chief Executive of the Aegis Trust, 18 August 2009.

[88] In Germany, groups of Rwandan genocide survivors did press for action, but in general the government was not under much pressure over Darfur. Interview with German Foreign Ministry officials, Berlin, 10 October 2008.

[89] Michael Shurkin, 'France and the Darfur Crisis', US-Europe Analysis Series, The Brookings Institution, Washington, DC (January 2005), p. 1. Shurkin thinks this, however, was not a decisive factor, and that rather France was more intent on building a multilateral response to the conflict.

want to call it genocide because this could invoke the social norm against genocide and pressure would increase on them to intervene, which they simply did not want to do. By not calling it a genocide, the principle of responsibility to protect is not undermined because of a consequent lack of action.[90]

Furthermore, the fact that the USA bumped the issue up to the UN level gave European governments a convenient way of deflecting any pressure on them to name the Darfur situation as a genocide: letting the UN have the final say on the matter fits comfortably with the legal norm and with the deep attachment to the UN and multilateralism in Europe. It also enabled European governments to avoid a repeat of a Kosovo-like scenario, in which they ran ahead of the international consensus on intervention.

Governments' response

First of all several governments noted that whether or not the situation in Darfur was a genocide, they would still respond the same way. The position in the USA was similar, but European governments cannot be accused of naming genocide as a substitute for action. In the House of Lords on 15 September 2004, Baroness Amos stated that

> A declaration [that it is genocide] would be a call on the international community to take greater action. We would support that action if it were taken by the UN. We have called for an international commission to investigate the allegations that have been made, but the action being taken by this Government would be no different if there were a declaration that genocide is happening in Sudan.[91]

Kerstin Müller told the Bundestag in March 2005 that 'from a political point of view, calling it genocide would not change the situation'. The matter has been referred to the ICC all the same.[92] In other words, European governments were acting perfectly in line with the legal norm: *if* it were to be decided that it was a genocide, *then* the

[90] I am grateful to Christian Schaller for this point.

[91] Hansard, House of Lords (15 September 2004), vol. 664, col. 1173.

[92] Plenary Protocol, 16 March 2005 (translation by DM). Similarly, one German MP told me that if it were genocide it would make no difference to government action. Interview in Berlin, 7 October 2008.

ICC would be responsible for prosecuting those individuals responsible for it; otherwise there is no further action required of them other than what they are already doing. And that entailed sending humanitarian aid, declaring concern, rhetorically supporting the ICC investigation, and above all backing AU 'leadership' on diplomacy and peacekeeping.

However, the line that 'naming genocide' would not change governments' response can be seen as an attempt to deflect pressure to do more. Chris Mullin clearly connected a 'finding of genocide' with military intervention. He has reported that Powell's declaration of genocide in September 2004 set 'alarm bells ringing' in the Foreign Office and that there was a feeling that as a result, 'British troops are going to end up in Darfur'.[93] But taking military action was out of the question. Although Blair reportedly considered the possibility of military intervention in July 2004, he quickly backed away from the notion, especially after the USA ruled out intervention but also because there was opposition from both the Foreign Office and the Ministry of Defence to intervention.[94] In November 2006, the German Foreign Minister Frank-Walter Steinmeier said that he could not envisage a deployment of European battle troops in Darfur and that is was an 'arrogant illusion' to think that European troops could achieve more than what the AU could.[95] The most that European governments would do militarily was eventually to send a small and limited mission in Chad and the Central African Republic. The EU mission lasted from January 2008 to March 2009, and was a 'bridging mission' before the UN could take over. As Gorm Rye Olsen notes, the mission allowed member states 'to do "something" and not least to

[93] Chris Mullin, *A View from the Foothills: The Diaries of Chris Mullin* (London: Profile Books, 2009), pp. 490–1. His entry for 7 April 2004 (anniversary of the Rwandan genocide) states that there was 'not a hope in hell of sending troops' and so there was little that could be done about Darfur (p. 462).

[94] Williams, 'The United Kingdom', p. 199. The Foreign Office was wary of intervention – and even strong condemnation of the Sudanese regime – because of its desire to keep the north–south peace process on track, to ensure that Sudan allowed aid to be delivered, and to encourage the country to 'deliver up' the head of the Lord's Resistance Army, which used bases in southern Sudan to attack Uganda. Mullin, *A View from the Foothills*, pp. 473–4.

[95] Interview with Frank-Walter Steinmeier, 'Unser Betrag wird respecktiert', *Frankfurter Rundschau* (28 November 2006) (translation by DM).

do something with an obvious humanitarian image, such as protecting the refugees who had fled as a result of the unresolved regional crisis.'[96]

The issue of humanitarian intervention was off the agenda not just because there was little African or international support for 'outside' intervention in Darfur. As Paul Williams argues, in the case of the UK, the Iraq War 'severely undermined Britain's credibility as a norm entrepreneur for an emerging doctrine of humanitarian intervention of the "responsibility to protect". In particular, the UK's "abuse" of humanitarian justifications for the invasion of Iraq reduced the scope for achieving a broad international consensus on the circumstances in which military force could be used to protect civilians being brutalised by their own governments.'[97]

European governments have not been under much pressure to intervene, although various activists have called for intervention. In any event, the deployment of European troops in Iraq (until recently) and then Afghanistan has strained both national resources and public support in several countries. Interestingly, however, the one public opinion poll we have on this issue shows public support in France for sending troops. This poll, conducted in several countries by the Chicago Council on Global Affairs and World Public Opinion in 2006–7, covers only one major European country, France, but the findings are interesting:

> France has the largest percentage of respondents who say the UN Security Council has a responsibility to intervene to stop the violence in Darfur and favor their country contributing troops to a peacekeeping operation there. France is the only country among 10 polled where a clear majority (55%) says the United Nations has a responsibility to authorize intervention in Darfur. Nearly a third (29%) believe the international body has the right, but not the responsibility to intervene and only 8 percent say it has no such right… Large numbers of French respondents (84%) are in favor of donating French troops to 'an international peacekeeping force to stop the killing in Darfur.'[98]

96 Gorm Rye Olsen, 'The European Union and Military Conflict Management in Africa', *CFSP Forum*, vol. 7, no. 1 (2009) (www.fornet.info).

97 Williams, 'The United Kingdom', p. 205. See also Bellamy, 'Responsibility to Protect or Trojan Horse?'.

98 The Chicago Council on Global Affairs and WorldPublicOpinion.org, 'Publics Around the world say UN has responsibility to protect against

Instead of intervention, and as was the case in most of the previous episodes of purported or proven genocide considered in this book, the primary and preferred response of European governments to the bloodshed in Darfur has been 'humanitarian' in nature. That is, the foremost concern has been to get humanitarian aid into Darfur and into the displaced persons and refugee camps in Darfur and Chad. European governments and the European Commission have been generous donors of humanitarian aid to Sudan.

Secondly, in line with the legal norm – and the precedents set by the Bosnia, Kosovo and Rwanda cases – the EU, and European governments, particularly the UK and France, supported the referral to the International Criminal Court, but there has been nervousness about the implications of the ICC indictment of al-Bashir. According to one account, France and the UK initially offered Sudan a deal whereby the ICC indictment would be suspended in exchange for Khartoum handing over the other two indicted Sudanese individuals, Harun and Kushayb, committing to the peace process, and allowing UNAMID to deploy fully.[99] But this deal went nowhere, and would in any event have been very controversial, undermining their traditional and long-standing support for the ICC in general.

Beyond humanitarian aid and ICC action, much activity of European governments vis-à-vis the Darfur conflict has been channeled through the European Union – but in support of UN and AU action. The EU has issued declaration after declaration: as of May 2007, it had issued fifty-four expressions of 'concern' about Darfur; more have been made since then.[100] The EU's stance was lambasted by former External Relations Commission Chris Patten who pointed out that there are few restrictions on Sudan, yet the 'horrors' there make the situations in Belarus, Uzbekistan or Liberia – which have been subjected to EU sanctions – 'pale into insignificance'.[101]

genocide' (4 April 2007), pp 8–9 (available at www.worldpublicopinion.org/ [last accessed 13 April 2010]).

99 Alex Duval Smith, 'Britain Blocks Prosecution of Sudan's Ruler; Human Rights Groups Criticise Strategy on Darfur', *The Observer* (14 September 2008).

100 Andrew Rettman, 'EU Giving Sudan Last Chance Amid Sanctions Threat', *EUobserver*.com (1 May 2007).

101 Andrew Rettman, 'Ex-Commissioner Attacks EU Verbalism on Darfur', *EUobserver.com* (20 March 2007).

European governments have willingly let the African Union take the lead. This was a classic case of ceding to 'African solutions to African problems', which Gérard Prunier asserts is just a politically correct way of saying 'we do not really care'.[102] European governments supported AU mediatory efforts.[103] Between 2004 and 2007 (when the UN stepped in), the EU bankrolled the AU mission in Sudan, providing about €500 million in cash, as well as equipment and assets, planning and technical assistance, and about thirty police officers, fifteen military experts and two military observers.[104] European governments have sent a handful of military and police personnel to UNAMID. The deference to the African position has been evident at the UN Human Rights Council in Geneva, where EU attempts to pass strong resolutions ensuring that the situation in Darfur is monitored by special rapporteurs or other experts, have frequently been watered down by the Africa Group.

Doing more than 'express concern', however, has been more controversial, and the EU has not tried to counter the African Union's opposition to coercive measures against the government of Sudan. It imposed an arms embargo on all of Sudan in early 2004, but has otherwise stuck to the limited sanctions approved by the UN Security Council in 2005. Going further, for the UK at least, would only 'inflame the situation in Darfur and undermine the [Naivaisha] peace agreement'.[105]

Conclusion

So in the case of Darfur, European governments – with the exception of a few wobbles – avoided the use of the term genocide. They justified their stance with reference to the 2005 UN commission on inquiry report which stated specifically that genocide was not ongoing in Darfur (though other serious crimes were). In this sense, Darfur marks a real departure in European practice: never before have European

102 Prunier, *Darfur*, p. 124.
103 Williams, 'The United Kingdom', p. 199.
104 Council of the EU, Secretariat, Fact sheet: EU support to the African Union mission in Darfur – AMIS', January 2008.
105 Cited in Alex J. Bellamy, 'Responsibility to Protect or Trojan Horse? The Crisis in Darfur and Humanitarian Intervention after Iraq', *Ethics and International Affairs*, vol. 19, no. 2 (2005), 43.

governments argued that another body was responsible for deciding on the genocide question. This is, in a way, an über-development of the legal norm: instead of national governments reaching their own determination on the question of genocide in a certain situation (whether on the basis of the 1948 Genocide Convention definition or not), the UN should be responsible for doing so. On one view this could be seen as an indication of the deep multilateral instincts of European governments; on another view, this could be seen as an abdication of responsibility. If the UN is to decide whether it is a genocide, then it is the UN's responsibility to respond. And if the UN can't or won't respond, well, then there's not much more to be done. Certainly at the very least this is a convenient way to deflect any domestic or international pressure to respond to a purported genocide.

Darfur is another departure in European practice because of the extent to which European governments asserted that it did not matter whether or not it was a genocide, their policy response would be the same regardless. On the one hand, this could be seen as putting war crimes and crimes against humanity on the same moral and legal footing as genocide, genocide therefore not being the most serious crime demanding an appropriately serious response. On the other, the actual policy response seems to show that in any event European governments will not do much in the name of the principle of responsibility to protect, which groups several serious crimes (genocide, ethnic cleansing, war crimes and crimes against humanity) together. There is little doubt that Sudan has not protected the civilians of Darfur for the past seven years; the eventual, slow response of the AU and UN has not made up for that lack of Sudanese responsibility. But European governments shied away from arguing that Sudan has actually failed to protect civilians in Darfur.[106] They have also deflected any responsibility to act to the African Union, and tangentially, to the UN. The mantra of 'African solutions for African problems' and of strong support for the UN justifies the Europeans' response. Again, it is not difficult to see this as a departure from the European rhetorical support for *their* responsibility to protect.

[106] On this see in particular Bellamy, 'Responsibility to Protect or Trojan Horse?'.

8 *Is there a European way of responding to genocide?*

This book has explored the European approach to genocide, beginning first with an analysis of European governments' attitudes towards the development of the legal norm against genocide, and then an analysis of their responses to various purported or proven genocides since the end of the Second World War, including four studies of the cases of Bosnia, Rwanda, Kosovo and Darfur. This chapter first reviews the main findings of this study, and then considers what European attitudes and practice might mean for the development of the legal and social norms against genocide.

The Europeans and genocide

As seen in Chapter 2, the attitude of European governments in the negotiations on the Genocide Convention were quite varied. The UK's hostility stands out, though the reticence of the Netherlands is also noteworthy. To be fair, some of the criticisms both governments made of the Convention do ring true, sixty years on, such as Shawcross's argument that 'genocide committed by States was punishable only by war' or Stikker's contention that 'the treaty would thus have little effect where it is most needed and would be abused for purposes of propaganda where it is needed least'. Many contemporary critics of the Convention might concur that is a 'useless' document and some might even agree that it was 'a complete waste of time' to negotiate it and that it added little to international human rights law.

But the Convention did – for all its faults – embody the promise of 'never again', a promise no 'civilised nation' could renounce, especially on the continent scarred by the Holocaust. And hence, once the troublesome problem of extradition was solved, European countries eventually fell into line and ratified or acceded to the Convention, and altered their domestic legislation accordingly. They accepted the legal norm, mostly because it was what 'civilised nations' do. Constructivist insights regarding the influence of international norms on states – and particularly the connection to state identity – seem especially pertinent here.

The rest of the book then considered the impact of the legal and social norms on European governments. To recap, the legal norm is that of the Genocide Convention, with the definition of genocide therein and the obligations on governments to prevent and punish the crime. The social norm encompasses a wider, more flexible, definition of genocide and requires states to try to stop genocide when it is occurring, including, if necessary, by intervening militarily.

Martha Finnemore has suggested that legal norms 'command compliance' because foreign policy-makers have legal training, or because there is a particular authority vested in law in Europe, or because they could face enforcement of the legal norm by other states.[1] But in the case of the legal norm against genocide, compliance is fairly easy and states do not fear they will face enforcement of the norm by other states. While not negligible, the obligations imposed on states by the legal norm are not that onerous – particularly because for four decades the obligation to punish fell largely on governments of states where genocide had taken place, as there were no international tribunals to prosecute the crime if those governments did not do so. Now there are such tribunals, and cooperation with them can pose difficulties for states. But in comparison with the social norm, the formal expectations of state behaviour in the Genocide Convention are low. Furthermore, European governments are confident of not having violated the inherent prohibition in the Convention on committing genocide, and have generally not feared being accused of perpetrating or abetting genocide themselves.[2]

So it is therefore puzzling that European governments are so clearly reluctant to use the term genocide to describe atrocities. Only occasionally have they 'named genocide'. They rarely invoke the Genocide Convention to enable action to prevent or punish genocide, or to call

[1] Finnemore, 'Are Legal Norms Distinctive?'.

[2] In 1992, Bosnia and Herzegovina did threaten to take the UK to the ICJ for failing to uphold the Genocide Convention, but did not do so; Serbia's later cases against ten NATO countries went nowhere. And the Rwandan government has accused the French government of complicity in the genocide there. Algerian rebels also accused France of genocide in the 1950s. Neither allegation has (yet) been pursued in legal fora.

on others to comply with its obligations, or to suggest that genocide *might* be ongoing.[3] Indeed, there has even been much ambivalence towards investigating and prosecuting genocide (as per the legal norm). Yet European governments do often point out that other countries are not fully respecting other human rights norms. Why, even where it is reasonable to suspect genocide, do they avoid or resist invoking the legal norm? This is even more puzzling when we consider the moral weight of the Holocaust in Europe, which makes 'never again Auschwitz' a profoundly-felt imperative across European governments.

The broad argument considered in this study suggests that governments resist naming a genocide not necessarily because they wish to avoid the obligations arising under the Genocide Convention, but because they wish to avoid the obligations arising from the social norm against genocide. Where it becomes impossible not to name a genocide, then governments can justify limiting their action to that required under the Genocide Convention. The legal norm can be useful to states. In particular, 'in an emergency' (when genocide has to be acknowledged) it allows them to evade pressures to do more than what is required under the Convention, as per the social norm against genocide.

In a series of cases, this study sought to understand the impact of the two norms against genocide on three European governments, France, Germany and the UK. Chapter 3 considered the situation during the Cold War. In general, governments almost never used the term genocide in public to describe atrocities and often did not view the legal norm as applicable. In contrast, the term genocide was widely used by journalists, NGOs, churches, MPs (opposition and backbench), and various commentators. The resultant cry to 'do something', however, did not extend to anything so radical as military intervention, but did entail measures that would have affected state interests, such as ceasing to sell arms to, or criticising a Cold War ally.

The responses of governments to purported genocides in the forty years after the Convention was concluded were heavily influenced by Cold War dynamics, though older rivalries between European powers

[3] Arguably European governments cannot be accused of using the term recklessly, though there are numerous other governments around the world that have used the term against opponents without presenting a solid objective case for doing so.

also played a role. In the case of Biafra, the UK had its economic and geopolitical reasons for supporting the Nigerian government in its fight to quell the secessionist rebellion, and because of them, it had every interest in proving that the Nigerian government was not pursuing a policy of genocide – hence the dispatch of an observer team instructed to do exactly that. Other European countries followed British leadership. In the case of Bangladesh, behind the closed doors of the Foreign and Commonwealth Office it was believed that genocide was indeed being perpetrated by Pakistani forces, but it was equally believed that there was nothing the UK could do about it – hence the British government never denounced the Pakistani government publicly and never used the term genocide to describe the atrocities. And no other European government had a motive for doing otherwise, given the Cold War line-up of forces in south Asia. In the case of Cambodia, there were doubts about whether it classified as a genocide under the Genocide Convention (and certainly it was difficult to know for certain what was going on in Cambodia under the Khmer Rouge) but this case in particular shows the extent to which Cold War politics militated against a strong response. Other cases of possible genocide were ignored or downplayed, and most often the government response was 'we do not think it is genocide'. The apparent conversion to the norm of non-interference by former colonial powers also allowed governments to put up their hands and say, 'tis none of our business. Even if it were to be admitted that human rights violations in one country should be of international concern, the Cold War, and post-colonial politics, had the effect of making meaningful action – even expressions of concern – too costly to envisage. Governments likely avoided using the term genocide because they wished to deflect the pressure stemming from the social norm.

The end of the Cold War had the effect of making meaningful action possible (though still rather costly). It also seemed to prove that the spread of democracy would make for a more peaceful world, and hence promoting democracy and human rights became an imperative. At least, that was the rhetoric (the debate about the extent to which any part of the preceding sentence is actually true or desirable will continue for years to come). And so former colonial powers that had previously professed respect for the non-interference norm now argued that violations of human rights should call into question that norm. These developments also had the effect of strengthening

Table 8.1. *Use of the term 'genocide' by European governments, while mass killings are ongoing 'yes' in bold indicates repeated usage by more than one minister; 'yes' in normal type indicates limited usage)*

	Bosnia	Rwanda	Kosovo	Darfur
France	no	**yes**	no	no
Germany	**yes**	yes	**yes**	yes → no
UK	no	yes	**yes**	no

the social norm against genocide, in that it was now possible, and expected, that governments would take action against gross violations of human rights, including genocide. With no existential need to maintain the balance of power or protect allies, no country could expect to get away with murdering its own citizens. Or at least, again, that was the rhetoric.

So in a situation in which pressure on governments to act in accordance with the social norm can be presumed to be greater, what was the response of European governments to four purported cases of genocide in the post-Cold War period? It should be recalled here that in all four cases, the term genocide was used by commentators, activists, backbench and opposition MPs, and journalists, and there were calls for 'strong action' (to a lesser or greater extent in particular cases and particular European countries). The existence of the social norm is clear. Table 8.1 summarises the position of our three key governments on using the term genocide in the four cases.

Of note first of all is that until the case of Darfur, there was no agreement between the three countries of whether a situation was genocide or not – there was no 'European way' of naming genocide. The British and German use of the term with respect to the Rwandan genocide occurred only in the context of the EU Declaration on Rwanda, issued in mid-May 1994, so there was really little agreement by the three governments on naming genocide in this case. With respect to Darfur, after an initial wobble by some German ministers, the official European position became that of 'let the UN decide' (and with a negative finding on that, the position was 'no genocide'). It is too early to tell whether the Darfur case will be the 'European model' for future cases or not.

The only country that (at least initially) used the term genocide in all four cases is Germany, which had a very low foreign policy profile during the Cold War. But with respect to Rwanda, its usage of the term was very limited (the EU declaration and little else), and with respect to Darfur, the official position soon fell into line with that of other European governments.

Why was Germany more willing to use the term than its European partners? Of all the European countries, Germany is the one where the social norm against genocide ('never again Auschwitz') is strongest. This imperative has been a core foundation of post-war German foreign policy. The revelations about 'concentration camps' in northern Bosnia in the summer of 1992 – with imagery so redolent of the Holocaust – clearly had a profound impact on the country. With respect to Kosovo, there was also similar imagery (trains crammed with refugees) and the person held responsible for such images, Milošević, was the same as in the Bosnia case. It is easy to see why the term 'genocide' would be used by politicians and commentators. As the Balkans are of particular interest in German foreign policy, Germany could be expected to take a strong stance on events there. In both the Bosnia and Kosovo cases, furthermore, the German government's usage of the term genocide was more in line with the social norm in that 'ethnic cleansing' was seen to be genocide.

The imperative of 'never again Auschwitz', however, conflicts with the equally strong imperative of 'never again war'. Fischer's controversial (within the Green Party) conversion after Srebrenica from attachment to pacifism to a belief that war could be necessary to stop genocide illustrates the kind of turmoil that the conflicting imperatives can create. Even as Germany has shed its self-imposed limitations on the use of force, 'never again war' looms large in public opinion.[4] In any event, 'never again war' balances any domestic pressure on the German government to take drastic action along the lines of humanitarian intervention. So the social norm against genocide takes a particular form in Germany which can be seen as leaving the

[4] The deep dilemma between 'never again Auschwitz' and 'never again war' was confirmed to me by German Foreign Ministry officials (interview, Berlin, 10 October 2008). Support for German participation in the Kosovo War is now interpreted as an anomaly, suggesting that only occasionally will the imperative of 'never again Auschwitz' justify disregarding that of 'never again war'. Miskimmon, 'Falling into Line?'.

government freer to use the term genocide. Naming genocide, however, is not quite a 'substitute for action',[5] because the German government was prepared to go along with *some* coercive measures in both cases (including air strikes against Serbia). But this argument still does not help explain why the government was so quiet about genocide in Rwanda – though of course it was in plenty of company on that one. Avoidance of the term in that case may have helped to justify taking little action, particularly when the role played by Germany's close ally, France, was so murky.

France has used the term the least. The only case in which it did so was that of Rwanda, from mid May 1994, when it was under quite intense domestic pressure to do so. Otherwise the government has consistently argued that the term does not apply, and has insisted on being precise about the terms it would use in the four cases. Furthermore, France has fully embraced the view that it should be the UN or international courts that decide on the question of genocide. An answer to a parliamentary question is revealing on this; in 2004, the MP Jean-Luc Warsmann asked the Foreign Minister to list the countries where war crimes or genocide had been committed since 1990. The answer only summarised the activities of the international criminal tribunals (ICTY, ICTR, ICC and the Special Tribunal for Sierra Leone).[6]

The proposition that France avoids the use of the term genocide in order to deflect pressure stemming from the social norm against genocide is possible: in Bosnia, for example, the Mitterrand government had little inclination to switch from a 'humanitarian policy' to a more coercive one, and thus every reason not to use laden terms such as genocide. It also notably went along with the proposals to create ICTY as a 'foil' for public opinion: it could limit its response to conforming with the legal norm. Likewise, in the case of Darfur, the government has little inclination to confront the Sudanese regime over the violence there. Rwanda, of course, created a maelstrom for France, and it did end up publicly justifying its unilateral intervention as a measure to stop genocide. But with respect to Kosovo, it had apparently little problem justifying intervention on the rationales

[5] Heinze, 'The Rhetoric of Genocide in U.S. Foreign Policy', 376.

[6] Assemblée Nationale, 12ème legislature, Question no. 98701, response published in the Official Journal of 7 November 2006 on p. 11568.

NATO was giving (which did not include stopping genocide), so had no need to deflect pressure associated with the social norm. However, France in general seems to be quite careful and precise about using the term genocide, and its non-use of the term may reflect a particular approach to law and language. It should also be recalled that France was uneasy with the term back in 1948.

The UK, the most hostile to the Convention during and after its negotiation, has remained for the most part reticent to use the term genocide, except with respect to Kosovo. It steadfastly refused to use the term vis-à-vis Bosnia, generally avoided its use in the Rwandan case, and has not used it vis-à-vis Darfur. It was very ambivalent about investigating whether genocide was being perpetrated in Bosnia, and about creating the international criminal tribunals for the former Yugoslavia and Rwanda. The Kosovo case is the exception – and quite a spectacular one – and the reasons why the government used the term genocide are hard to discern, leaving us with the possibility that it was actually seen as an appropriate descriptive term. It coincided with quite forthright 'moral leadership' by the Blair government – pursuing 'foreign policy with an ethical dimension' – so it rather fits the moment. The Labour government then reverted to type in the Darfur case. The proposition that governments avoid using the term genocide because they wish to avoid the pressures generated by the social norm seems to fit the British experience, but the UK's stance may also reflect its historical animosity towards the Genocide Convention.

There are two other possible reasons why there is such reluctance by European governments, much of the time, to use the term 'genocide'. One is that using the term could be seen as debasing the experience of the Holocaust. Genocide is therefore a term that could never be used lightly. Of the three European countries considered here, the debate in France has more often shown elements of this argument. But it has clearly not played much of a role in Germany (as Germany has used the term the most) and there is little evidence that it played a role in UK debates.

The second reason is perhaps an unintended consequence of Lemkin's approach to combating genocide via international criminal law. Genocide is a crime, not (just) a violation of human rights. It is therefore an act to be punished in courts, which means that there is the burden of proving individuals are guilty of engaging in it. As a result, even though governments themselves may not have to take on that burden, reverence for the rule of law means that the approach to genocide is principally a legal one. Certainly we have seen elements of this argument often in European governments' responses to purported genocides: courts are to judge whether it *was* a genocide.[7] And governments should not sway courts by declaring beforehand that it was. However, this somewhat excessive legalistic approach can also be seen as a 'foil', allowing governments to avoid pressure to take action to prevent or stop genocide.

It is nonetheless the case that until Darfur, the practice of European governments regarding the use of the term genocide has actually been quite varied. What about policy responses? Table 8.2 summarises the actions taken by European governments together in response to the four cases in which genocide was alleged to be taking place.

The revelations about 'concentration camps' in northern Bosnia in the summer of 1992 sparked concerns that Bosnian Serbs, backed by the Yugoslav army, were engaging in genocide. Certainly the German government was convinced that they were. But Germany was hobbled by its self-imposed restraints on using force ('never again war') as well as by the suspicions of German policy prevalent not only in the Balkans but in western Europe as well. Hence Germany named it a genocide, called for stronger action, but was unwilling and/or unable to do much itself. The UK and France, on the other hand, insisted it was not genocide, but 'merely' ethnic cleansing, and that all of the 'warring parties' were behaving badly. Protecting deliveries of humanitarian aid was the most they were prepared to do – until the summer of 1995, when the USA also swung its weight behind a more coercive approach. The murder of over 7000 Muslim men in Srebrenica in July 1995 – so far the only 'proven' (that is, in a court of law) case of genocide in Bosnia – in and of itself did not prompt the air strikes that contributed to ending the war. 'Genocide' as such played a minimal part in determining the European response.

[7] One NGO, the Aegis Trust, has suggested that governments could instead use the term 'genocidal crisis' as a 'risk assessment' thus avoiding a 'legal conclusion'. 'Memorandum submitted by the Aegis Trust: Darfur', in UK House of Commons, 'Darfur, Sudan: the responsibility to protect', p. Ev97. It should be recalled that Joschka Fischer did use this sort of language with respect to Darfur, before the international commission of inquiry had published its report.

Table 8.2. *Collective policy responses by European states, through EU, NATO or UN, while mass killings and/or ethnic cleansing are ongoing.*

	Bosnia (1 of 3 governments named it as genocide)	Rwanda (all named it as genocide)	Kosovo (2 of 3 governments named it as genocide)	Darfur (no government names it as genocide)
Support for investigation into whether crime of genocide is occurring	x	x (though actually launched after genocide)		x
Clear identification and condemnation of one side as *primarily* responsible for killings			x	
Support for *ad hoc* international criminal tribunals, or prosecution by ICC	x	x	x	x
Arms embargo	x	x	x	x
'Smart' sanctions on individuals (visa bans; asset freezes)			x	x (limited)
Extensive sanctions (oil embargo; suspension of aid, etc)	x		x	

Table 8.2 (*cont.*)

	Bosnia (1 of 3 governments named it as genocide)	Rwanda (all named it as genocide)	Kosovo (2 of 3 governments named it as genocide)	Darfur (no government names it as genocide)
Support for peace-keeping by regional organisation and/or UN (but few if any troops supplied)		x (eventually)		x
Participation in multilateral peacekeeping mission (with substantial numbers of troops)	x			
Participation in coercive multilateral intervention against identified perpetrators			x	

The Bosnian case did, however, prompt the development of the legal machinery for punishing genocide, a remarkable development of international criminal law. The role of European governments in creating the International Criminal Tribunal for the former Yugoslavia is significant, though the British were not at all keen to see it created, and the British and the French stymied its operation in the first couple of years after the war. Creating ICTY had the effect of allowing

European governments to argue that it was up to ICTY to make a determination about whether genocide had been committed in Bosnia or not, and take the appropriate action to punish individuals for the crime.

The case of Rwanda is the first clear case of obvious governmental unease with the implications of naming genocide. Although the Council of the EU was actually relatively quick off the mark in calling it a genocide in mid May 1994, most EU governments chose to keep quiet about 'genocide' after that, and they steadfastly avoided identifying the side actually carrying out the genocide. This stance helped to justify a 'humanitarian policy', centred on delivering humanitarian aid and encouraging peace negotiations between all the parties on the ground. There was no appetite to intervene with military force, and the French intervention in June was (and remains) extremely controversial – as well as of dubious relevance to stopping genocide. Again in this case there was not much initial enthusiasm for creating an ad hoc international tribunal to try individuals for violating the Genocide Convention, but eventually European governments came round to supporting it. The Rwanda case has, however, cast a long shadow, sparking an exceptional outburst of the 'never again' rhetoric.

It is perhaps therefore not surprising that the eruption of violence in Kosovo in 1998–9 was met with a robust response. Contrary to some accounts, NATO governments did not justify the launching of air strikes by arguing that they were preventing or stopping a genocide. After air strikes began and after the violence and ethnic cleansing on the ground in Kosovo had accelerated, then two European governments, the German and the British, did use the term genocide to describe the atrocities. But neither of them linked their use of the term to a change of military strategy. In the British case, it was not explicitly linked to the conviction that ground troops were needed; in the German case, the option of sending in ground troops was dismissed outright. In other words, a 'finding' of genocide did not alter their behaviour, though they did repeatedly state that what they were doing was stopping genocide (even when it was clear that air strikes were not having that effect). But the use of the term was nonetheless controversial, and combined with the controversies surrounding the use of force in Kosovo (and the aftermath), has led to something of a backlash against intervention and increased suspicion that use of the term 'genocide' is inherently politicised (a backlash made stronger by the Iraq War).

The war over Kosovo led to an attempt to set out guidelines for legitimising humanitarian intervention, and thus to the elaboration of the principle of the responsibility to protect at the UN world summit in September 2005. On the face of it, the principle appears almost to 'codify' the social norm against genocide. On closer inspection, it allows governments enough wiggle room to justify not assuming a collective responsibility to protect populations from atrocities. And while the principle seems to 'level out' genocide, ethnic cleansing, war crimes and crimes against humanity, the Darfur case has tragically illustrated that even where crimes 'no less serious' than genocide, but not genocide, have been shown to be committed (by a UN commission itself) the pressure to 'do something drastic' is much reduced.

The response by European governments to Darfur is similar to the Bosnia and Rwanda cases, in that the first impulse is to respond with humanitarian aid; coercive measures – even just sanctions on more than the four individuals targeted thus far – have been rejected as infeasible or undesirable (for a host of material and geopolitical reasons). The response to Darfur is also similar to Rwanda in the preference for 'African solutions to African problems', which represents a step back from the cosmopolitan notion – proclaimed at the end of the Cold War – that human rights violations everywhere should be of concern to us all.

All four cases illustrate the influence on governments of the legal norm against genocide in the reliance on international criminal tribunals to punish individuals for the crime of genocide (and others). While there was not always enthusiasm for, in fact sometimes there was obstruction of, the tribunals, the development of the international legal machinery to punish genocide is a clear example of the effect of the legal norm. Furthermore, in most of the cases there has been support for investigation by the UN into the question of which crimes have been committed – again, this can be seen as conforming perfectly with the legal norm. But while European governments have (at times reluctantly) taken action required by the legal norm, they have not used the legal norm to enable action to prevent – much less halt – purported ongoing genocides.

The social norm against genocide has played a more subtle role in policy responses. In most cases, barring Kosovo, governments did not want to intervene coercively, and even in Kosovo, most preferred to rely on (safe) air power and not to use ground troops. This held even in the most clear-cut case of genocide, Rwanda. So the social norm against genocide rarely if ever has enough force to counter resistance to do more than what the legal norm requires; the countervailing economic and political interests are often simply too strong. If governments do not want to intervene in, or criticise, or impose sanctions on states suspected of or clearly engaged in genocide, then they will not. And governments have not paid a domestic price (the loss of our support) for not complying with the social norm.

But the social norm is not without influence. As Alex Bellamy has argued, 'there is little evidence to suggest that states intervene in foreign emergencies because they are in some sense morally shamed into doing so by either domestic or global public opinion.'[8] But they can still be shamed by *not* intervening. The moral force of 'never again' operates not just at the level of domestic or international opinion, but within governments as well. Policy-makers are stuck between a rock and a hard place: the costs of doing something (including but not limited to the possible negative impact on domestic public opinion if intervention should prove unsuccessful and costly in terms of blood and treasure, and possible negative impact on economic and geopolitical interests) versus the 'moral imperative' to stop genocide. Avoiding this dilemma could lead them to reframe the debate into one about whether it is a genocide. It is sad but apparent, especially from the Darfur case, that classifying atrocities as war crimes or crimes against humanity does skirt round that 'moral imperative'. These are run-of-the-mill humanitarian emergencies, which can be addressed with fairly conventional strategies (infusions of humanitarian aid here, pressure to negotiate a solution to the conflict there). They evidently do not create the sort of moral pressure to 'do something' potentially drastic (like use military force) that genocide does. There is much less reluctance by governments to use the terms 'war crimes' or 'crimes

[8] Alex J. Bellamy, 'Whither the Responsibility to Protect? Humanitarian Intervention and the 2005 World Summit', *Ethics and International Affairs*, vol. 20, no. 2 (2006), 149–50.

against humanity' (as in the Darfur debate) and such terms are not automatically connected to calls to 'do something', such as intervene militarily, as is the case with genocide.

Thus to avoid appearing not to do anything in response to purported genocides, governments can point to compliance with the legal norm and/or they can show that 'genocide' is not the appropriate descriptive term. The debates about naming a genocide are crucial in determining governments' responses to atrocities, and therefore are inextricably linked to considerations of what governments are prepared to do. Naming genocide is controversial not just because it could seem disrespectful of the suffering endured during the Holocaust, or because a legal approach dictates that courts should be responsible for naming genocide. It is controversial also because it raises the pressure on governments, stemming from the social norm, to 'do something' to stop the killing.

Whither the norms against genocide?

Sixty-odd years on from the Genocide Convention, and it is clear that the 'odious scourge' has not been eliminated. As numerous commentators have noted, the promise of 'never again' has usually been honoured only in the breach. Since the end of the Cold War, however, the legal machinery for punishing genocide – at both national and international levels – has been reinforced and individuals have been imprisoned for the crime of genocide. Over time, holding more individuals accountable for perpetrating serious international crimes may have the effect of reducing the incidence of such crimes, though the experiences of crime-fighting at the domestic level suggest it cannot just be about dispensing justice through the court system. There have also been numerous reports and recommendations on preventing genocide, some with quite detailed proposals for action by national governments, regional and international organisations and NGOs. We are not lacking suggestions on how to prevent and respond to mass atrocities. And at least at the rhetorical level, the various controversies about the legality and legitimacy of intervention to prevent or stop genocide have culminated in a (shaky) consensus that the UN Security Council can authorise – as a measure of last resort – intervention to protect populations from genocide, war crimes, ethnic cleansing and crimes against humanity. But people continue to die at the hands of their own governments in alarming numbers.

Moreover, the reluctance by European governments to use the term 'genocide' to describe atrocities has not diminished over time. This study has suggested why that is the case; in this final section, the implications of the European practice with respect to naming genocide in the Darfur case are explored further.

Naming genocide is a political act, and contestation is bound to follow. In that sense, the apparent new 'European way' of deciding whether it is a genocide – bump the problem up to the UN – has some merit (putting aside for now that it could also be seen as an evasion of responsibility). If a respected and legitimate UN mechanism for determining whether a genocide is ongoing could be devised – perhaps building up the resources around the Secretary-General's Special Adviser for the Prevention of Genocide – then this might help eliminate suspicions of 'politicisation' regarding the use of the term. Governments would still be free to name genocides and to present evidence to back up their assertions, but the 'definitive' finding would be done through the UN.

However, if the problem is bumped up to the UN, then the UN has to be empowered to respond appropriately. And therein lies the nub of the problem. European governments may be the best friends the UN has, but as can be seen in their unwillingness to contribute 'Blue Helmets' to peacekeeping missions, their contribution to strengthening the UN itself is not above criticism. As Gérard Prunier has suggested, Kofi Annan knew that if he uttered the word genocide in respect of Darfur, governments would dump the whole problem in the UN's lap and almost certainly not provide it with the resources needed to try to suppress the genocide. Hence the suspicions that the UN commission of inquiry could really only arrive at one conclusion – Darfur is not a case of genocide – or else contribute to yet another morale-sapping, legitimacy-draining crisis in the UN itself.

So the question of empowering the UN to act becomes critical – but also difficult (if not impossible) to achieve not just in the current divisive climate at the UN but because few states are willing to cede much autonomy to the international organisation. Henry Shue has argued that powerful states have to be forced to act to protect populations from genocide.[9] Who or what would force them to do so is the

[9] Shue, 'Limiting Sovereignty', p. 28,

problem: the social norm against genocide, as we have seen, has not been powerful enough to do so.

The development of the principle of responsibility to protect is arguably an encouraging step, no matter how hedged it is. It is a start, at least, in developing an international consensus on protecting populations from atrocities, or 'saving strangers', to use Nick Wheeler's term. But the principle is under sustained attack at the UN by states that consider the principle of non-intervention to be absolute.[10] The debate could be improved if European states were to acknowledge that fears of interference by rich powers have some foundation (it is, after all, within living memory that European governments were perpetrating atrocities in their colonies, often while shouting racist abuse). But *mea culpas* alone are certainly not going to 'convert' states bent on protecting their rights to do as they please within their borders.

The spirit of the 'responsibility to protect' is also not wholeheartedly embraced by European governments. Certainly there has been a backlash against the notion that in cases of gross violations of human rights (such as possible genocide) states should intervene without UN Security Council authorisation. Support for the principle of the responsibility to protect reiterates that the responsibility is collective, of the international community as a whole. And we all know how difficult it is for the entire community to agree to act quickly, resolutely, decisively. European governments have not tried to assume a leadership role in building support for action under the principle of the responsibility to protect; arguably, in fact, their policies on Darfur demonstrate quite the opposite: responsibility is passed to other bodies such as the African Union.

Thus we are left with the unhappy conclusion that implementation of the social norm against genocide faces both countervailing economic and geopolitical interests on the one hand, and professed respect for multilateral practices and principles on the other. Further, the legal norm is not enough to enable action to prevent, much less stop, genocide. 'Never again' is quite likely to be a hollow promise, for all the moral agonising this produces.

[10] Except in the case of apartheid South Africa or Israel. Hypocrisy in debates about intervention abounds.

Appendix 1: United Nations General Assembly Resolution 96 (I), 11 December 1946

The Crime of Genocide

Genocide is a denial of the right of existence of entire human groups, as homicide is the denial of the right to live of individual human beings; such denial of the right of existence shocks the conscience of mankind, results in great losses to humanity in the form of cultural and other contributions represented by these human groups, and is contrary to moral law and to the spirit and aims of the United Nations.

Many instances of such crimes of genocide have occurred, when racial, religious, political and other groups have been destroyed, entirely or in part.

The punishment of the crime of genocide is a matter of international concern.

The General Assembly, therefore,

Affirms that genocide is a crime under international law which the civilized world condemns, and for the commission of which principals and accomplices – whether private individuals, public officials or statesmen, and whether the crime is committed on religious, racial, political or any other grounds – are punishable;

Invites the Member States to enact the necessary legislation for the prevention and punishment of this crime;

Recommends that international co-operation be organized between States with a view to facilitating the speedy prevention and punishment of the crime of genocide, and, to this end,

Requests the Economic and Social Council to undertake the necessary studies, with a view to drawing up a draft convention on the crime of genocide to be submitted to the next regular session of the General Assembly.

Appendix 2: Convention on the Prevention and Punishment of the Crime of Genocide

Approved and proposed for signature and ratification or accession by General Assembly resolution 260 A (III) of 9 December 1948

Entry into force: 12 January 1951, in accordance with article XIII

The Contracting Parties,

Having considered the declaration made by the General Assembly of the United Nations in its resolution 96 (I) dated 11 December 1946 that genocide is a crime under international law, contrary to the spirit and aims of the United Nations and condemned by the civilized world,

Recognizing that at all periods of history genocide has inflicted great losses on humanity, and

Being convinced that, in order to liberate mankind from such an odious scourge, international co-operation is required,

Hereby agree as hereinafter provided:

Article I

The Contracting Parties confirm that genocide, whether committed in time of peace or in time of war, is a crime under international law which they undertake to prevent and to punish.

Article II

In the present Convention, genocide means any of the following acts committed with intent to destroy, in whole or in part, a national, ethnical, racial or religious group, as such:

(a) Killing members of the group;

(b) Causing serious bodily or mental harm to members of the group;
(c) Deliberately inflicting on the group conditions of life calculated to bring about its physical destruction in whole or in part;
(d) Imposing measures intended to prevent births within the group;
(e) Forcibly transferring children of the group to another group.

Article III

The following acts shall be punishable:

(a) Genocide;
(b) Conspiracy to commit genocide;
(c) Direct and public incitement to commit genocide;
(d) Attempt to commit genocide;
(e) Complicity in genocide.

Article IV

Persons committing genocide or any of the other acts enumerated in article III shall be punished, whether they are constitutionally responsible rulers, public officials or private individuals.

Article V

The Contracting Parties undertake to enact, in accordance with their respective Constitutions, the necessary legislation to give effect to the provisions of the present Convention, and, in particular, to provide effective penalties for persons guilty of genocide or any of the other acts enumerated in article III.

Article VI

Persons charged with genocide or any of the other acts enumerated in article III shall be tried by a competent tribunal of the State in the territory of which the act was committed, or by such international penal tribunal as may have jurisdiction with respect to those Contracting Parties which shall have accepted its jurisdiction.

Article VII

Genocide and the other acts enumerated in article III shall not be considered as political crimes for the purpose of extradition.

The Contracting Parties pledge themselves in such cases to grant extradition in accordance with their laws and treaties in force.

Article VIII

Any Contracting Party may call upon the competent organs of the United Nations to take such action under the Charter of the United Nations as they consider appropriate for the prevention and suppression of acts of genocide or any of the other acts enumerated in article III.

Article IX

Disputes between the Contracting Parties relating to the interpretation, application or fulfilment of the present Convention, including those relating to the responsibility of a State for genocide or for any of the other acts enumerated in article III, shall be submitted to the International Court of Justice at the request of any of the parties to the dispute.

Article X

The present Convention, of which the Chinese, English, French, Russian and Spanish texts are equally authentic, shall bear the date of 9 December 1948.

Article XI

The present Convention shall be open until 31 December 1949 for signature on behalf of any Member of the United Nations and of any non-member State to which an invitation to sign has been addressed by the General Assembly.

The present Convention shall be ratified, and the instruments of ratification shall be deposited with the Secretary-General of the United Nations.

After 1 January 1950, the present Convention may be acceded to on behalf of any Member of the United Nations and of any non-member State which has received an invitation as aforesaid.

Instruments of accession shall be deposited with the Secretary-General of the United Nations.

Article XII

Any Contracting Party may at any time, by notification addressed to the Secretary-General of the United Nations, extend the application of the present Convention to all or any of the territories for the conduct of whose foreign relations that Contracting Party is responsible.

Article XIII

On the day when the first twenty instruments of ratification or accession have been deposited, the Secretary-General shall draw up a procès-verbal and transmit a copy thereof to each Member of the United Nations and to each of the non-member States contemplated in article XI.

The present Convention shall come into force on the ninetieth day following the date of deposit of the twentieth instrument of ratification or accession.

Any ratification or accession effected subsequent to the latter date shall become effective on the ninetieth day following the deposit of the instrument of ratification or accession.

Article XIV

The present Convention shall remain in effect for a period of ten years as from the date of its coming into force.

It shall thereafter remain in force for successive periods of five years for such Contracting Parties as have not denounced it at least six months before the expiration of the current period.

Denunciation shall be effected by a written notification addressed to the Secretary-General of the United Nations.

Article XV

If, as a result of denunciations, the number of Parties to the present Convention should become less than sixteen, the Convention shall cease to be in force as from the date on which the last of these denunciations shall become effective.

Article XVI

A request for the revision of the present Convention may be made at any time by any Contracting Party by means of a notification in writing addressed to the Secretary-General.

The General Assembly shall decide upon the steps, if any, to be taken in respect of such request.

Article XVII

The Secretary-General of the United Nations shall notify all Members of the United Nations and the non-member States contemplated in article XI of the following:

(a) Signatures, ratifications and accessions received in accordance with article XI;
(b) Notifications received in accordance with article XII;
(c) The date upon which the present Convention comes into force in accordance with article XIII;
(d) Denunciations received in accordance with article XIV;
(e) The abrogation of the Convention in accordance with article XV;
(f) Notifications received in accordance with article XVI.

Article XVIII

The original of the present Convention shall be deposited in the archives of the United Nations.

A certified copy of the Convention shall be transmitted to each Member of the United Nations and to each of the non-member States contemplated in article XI.

Article XIX

The present Convention shall be registered by the Secretary-General of the United Nations on the date of its coming into force.

Bibliography

Abrams, Jason, 'The Atrocities in Cambodia and Kosovo: Observations on the Codification of Genocide', *New England Law Review*, vol. 35, no. 2 (2001).

Akhavan, Payam, 'Punishing War Crimes in the Former Yugoslavia: A Critical Juncture for the New World Order', *Human Rights Quarterly*, vol. 15, no. 2 (1993).

Allen, Tim and David Styan, 'A Right to Interfere? Bernard Kouchner and the New Humanitarianism', *Journal of International Development*, vol. 12, no. 6 (2000).

Annan, Kofi, 'Intervention', Ditchley Foundation Lecture XXXV (26 June 1998).

Arbour, Louise, 'The Responsibility to Protect as a Duty of Care in International Law and Practice', *Review of International Studies*, vol. 34, no. 3 (2008).

Arend, Anthony Clark, 'Do Legal Rules Matter? International Law and International Politics', *Virginia Journal of International Law*, vol. 38, no. 2 (1998).

Assemblée Nationale de France, Mission d'information commune, Enquête sur la tragédie rwandaise (1990–1994), rapport no. 1271, vol. 1 (15 December 1998).

Assemblée Nationale de France, Mission d'information commune sur les événements de Srebrenica, rapport d'Information no. 3413 (22 November 2001).

Barnett, Michael, *Eyewitness to a Genocide: The United Nations and Rwanda* (Ithaca: Cornell University Press, 2002).

Beigbeder, Yves, *Judging Criminal Leaders: The Slow Erosion of Impunity* (The Hague: Martinus Nijhoff Publishers, 2002).

Judging War Crimes and Torture: French Justice and International Criminal Tribunals and Commissions (1940–2005) (Leiden: Martinus Nijhoff, 2006).

Belgian Senate, Commission d'enquête parlementaire concernant les événements du Rwanda, 1–611/7 (6 December 1997).

Bellamy, Alex J., Responsibility to Protect or Trojan Horse? The Crisis in Darfur and Humanitarian Intervention after Iraq, *Ethics and International Affairs*, vol. 19, no. 2 (2005).

'Whither the Responsibility to Protect? Humanitarian Intervention and the 2005 World Summit', *Ethics and International Affairs*, vol. 20, no. 2 (2006).

Responsibility to Protect (Cambridge: Polity, 2009).

Berman, Paul, *Power and the Idealists or, the Passion of Joschka Fischer and its Aftermath* (Brooklyn, NY: Soft Skull Press, 2005).

Bloxham, Donald, *The Great Game of Genocide: Imperialism, Nationalism and the Destruction of the Ottoman Armenians* (Oxford: Oxford University Press, 2005).

Braunstein, Matheiu, *François Mitterrand à Sarajevo, 28 Juin 1992: Le rendez-vouz manqué* (Paris: L'Harmattan, 2001).

Brendon, Piers, *The Decline and Fall of the British Empire 1781–1997* (London: Vintage, 2008).

Brierly, J.L., 'The Genocide Convention', *The Listener* (10 March 1949).

Bruns, Wilhelm, *Die UNO-Politik der DDR* (Stuttgart: Verlag Bonn Aktuell, 1978).

Bruun, Lori Lyman, 'Beyond the 1948 Convention: Emerging Principles of Genocide in Customary Law', *Maryland Journal of International Law and Trade*, vol. 17, no. 2 (1993).

Calic, Marie-Janine, 'German Perspectives', in Alex Danchev and Thomas Halverson, eds., *International Perspectives on the Yugoslav Conflict* (Houndmills: Macmillan, 1996).

Caplan, Richard, 'International Diplomacy and the Crisis in Kosovo', *International Affairs*, vol. 74, no. 4 (1998).

Europe and the Recognition of New States in Yugoslavia (Cambridge: Cambridge University Press, 2005).

Chandler, David, *From Kosovo to Kabul: Human Rights and International Intervention* (London: Pluto Press, 2002).

Chicago Council on Global Affairs and WorldPublicOpinion.org, 'Publics Around the World Say UN Has Responsibility to Protect Against Genocide', 4 April 2007 (available at www.worldpublicopinion.org (last accessed 13 April 2010)).

Churchill, Ward, *A Little Matter of Genocide* (San Francisco: City Lights Books, 1997).

Cigar, Norman, *Genocide in Bosnia: The Policy of 'Ethnic Cleansing'* (College Station: Texas A&M University Press, 1995).

Conversi, Daniele, 'Moral Relativism and Equidistance in British Attitudes to the War in the Former Yugoslavia', in Thomas Cushman and

Stjepan G. Meštrović, eds., *This Time We Knew: Western Responses to Genocide in Bosnia* (New York: New York University Press, 1996).

Cooper, John, *Raphael Lemkin and the Struggle for the Genocide Convention* (Houndmills: Palgrave, 2008).

Cot, Jean, 'La France e le conflit de Bosnie-Herzégovine', *Défense Nationale*, vol. 55, part 11 (1999).

Council of the European Union, press release, 'General Affairs Council, 18–19 April 1994', document no. 6294/94 (Presse 70).

Press release, 'General Affairs Council, 16–17 May 1994', document no. 6883/94 (Presse 88-G).

'Common position of 10 May 1999 concerning additional restrictive measures against the Federal Republic of Yugoslavia (99/318/CFSP)', in Official Journal of the European Union L123 (13 May 1999).

Press release, 'External Relations, 13 September 2004', 12068/04 (Presse 251).

'Declaration by the Presidency on behalf of the European Union on the report by the International Commission of Inquiry on Darfur', document no. 6072/2/05 REV 2 (Presse 19) (7 February 2005).

'Council conclusions on Sudan' (30 March 2006), document no. 7035/06 (Presse 69).

Secretariat, fact sheet: EU support to the African Union mission in Darfur – AMIS' (January 2008).

Cronje, Suzanne, *The World and Nigeria: The Diplomatic History of the Biafran War 1967–1970* (London: Sidgwick and Jackson, 1972).

Cushman, Thomas and Stjepan G. Meštrović, 'Introduction', in Thomas Cushman and Stjepan G. Meštrović, eds., *This Time We Knew: Western Responses to Genocide in Bosnia* (New York: New York University Press, 1996).

Daalder, Ivo H. and Michael E. O'Hanlon, *Winning Ugly: NATO's War to Save Kosovo* (Washington, DC: Brookings Institution Press, 2000).

Dallaire, Roméo, *Shake Hands with the Devil: The Failure of Humanity in Rwanda* (London: Arrow Books, 2003).

de Graaff, Bob, 'Activist and Catalyst: Dutch Moralistic Decision-making Regarding (former) Yugoslavia, 1991–1994', *Journal of European Integration History*, vol. 10, no. 1 (2004).

'The Difference between Legal Proof and Historical Evidence: The Trial of Slobodan Milosevic and the Case of Srebrenica', *European Review*, vol. 14, no. 4 (2006).

de Saint-Exupéry, Patrick, *L'Inavouable: La France au Rwanda* (Paris: les Arènes, 2004).

des Forges, Alison, *Leave None to Tell the Story: Genocide in Rwanda* (New York: Human Rights Watch and Fédération Internationale des Ligues de Droits de l'Homme, 1999).

Destexhe, Alain, 'The Third Genocide', *Foreign Policy*, no. 97 (Winter 1994/95).

Drost, Pieter N., *The Crime of State: Penal Protection for Fundamental Freedoms of Persons and Peoples, Book II Genocide* (Leyden: A. W. Sythoff, 1959).

Elder, Tanya, 'What You See Before Your Eyes; Documenting Raphael Lemkin's Life by Exploring his Archival Papers, 1900–1959', *Journal of Genocide Research*, vol. 7, no. 4 (2005).

European Communities, *Bulletin of the European Communities* (Luxembourg: Office of the Official Publications of the European Communities), various issues.

European Council, Presidency conclusions on Rwanda, Corfu (24–25 June 1994).

'Report on the implementation of the European Security Strategy: providing security in a changing world', document S407/08, Brussels (11 December 2008)

European Parliament, Resolution on the Darfur region in the Sudan, 16 September 2004, in Official Journal of the European Union C 140E (9 June 2005).

European Union, Press release, 'Declaration by the Presidency on behalf of the European Union on the occasion of the 10th anniversary of the genocide in Rwanda: NEVER AGAIN', document no. 8219/1/04 REV 1 (Presse 102), Brussels (8 April 2004).

Evans, Gareth, 'The Responsibility to Protect: An Idea Whose Time Has Come ... and Gone?', *International Relations*, vol. 22, no. 3 (2008).

Everts, Philip 'War without Bloodshed? Public Opinion and the Conflict over Kosovo', in Philip Everts and Pierangelo Isernia, eds., *Public Opinion and the International Use of Force* (London: Routledge, 2001).

'Innocence Lost: The Netherlands and the Yugoslav Conflict', in Richard Sobel and Eric Shiraev, eds., *International Public Opinion and the Bosnia Crisis* (Lanham, MD: Lexington Books, 2003).

Finnemore, Martha, 'Are Legal Norms Distinctive?', *New York University Journal of International Law and Politics*, vol. 32, no. 3 (2000).

Flint, Julie and Alex de Waal, *Darfur: A New History of a Long War*, revised edition (London: Zed Books, 2008).

Fournet, Caroline, 'Reflection on the Separation of Powers: The Law of Genocide and the Symptomatic French Paradox', in Ralph Henham and Paul Behrens, eds., *The Criminal Law of Genocide: International, Comparative and Contextual Aspects* (Aldershot: Ashgate, 2007).

The Crime of Destruction and the Law of Genocide: Their Impact on Collective Memory (Aldershot: Ashgate, 2007)

Fowler, Jerry, 'A New Chapter of Irony: The Legal Implications of the Darfur Genocide Determination', *Genocide Studies and Prevention*, vol. 1, no. 1 (2006).

Franck, Christian, 'Belgium: Committed Multilateralism', in Christopher Hill, ed., *National Foreign Policies and European Political Cooperation* (London: George Allen & Unwin, 1983).

Freedman, Lawrence, 'Victims and Victors: Reflections on the Kosovo War', *Review of International Studies*, vol. 26, no. 3 (2000).

French Foreign Ministry, *La Politique Étrangère de la France: Textes et Documents* (Paris: Ministère des Affaires Étrangères), various issues.

'Genocide: A Commentary on the Convention', *The Yale Law Journal*, vol. 58, no. 7 (1949).

Genocide Prevention Task Force, *Preventing Genocide: A Blueprint for U.S. Policymakers* (United States Holocaust Memorial Museum, the American Academy of Diplomacy and the Endowment of the United States Institute of Peace, 2008).

Gow, James, *Triumph of the Lack of Will: International Diplomacy and the Yugoslav War* (London: Hurst & Company, 1997).

Grundmann, Reiner, Dennis Smith, and Sue Wright, 'National Elites and Transnational Discourses in the Balkan War: A Comparison between the French, German and British Press', *European Journal of Communication*, vol. 15, no. 3 (2000).

Gutman, Roy, *A Witness to Genocide: The First Inside Account of the Horrors of 'Ethnic Cleansing' in Bosnia* (Shaftesbury: Element, 1993).

Hansen, Lene, *Security as Practice: Discourse Analysis and the Bosnian War* (London: Routledge, 2006).

Heinze, Eric A., 'The Rhetoric of Genocide in U.S. Foreign Policy: Rwanda and Darfur Compared', *Political Science Quarterly*, vol. 122, no. 3 (2007).

Henham, Ralph **and** Paul Behrens, eds., *The Criminal Law of Genocide: International, Comparative and Contextual Aspects* (Aldershot: Ashgate, 2007).

Honig, Jan Willem and Norbert Both, *Srebrenica: Record of a War Crime* (London: Penguin, 1996).

Independent International Commission on Kosovo, *The Kosovo Report* (Oxford: Oxford University Press, 2000).

International Commission of Inquiry on Darfur, Report of the International Commission of Inquiry on Darfur to the United Nations Secretary-General, pursuant to Security Council Resolution 1564 of 18 September 2004 (Geneva, 25 January 2005).

International Court of Justice, Application of the Convention on the Prevention and Punishment of the Crime of Genocide (*Bosnia and*

Herzegovina v. *Serbia and Montenegro*), summary of the judgment of 26 February 2007, summary 2007/2 (26 February 2007).

International Criminal Court, 'Situation in Darfur, The Sudan: public summary of Prosecutor's application under Article 58', document no. ICC-02/05 (14 July 2008).

International Criminal Tribunal for the former Yugoslavia, Case No. IT-02–54-T, *Prosecutor* v. *Slobodan Milosevic*, decision on motion for acquittal (16 June 2004).

Case No. IT-95–5/18-PT, The Prosecutor of the Tribunal against Radovan Karadžić, Third Amended Indictment (27 February 2009).

International Panel of Eminent Personalities, 'Rwanda: the preventable genocide', Organisation of African Unity (7 July 2000).

Jahan, Rounaq, 'Genocide in Bangladesh', in Samuel Totten, William S. Parsons and Israel W. Charney, eds., *Century of Genocide*, 2nd edition (London: Routledge, 2004).

Jepperson, Ronald L., Alexander Wendt and Peter J. Katzenstein, 'Norms, Identity, and Culture in National Security', in Peter J. Katzenstein, ed., *The Culture of National Security: Norms and Identity in World Politics* (New York: Columbia University Press, 1996).

Johnston, Karin, 'German Public Opinion and the Crisis in Bosnia', in Richard Sobel and Eric Shiraev, eds., *International Public Opinion and the Bosnia Crisis* (Lanham, MD: Lexington Books, 2003).

Joint Evaluation of Emergency Assistance to Rwanda, 'The international response to conflict and genocide: lessons from the Rwanda experience', synthesis report (March 1996).

Jones, Adam, ed., *Genocide, War Crimes and the West: History and Complicity* (London: Zed Books, 2004).

Kampfner, John, *Blair's Wars* (London: Free Press, 2003).

Kent, Gregory, *Framing War and Genocide; British Policy and News Media Reaction to the War in Bosnia* (Cresskill, NJ: Hampton Press, 2006).

Keohane, Dan, 'The Debate on British Policy in the Kosovo Conflict: An Assessment', *Contemporary Security Policy*, vol. 21, no. 3 (2000).

Kiernan, Ben, 'The Inclusion of the Khmer Rouge in the Cambodian Peace Process: Causes and Consequences', in Ben Kiernan, ed., *Genocide and Democracy in Cambodia: The Khmer Rouge, the United Nations, and the International Community* (New Haven: Yale University South East Asian Studies, 1993).

'The Cambodian Genocide – 1975–1979', in Samuel Totten, William S. Parsons and Israel W. Charney, eds., *Century of Genocide*, 2nd edition (London: Routledge, 2004).

Korey, William, *Epitaph for Raphael Lemkin* (New York: Jacob Blaustein Institute for the Advancement of Human Rights of the American Jewish Committee, 2001).

Kreicker, Helmut, 'National Prosecution of Genocide from a Comparative Perspective', *International Criminal Law Review*, vol. 5, no. 3 (2005).

Kroslak, Daniela, *The Role of France in the Rwandan Genocide* (London: Hurst & Company, 2007).

Kunz, Josef, 'The United Nations Convention on Genocide', *The American Journal of International Law*, vol. 43, no. 4 (1949).

Kuper, Leo, *Genocide* (Harmondsworth: Penguin, 1981).

Kuperman, Alan J., *The Limits of Humanitarian Intervention: Genocide in Rwanda* (Washington, DC: Brookings Institution Press, 2001).

Kurlic, Joseph, 'La France et la crise yougoslave jusqu'au traité d l'Elysée (1991–1995)', *Journal of European Integration History*, vol. 10, no. 1 (2004).

Lagrou, Pieter, 'Victims of Genocide and National Memory: Belgium, France and the Netherlands, 1945–65', in Gordon Martel, ed., *The World War Two Reader* (London: Routledge, 2004).

LeBlanc, Lawrence J., *The United States and the Genocide Convention* (Durham: Duke University Press, 1991).

Lebor, Adam, *'Complicity with Evil' The United Nations in the Age of Modern Genocide* (New Haven: Yale University Press, 2006).

Lemarchand, René, 'The Burundi Genocide', in Samuel Totten, William S. Parsons and Israel W. Charney, eds., *Century of Genocide*, 2nd edition (London: Routledge, 2004).

'Unsimplifying Darfur', *Genocide Studies and Prevention*, vol. 1, no. 1 (2006).

Lemkin, Raphael, *Axis Rule in Occupied Europe: Laws of Occupation; Analysis of Government: Proposals for Redress* (Washington, DC: Carnegie Endowment for International Peace, 1944).

'Genocide', *The American Scholar*, vol. 15, part 2 (1946).

'Genocide as a Crime under International Law', *The American Journal of International Law*, vol. 41, no.1 (1947).

Levene, Mark, *The Meaning of Genocide* (London: I.B.Tauris, 2005).

Macdonald, Anna, 'Strengthening UK Law on Genocide, War Crimes and Crimes against Humanity', in Nick Donovan, ed., *The Enforcement of International Criminal Law* (Laxton, Nottinghamshire: Aegis Trust, 2009).

Markusen, Eric, 'Three Empirical Investigations of Alleged Genocide in Darfur', in Amanda Grzyb, ed., *The World and Darfur: International Response to Crimes against Humanity in Western Sudan* (Montreal and Kingston: McGill-Queen's University Press, 2009).

Martin, James J., *The Man Who Invented Genocide: The Public Career and Consequences of Raphael Lemkin* (Torrance, CA: Institute for Historical Review, 1984).

MccGwire, Michael, 'Why did we Bomb Belgrade?', *International Affairs*, vol. 76, no. 1 (2000).

Melvern, Linda, *A People Betrayed: The Role of the West in Rwanda's Genocide* (London: Zed Books, 2000).

Conspiracy to Murder: The Rwandan Genocide (London: Verso, 2004).

'The UK Government and the 1994 Genocide in Rwanda' *Genocide Studies and Prevention*, vol. 2, no. 3 (2007).

Melvern, Linda and Paul Williams, 'Britannia Waived the Rules: The Major Government and the 1994 Rwandan Genocide', *African Affairs*, vol. 103, no. 410 (2004).

Mendez, Juan E., 'The United Nations and the Prevention of Genocide', in Ralph Henham and Paul Behrens, eds., *The Criminal Law of Genocide: International, Comparative and Contextual Aspects* (Aldershot: Ashgate, 2007).

Mennecke, Martin, 'Genocide in Kosovo?', in Samuel Totten, William S. Parsons and Israel W. Charny, eds., *Century of Genocide*, 2nd edition (London: Routledge, 2004).

Mennecke, Martin and Eric Markusen, 'Genocide in Bosnia and Herzegovina', in Samuel Totten, William S. Parsons and Israel W. Charny, eds., *Century of Genocide*, 2nd edition (London: Routledge, 2004).

Metzl, Jamie Frederic *Western Responses to Human Rights Abuses in Cambodia, 1975–80* (Houndmills: Palgrave, 1996).

Miles, William, 'Labelling "Genocide" in Sudan: A Constructionist Analysis of Darfur', *Genocide Studies and Prevention*, vol. 1, no. 3 (2006).

Miraglia, Michela, 'Genocide: The Italian Perspective', *International Criminal Law Review*, vol. 5, no. 3 (2005).

Miskimmon, Alister, 'Falling into Line? Kosovo and the Course of German Foreign Policy', *International Affairs*, vol. 85, no. 3 (2009).

Moghalu, Kinglsey, *Rwanda's Genocide: The Politics of Global Justice* (Houndmills: Palgrave, 2005).

Morjé Howard, Marc and Lise Morjé Howard, 'Raison d'état or Raison populaire? The Influence of Public Opinion on France's Bosnia Policy', in Richard Sobel and Eric Shiraev, eds., *International Public Opinion and the Bosnia Crisis* (Lanham, MD: Lexington Books, 2003).

Morris, Nicholas, 'Humanitarian Intervention in the Balkans', in Jennifer M. Welsh, ed., *Humanitarian Intervention and International Relations* (Oxford: Oxford University Press, 2004).

Mullin, Chris, *A View from the Foothills: The Diaries of Chris Mullin* (London: Profile Books, 2009).

Nardin, Terry, 'International Political Theory and the Question of Justice', *International Affairs*, vol. 82, no. 3 (2006).

Netherlands Institute for War Documentation, 'Srebrenica, A 'Safe' Area: Reconstruction, Background, Consequences and Analyses of the Fall of a Safe Area', (Amsterdam 2002).

North Atlantic Council, 'The situation in and around Kosovo', statement issued at the extraordinary ministerial meeting of the North Atlantic Council held at NATO headquarters, Brussels, on 12 April 1999, press release M-NAC-1(99)51.

Olsen, Gorm Rye, 'The European Union and Military Conflict Management in Africa', *CFSP Forum*, vol. 7, no. 1 (2009).

Organization for Security and Cooperation in Europe, 'Kosovo/ Kosova: as seen, as told. An analysis of the human rights findings of the OSCE Kosovo verification mission, October 1998 to June 1999', (1999).

Power, Samantha, 'Bystanders to Genocide', *The Atlantic Monthly* (September 2001).

'A Problem from Hell': America and the Age of Genocide (New York: Perennial, 2002).

'Dying in Darfur: Can the Ethnic Cleansing in Sudan be Stopped?', *The New Yorker* (30 August 2004).

Press and Information Office, Federal Government Bonn, *European Political Co-operation (EPC)*, 1982.

Price, Richard, 'Emerging Customary Norms and Anti-Personnel Landmines', in Christian Reus-Smit, ed., *The Politics of International Law* (Cambridge: Cambridge University Press, 2004).

Prunier, Gérard, *The Rwanda Crisis: History of a Genocide* (London: Hurst & Company, 1995).

'The Politics of Death in Darfur', *Current History* (May 2006).

Darfur: The Ambiguous Genocide (London: Hurst & Company, 2007).

Puhl, Detlef, 'Addendum: Kosovo and German Public Opinion', in Wolfgang-Uwe Friedrich, ed., *The Legacy of Kosovo: German Politics and Policies in the Balkans*, German Issues no. 22 (American Institute for Contemporary German Studies, The Johns Hopkins University, 2000).

Quayle, Peter, 'Unimaginable Evil: The Legislative Limitations of the Genocide Convention', *International Criminal Law Review*, vol. 5, no. 3 (2005).

Quigley, John, *The Genocide Convention: An International Legal Analysis* (Aldershot: Ashgate, 2006).

Reeves, Eric, Report of the International Commission of Inquiry on Darfur: a critical analysis (Part II), February 6, 2005 (www.sudan-reeves.org (last accessed 13 April 2010)).

Reiding, Hilde, *The Netherlands and the Development of International Human Rights Instruments* (Antwerp and Oxford: Intersentia, 2007).

Reus-Smit, Christian, 'The Politics of International Law', in Christian Reus-Smit, ed., *The Politics of International Law* (Cambridge: Cambridge University Press, 2004).

Rieff, David *Slaughterhouse: Bosnia and the Failure of the West* (New York: Touchstone, 1996).

Roberts, Adam, 'NATO's "Humanitarian War" over Kosovo', *Survival*, vol. 41, no. 3 (Autumn 1999).

Robertson, Geoffrey, *Crimes against Humanity: The Struggle for Global Justice*, 2nd edition, (London: Penguin Books, 2002).

Sadat, Leila, 'The Crime Against Humanity Initiative', in Nick Donovan, ed., *The Enforcement of International Criminal Law* (Laxton, Nottinghamshire: Aegis Trust, 2009).

Schabas, William A., 'Problems of International Codification – Were the Atrocities in Cambodia and Kosovo Genocide?', *New England Law Review*, vol. 35, no. 2 (2001).

'The "Odious Scourge": Evolving Interpretations of the Crime of Genocide', *Genocide Studies and Prevention*, vol. 1, no. 2 (2006).

'Semantics or Substance? David Scheffer's Welcome Proposal to Strengthen Criminal Accountability for Atrocities', *Genocide Studies and Prevention*, vol. 2, no. 1 (2007).

'Genocide and the International Court of Justice: Finally a Duty to Prevent the Crime of Crimes', *Genocide Studies and Prevention*, vol. 2, no. 2 (2007).

'Origins of the Genocide Convention: From Nuremberg to Paris', *Case Western Reserve Journal of International Law*, vol. 40 (2007–08).

Genocide in International Law, 2nd edition (Cambridge: Cambridge University Press), 2009.

Scharf, Michael P., *Balkan Justice: The Story Behind the First International War Crimes Trial Since Nuremberg* (Durham, NC: Carolina Academic Press, 1997)

Scheffer, David, 'Genocide and Atrocity Crimes', *Genocide Studies and Prevention*, vol. 1, no. 3 (2006).

'The World Court's Fractured Ruling on Genocide', *Genocide Studies and Prevention*, vol. 2, no. 2 (2007).

Semelin, Jacques, 'What is "Genocide"?', *European Review of History – Revue Européenne d'Histoire*, vol. 12, no. 1 (2005).

Shaw, Martin, *What is Genocide?* (Cambridge: Polity Press, 2007).

Shue, Henry, 'Bombing to Rescue? NATO's 1999 Bombing of Serbia', in Deen K. Chatterjee and Don E. Scheid, eds., *Ethics and Foreign Intervention* (Cambridge: Cambridge University Press, 2003).

'Limiting Sovereignty', in Jennifer Welsh, ed., *Humanitarian Intervention and International Relations* (Oxford: Oxford University Press, 2004).

Shurkin, Michael, 'France and the Darfur Crisis', US-Europe Analysis Series, The Brookings Institution, Washington, DC (January 2005).

Silber, Laura and Allan Little, *The Death of Yugoslavia*, revised edition (London: Penguin Books, 1996).

Simms, Brendan, *Unfinest Hour: Britain and the Destruction of Bosnia* (London: Penguin Books, 2002).

'From the Kohl to the Fischer Doctrine: Germany and the Wars of the Yugoslav Succession, 1991–1999', *German History*, vol. 21, no. 3 (2003).

Simpson, A. W. Brian, 'Britain and the Genocide Convention', *British Yearbook of International Law*, vol. 73 (2003).

Slim, Hugo, 'Dithering over Darfur? A Preliminary Review of the International Response', *International Affairs*, vol. 80, no. 5 (2004).

Sobel, Richard and Eric Shiraev, eds., *International Public Opinion and the Bosnia Crisis* (Lanham, MD: Lexington Books, 2003).

Staunton, Enda, 'The Case of Biafra: Ireland and the Nigerian Civil War', *Irish Historical Studies*, vol. 31, no. 124 (November 1999).

Straus, Scott, 'Darfur and the Genocide Debate', *Foreign Affairs*, vol. 84, no. 1 (January/February 2005).

Stremlau, John J., *The International Politics of the Nigerian Civil War 1967–1970* (Princeton: Princeton University Press, 1977)

Tabeau, Ewa and Jakub Bijak, 'War-related Deaths in the 1992–1995 Armed Conflicts in Bosnia and Hezegovina: A Critique of Previous Estimates and Recent Results', *European Journal of Population*, vol. 21, nos. 2–3 (2005).

Tardy, Thierry, *La France et la gestion des conflits yougoslaves (1991–1995): Enjeux et leçons d'une opération de maintien de la paix de l'ONU* (Brussels: Bruylant, 1999).

Thompson, Allan, ed., *The Media and the Rwanda Genocide* (London: Pluto Press, Fountain Publishers and International Development Research Centre, 2007).

Thompson, Joseph E., *American Policy and African Famine: The Nigeria-Biafra War, 1966–1970* (New York: Greenwood Press, 1990).

Totten, Samuel, 'Saving Lives in Darfur, 2003–06?: Lots of Talk, Little to No Action', in Amanda Grzyb, ed., *The World and Darfur: International Response to Crimes against Humanity in Western Sudan* (Montreal and Kingston: McGill-Queen's University Press, 2009).

Totten, Samuel, William S. Parsons and Israel W. Charney, eds., *Century of Genocide*, 2nd edition (London: Routledge, 2004).

Totten, Samuel and Eric Markusen, 'The US Government Darfur Genocide Investigation', *Journal of Genocide Research*, vol. 7, no. 2 (2005).

Trahan, Jennifer, 'Why the Killing in Darfur is Genocide', *Fordham International Law Journal*, vol. 31, no.4 (2008).

United Kingdom House of Commons, Select Committee on Foreign Affairs, fourth report: Kosovo (23 May 2000).

International Development Committee, 'Darfur, Sudan: the responsibility to protect', fifth report of session 2004–05, vol. I, HC-67 (30 March 2005).

International Development Committee, 'Darfur, Sudan: the responsibility to protect', fifth report of session 2004–05, vol. II, HC-67-II (30 March 2005).

United Nations Commission on Human Rights, First special session, summary record of the second meeting (First Part), E/CN.4/1992/S-1/SR.2 (22 October 1992).

Report on the second special session (30 November – 1 December 1992), E/1992/22/Add.2 and E/CN.4/1992/84/Add.2.

Second special session, summary record of the first meeting (30 November 1992), E/CN.4/1992/S-2/SR.1.

United Nations Economic and Social Council, Analysis prepared on behalf of the Sub-Commission by its chairman of materials submitted to it and the Commission on Human Rights under decision 9 (XXXIV) of the Commission on Human Rights, document E/CN.4/1335 (30 January 1979).

Revised and updated report on the question of the prevention and punishment of genocide prepared by Mr B. Whitaker, (2 July 1985), E/CN.4/Sub.2/1985/6.

Report of the Commission on Human Rights on its first special session (Geneva, 13 and 14 August 1992), E/CN.4/1992/S-1/8.

Report by Mr B W Ndiaye, Special Rapporteur, on his mission to Rwanda from 8 to 17 April 1993, E/CN.4/1994/7/Add.1 (11 August 1993).

Report of the Commission on Human Rights on its third special session (Geneva, 24 and 25 May 1994), E/CN.4/S-3/4 (30 May 1994).

Summary Record of the second meeting, third special session, Commission on Human Rights, E/CN.4/S-3/SR.2 (1 June 1994).

Summary record of the third meeting, third special session, Commission on Human Rights, E/CN.4/S-3/SR.3 (16 June 1994).
Summary record of the first meeting, third special session, Commission on Human Rights, E/CN.4/S-3/SR.1 (21 June 1994).
Commission on Human Rights, fifty-fifth session, summary record of the 19th meeting held at the Palais de Nations, Geneva, on Wednesday, 7 April 1999 at 10 a.m. E/CN.4/1999/S.R.19 (9 July 1999)
Report of the United Nations High Commission for Human Rights and follow-up to the world conference on human rights: situation of human rights in the Darfur region of the Sudan, E/CN.4/2005/3 (7 May 2004).
United Nations General Assembly, Sixth Committee, Sixty-fourth meeting (1 October 1948), A/C.6/SR.64.
Sixth Committee, Seventy-fifth meeting (15 October 1948), A/C.6/ SR.75.
Sixth Committee, Hundred and twenty-eighth meeting (29 November 1948), A/C.6/SR.128.
Sixth Committee, Hundred and thirty-third meeting (2 December 1948), A/C.6/SR.133.
Provisional verbatim record of the 92nd meeting, held on 18 December 1992, A/47/PV.92 (22 January 1993).
Report of the Group of Experts for Cambodia established pursuant to General Assembly Resolution 52/135, document no. A/53/850 and S/1999/231 (16 March 1999).
Report of the Secretary-General pursuant to General Assembly Resolution 53/35: the fall of Srebrenica, A/54/549 (15 November 1999).
Resolution 60/1, 2005 World Summit outcome, A/RES/60/1 (24 October 2005)
United Nations Human Rights Council, Report of the high-level mission on the situation of human rights in Darfur pursuant to Human Rights Council Decision S-4/101, A/HRC/4/80 (9 March 2007).
Report of the Special Rapporteur on the situation of human rights in the Sudan, Sima Samar, A/HRC/1114 (June 2009).
United Nations Security Council, Interim report of the Commission of Experts established pursuant to Security Council Resolution 780 (1992), S/25274 (10 February 1993).
Letter dated 10 February 1993 from the Permanent Representative of France to the United Nations addressed to the Secretary-General, S/ 25266 (10 February 1993).
Letter dated 18 February 1993 from the Permanent Representative of Sweden to the United Nations addressed to the Secretary-General, S/ 25307 (18 February 1993).

Letter dated 16 February 1993 from the Permanent Representative of Italy to the United Nations addressed to the Secretary-General, S/ 25300 (17 February 1993).
Note verbale dated 30 April 1993 from the Permanent Representative of the Netherlands to the United Nations addressed to the Secretary-General, S/25716 (4 May 1993).
Statement by the President of the Security Council (30 April 1994), S/PRST/1994/21.
Record of the 3377th meeting (16 May 1994), S/PV.3377.
Final report of the Commission of Experts established pursuant to Security Council Resolution 80 (1992), S/1994/674 (27 May 1994).
Report of the Secretary-General on the situation in Rwanda, S/1994/640 (31 May 1994).
Record of the 3388th meeting (8 June 1994), S/PV.3388.
Preliminary report of the Independent Commission of Experts established in accordance with Security Council Resolution 935 (1994), S/1994/1125 (4 October 1994).
Final report of the Commission of Experts established pursuant to Security Council Resolution 935 (1994), S/1994/1504 (9 December 1994).
Report of the Independent Inquiry into the actions of the United Nations during the 1994 Genocide in Rwanda, S/1999/1257 (16 December 1999).

Uvin, Peter, 'Reading the Rwandan Genocide', *International Studies Review*, vol. 3, no. 3 (2001).

van den Herik, Larissa, 'The Schism Between the Legal and Social Concept of Genocide in Light of the Responsibility to Protect' in Ralph Henham and Paul Behrens, eds., *The Criminal Law of Genocide: International, Comparative and Contextual Aspects* (Aldershot: Ashgate, 2007).

Weiss, Thomas, 'Halting Genocide: Rhetoric versus Reality', *Genocide Studies and Prevention*, vol. 2, no. 1 (2007).
Humanitarian Intervention (Cambridge: Polity Press, 2007).

Wendt, Alexander, 'Anarchy is What States Make of It: The Social Construction of Power Politics', *International Organization*, vol. 46, no. 2 (1992).

Wheeler, Nicholas J., *Saving Strangers: Humanitarian Intervention in International Society* (Oxford: Oxford University Press, 2000).
'The Kosovo Bombing Campaign', in Christian Reus-Smit, ed., *The Politics of International Law* (Cambridge: Cambridge University Press, 2004).

Wiener, Antje, 'Enacting Meaning-In-Use: Qualitative Research on Norms and International Relations', *Review of International Studies*, vol. 35, no. 1 (2009).

Williams, Paul D., 'The Peacekeeping System, Britain and the 1994 Rwandan Genocide', in Phil Clark and Zachary D. Kaufman, eds., *After Genocide: Transitional Justice, Post-Conflict Reconstruction and Reconciliation in Rwanda and Beyond* (London: Hurst & Company, 2008).

'The United Kingdom', in David R. Black and Paul D. Williams, eds., *The International Politics of Mass Atrocities: The Case of Darfur* (London: Routledge, 2009).

Wilson, Harold, *The Labour Government 1964–1970: A Personal Record* (London: Weidenfeld and Nicolson, and Michael Joseph Ltd, 1971).

Wouters, Jan and Sten Verhoeven, 'The Prosecution of Genocide – In Search of a European Persepective', in Ralph Henham and Paul Behrens, eds., *The Criminal Law of Genocide: International, Comparative and Contextual Aspects* (Aldershot: Ashgate, 2007).

'The Prohibition of Genocide as a Norm of *Ius Cogens* and its Implications for Enforcement of the Law of Genocide', *International Criminal Law Review*, vol. 5, no. 3 (2005).

Wybrow, Robert J., 'British Attitudes Toward the Bosnian Situation', in Richard Sobel and Eric Shiraev, eds., *International Public Opinion and the Bosnia Crisis* (Lanham, MD: Lexington Books, 2003).

Youngs, Tim and Tom Dodd, 'Kosovo', House of Commons Research Paper, 98/73 (7 July 1998).

Youngs, Tim, Mark Oakes and Paul Bowers, 'Kosovo: Operation "Allied Force"', House of Commons Library Research Paper 99/48 (29 April 1999).

Archives consulted:

The National Archives, UK (UKNA)

Irish National Archives (INA)

Raphael Lemkin papers, New York Public Library (NYPL), US

Raphael Lemkin papers, American Jewish Historical Society, New York, US

Nigerian Civil War Collection (archives of Suzanne Cronje), School of Oriental and African Studies, London

Index